Fearless Philanthropy

Fearless Philanthropy

EDITH
ROSENWALD
STERN'S
CAMPAIGNS TO
TRANSFORM LIVES
IN NEW ORLEANS

ROBERTA BRANDES GRATZ

LOUISIANA STATE
UNIVERSITY PRESS
BATON ROUGE

Published with the assistance of the V. Ray Cardozier Fund

Published by Louisiana State University Press
lsupress.org

Manufactured in the United States of America
First printing

DESIGNER: Michelle A. Neustrom
TYPEFACE: Fournier MT Pro
PRINTER AND BINDER: Sheridan Books, Inc.

The manufacturer's authorized representative in the EU for product safety is Mare Nostrum Group B.V., Doelen 72, 4831 GR Breda, The Netherlands.
Email: gpsr@mare-nostrum.co.uk.

JACKET PHOTOGRAPH: Portrait of Edith Rosenwald Stern taken by Dorothy Wilding, 1936, courtesy of Longue Vue House and Gardens.

All interior illustrations appear courtesy of Longue Vue House and Gardens.

Portions of chapter 1 were first published, in different form, in "The Making of Pontchartrain Park in New Orleans," *Common/Edge*, March 7, 2024.

LIBRARY OF CONGRESS CATALOGING-IN-PUBLICATION DATA

Names: Gratz, Roberta Brandes, author.
Title: Fearless philanthropy : Edith Rosenwald Stern's campaigns to transform lives in New Orleans / Roberta Brandes Gratz.
Description: Baton Rouge : Louisiana State University Press, [2026] | Includes bibliographical references and index.
Identifiers: LCCN 2026020910 (print) | LCCN 2026020911 (ebook) | ISBN 978-0-8071-8653-4 (cloth) | ISBN 978-0-8071-8743-2 (epub) | ISBN 978-0-8071-8744-9 (pdf)
Subjects: LCSH: Stern, Edith Rosenwald, 1895–1980 | Jewish women philanthropists—Louisiana—New Orleans | African Americans—Education—Louisiana—New Orleans—History—20th century | Women civic leaders—Louisiana—New Orleans | Women social reformers—Louisiana—New Orleans | Community development, Urban—Louisiana—New Orleans | New Orleans (La.)—Social conditions—20th century | New Orleans (La.)—Ethnic relations | LCGFT: Biographies
Classification: LCC HV28.S76 G73 2026 (print) | LCC HV28.S76 (ebook) | DDC 361.7/4092—dc23/eng/20260513
LC record available at https://lccn.loc.gov/2026020910
LC ebook record available at https://lccn.loc.gov/2026020911

For the late Bill Borah,
the inspiration for this book

Contents

PREFACE ix

ACKNOWLEDGMENTS xiii

Introduction 1

1. Pontchartrain Park 7

2. Behind the Masque 24

3. Fitting In 45

4. Like Father, Like Daughter 67

5. A Place to Live and a Place to Learn 100

6. A University Is Born 131

7. Renewing the French Quarter 146

8. Legal Pathbreakers 155

9. An Upfront Activist 174

10. Edith and the Arts 184

11. Overcoming the Masque 201

Conclusion 219

NOTES 231

SELECTED BIBLIOGRAPHY 245

INDEX 251

Illustrations follow page 116.

Preface

In 2015, I wrote a book about New Orleans, *We're Still Here Ya Bastards: How the People of New Orleans Rebuilt Their City*. This was not my first book about cities—how they grow, fall apart, and get rebuilt from the bottom up, not by the experts at the top. In all my books I showed that cities recover most effectively when community leaders are the primary guides to genuine revitalization.

We're Still Here Ya Bastards was my first book about New Orleans. I visited New Orleans just three weeks after Hurricane Katrina devastated the city in August 2005. I had watched the storm ravaging the city on television and knew I had to write about New Orleans and its recovery—but I never expected to fall in love with it. Many visitors become enamored of the French Quarter, the music, the food. That is a given. But I fell in love with the city's blemished but authentic urbanism.

I am a passionate urbanist. I love cities. I love cities especially when their basic urbanism is intact: where a traditional street grid has not been destroyed by car-centric boulevards and highways; the building scape has not been erased by the overaggressive days of urban renewal; the parking lot or enlarged driveway is not the dominant design form; a mix of architectural styles reflect the art, the culture, the people and their social foundations; the urban scape blends the new and the old over time without one overwhelming the other; and there is an urban panorama—not just a random few historic sites isolated from their demolished surroundings—emblematic of the city's history and people. A place where all the elements of a living, breathing city are not swept away by the excessive-scaled investor style of the moment that exhibits all the charm of a steel totem pole or windowed box. All these positive attributes dominate New Orleans. The quick-buck style of the moment, of course, is present and increasing, but it does not yet overwhelm the city's authentic appeal.

While writing *We're Still Here Ya Bastards*, I was inspired by the people I met whose passion for their place overcame the hardships that come with a city run by the elites. After Katrina, neighborhood groups organized, defended, and then rebuilt their turf. They came in all colors and backgrounds.

During my research for that book and the scores of interviews I conducted with New Orleanians, I met a fabulous activist named Bill Borah, with sparkling blue eyes, white hair, and a great sense of humor. He was born into the upper crust of this class-conscious city but rejected its social rules. Instead, Bill lived on the fringe of the French Quarter and fought for good planning and historic preservation. He understood better than most how valuable the urban texture of the whole city is and how easily it could be lost.

In one of our many conversations, Bill told me about the fight to stop the Riverfront Expressway, which was designed by Robert Moses to go along the Mississippi River, thereby decimating the French Quarter, the jewel of the city. Highways have been the most destructive force in cities across the country, and Bill understood this well. He and I seriously bonded over the expressway issue. Jane Jacobs, my friend and mentor, was one of the successful leaders against a similar Robert Moses–planned highway in New York City that would have destroyed most of Greenwich Village, SoHo, and Chinatown, as I chronicled in *Battle for Gotham: New York in the Shadow of Robert Moses and Jane Jacobs*. Bill told me about a man named Edgar Stern who hired him and his colleague Richard Baumbach to help lead the fight against the road. The passionate group of smart New Orleanians who started the fight found it very tough going at first. There is nothing so difficult in any city as a fight against a proposed highway. Their eventual victory changed the city in a most positive way.

Edgar Stern, Bill explained, was very rich, Jewish, and an opponent of many of the positions taken by the ruling class, not just the building of the highway. At first, I did not realize there were two Edgar Sterns, Sr. and Jr., and that Bill was primarily talking about Edgar Jr.'s support for the effort to fight the highway.

But Edgar Sr., as Bill explained, was similarly independent and his wife Edith even more so. In fact, as Bill made clear, it was Edith who brought her husband along on a progressive, if not liberal, path. Together they set the pattern of standing up to the Establishment, a pattern that Edgar Jr. followed.

Edith and Edgar married in 1921. Although women had gotten the right to vote the year before, they were still expected to focus only on hearth and home, and in New Orleans they had an even more decorative function. This was not an easy time for ambitious women anywhere, even those with endless funds and the desire to go where others feared to tread. I was most fascinated by Edith's willingness to break out of those social limits and to go so far as to violate New Orleans's social rules. Edgar Sr.'s willingness to follow her lead, especially in support of the Black community, was also out of step with convention. People with such courage intrigued me. As I started to research their lives, I found an interesting group of change agents: Judge J. Skelly Wright, lawyer A. P. Tureaud, activist Rosa Freeman Keller, and Judge John Minor Wisdom. They were all, individually and collectively, an incredible force for change. One cannot fully appreciate the progress in the city without their contributions to it.

The more I learned about the Sterns and others, the more I wanted to know, especially about Edith. I had experienced the fight for women's rights in the 1970s. I knew how hard it was then, a full forty years after Edith's time. I have always been intrigued by women who forge their own path and overcome the expected norms. I told Bill that I had to write a book about Edith Stern. This is the book I promised. Sadly, Bill did not live to read it.

Acknowledgments

Many people contributed to this book through interviews, observations, and comments. I am indebted to them all, but a few were particularly helpful. Lawrence N. Powell, Jacques Morial, and Gwen Thompkins offered insights into New Orleans history that were extremely valuable. Members of the Stern family—Bill Hess, Anne Hess, Susan Hess, Sandra McIver, Walter C. Stern, Lessing Stern, Charles Stern, Eve Stern, and David Stern—shared memories that shed light on the family in critical ways. Lenora Costa, deputy director of collections at Longue Vue House and Gardens, was exceedingly generous with her time and knowledge of family history, letting me spend days and days in the Longue Vue Archives and sharing invaluable details and observations. Lisa C. Moore at the Amistad Research Center at Tulane University helped me comb through numerous archives. I am grateful to Alessandra Seiter at the John F. Kennedy Library in Boston for helping me long-distance. The staff at the Wisconsin Historical Society, Division of Libraries, Archives and Museum Collections, and at the University of Wisconsin Archives, both in in Madison, Wisconsin, also deserve much thanks. The staff at Tulane University Special Collections were helpful as well. I am particularly grateful to the New Orleans Center for the Gulf South at Tulane University for its Monroe Fellowship.

I reached out for interviews to anyone and everyone who either had their own memories of the Sterns or had them passed down from a parent who was a friend or associate of the Sterns. Also helpful were those I interviewed about various aspects of New Orleans history and culture, as well as friends who, at various times, read a portion of my work in progress. I am grateful to all of them: Peter Ascoli, Linda Aubert, John Berendt, Daniel Bluestone, Bill

Borah, John Bullard, Vivian Cahn, Richard Campanella, Ralph Cassimere, Katherine Cecil, Leah Chase, Ellen Heller Cohen, Rabbi Edward P. Cohn, Dawn DeDeaux, Lolis Elie, William A. Fagaly, Ribby Ferguson, Randy Fertel, Norman Francis, Tina Freeman, Trip Friedler, Karen Gadbois, Mara Gay, William A. Goldring, Sally Heller, Sandra Heller, Ken Hoffman, Jed Horne, Mary Howell, Howard Hunter, Pres Kabacoff, Henry Kelleher, Susan Kierr, Herman Kohlmeyer, Dr. Stella Baty Landis, Moon Landrieu, Verna Landrieu, Nicholas Lemann, Tommy Lemann, Anthony Mancini, Jerry Majzlin, Leonard Majzlin, Bobby Malone, Kevin Mercadel, Lee Miller, Sybil Morial, Stephen Moses, Jeanne Nathan, Marcy Planer, Richard Rabinowitz, Caroline Reily, Taylor Segue, Kathy Seligman, Stephen Sontheimer, Sandra Stokes, Harvey M. Stone, Richard Stone, Dorothy Shushan, Robert Tannen, Jeff Thomas, Alexander P. Tureaud Jr., Pam Tyler, David Torkanowsky, Linda Usdin, Darren Walker, Dr. Michael White, James E. Wright III, James S. Wright, Andrew Young, and Mary Freeman Keller Zervigon. And a big thanks to LSU editor in chief Rand Dotson and managing editor Catherine L. Kadair for putting this manuscript into printable format. Without them there would be no book.

Fearless Philanthropy

INTRODUCTION

> From the moment she arrived, her presence was felt. I first saw her at a reception given by mutual friends. The spacious drawing rooms were filled with guests when the newlyweds made their appearance. Edgar very proudly introduced his bride, who immediately charmed everyone by her gracious and cordial manner. She was perfectly groomed from the top of her stylish, perky hat to the fingertips of her white kid gloves. Clearly, the handsome couple emanated an aura of happiness: [This indeed contrasted to what was apparently expected,] a flashy Eastern heiress, dressed to her teeth and flaunting her wealth.[1]

Edith Rosenwald Stern was indeed attractive, but beneath that glitz and glamour was a tough and determined woman. It would take her a while to understand the nuances of the society she had married into, but she would learn—and she would act. Usually, her actions were quiet and behind the scenes. Her philanthropy, like that of her father before her, was targeted and not publicized—but it had a significant impact on New Orleans. One of her most impactful contributions had nothing to do with her generous donations. Instead, it had everything to do with principle and justice and resulted in a deep friendship with the judge who probably did the most to drag the state of Louisiana and the city of New Orleans away from its unlawful commitment to segregation.

In 1984, J. Skelly Wright was a nationally renowned federal judge. More than two decades earlier, then-president John F. Kennedy had nominated him to serve as a circuit judge of the Court of Appeals for the District of Columbia. There, he dissented in a landmark ruling in favor of the freedom of the press. But earlier in the 1950s and 1960s as a judge of the US District Court for the Eastern District of Louisiana, he had staved off twenty-nine separate attempts of the Louisiana legislature to prevent integration in New Orleans. Those decisions angered many Louisianans and threatened the safety of him and his family then living in the city. Wright and his wife were social outcasts for his efforts to upend the segregationist status quo, and a cross was burned on his lawn.

Wright's rulings over the years involved the great issues of his time. They were key not only to school integration in New Orleans but also to the integration of universities, public buses, parks, and sporting events, as well as to voter rights. Over the course of his judicial career, he received honorary degrees of law from five universities, including Yale. After he left New Orleans for the US Court of Appeals, his decisions expanded his significant place in history. Skelly Wright was a judicial giant and a fan of Edith Rosenwald Stern: he saw her standing up for social justice issues as controversial as the ones he ruled on. In turn, she befriended Wright and his wife when things were at their darkest for them.

Chicago born and raised, Edith was a formidable force for civil rights and other justice issues in her adopted city of New Orleans. Four years after her death in 1980, a biography of Edith was published. Titled *A Passion for Sharing*, it was commissioned by the National Council of Jewish Women, and Judge Wright had been interviewed for the book by its author, Gerda Weissman Klein.[2] Its publication was an occasion for celebrating Edith's life. At the book launch, Judge Wright spoke about Edith, highlighting her achievements, particularly in support of civil rights and voter registration of Black citizens. He described his admiration for Edith Stern and for her efforts to stand up against hostility from New Orleans's social elites and often vicious hate from white segregationists. He spoke of her commitment to justice and her fight against entrenched segregation.

This celebration was held at Edith and Edgar's most artful achievement, Longue Vue House and Gardens. It is considered the last important private house built in the United States before World War II. Designed in partnership with renowned architect William Platt and celebrated garden designer Ellen Biddle Shipman, Longue Vue and its gardens are a jewel among New

Orleans's many beautiful homes. Attached to the house is the well-used Playhouse, where the book launch was held.

The Playhouse was designed for all kinds of occasions from weddings to New Year's Eve parties to celebrations like this book launch. With its two-story open interior that had a balcony for an occasional musical ensemble, the Playhouse was the perfect setting for friends and family to gather to honor Edith. Wright's stature as a nationally respected jurist underscored the significance of Edith's extensive achievements.

School integration may be the best known of Edith's commitments, most of which she expressed anonymously. Already an outsider as a Jew, Edith often defied convention; for instance, she invited Marian Anderson, at the beginning of her singing career, to perform at her New Orleans home for her guests when it was still illegal for Blacks and whites to socialize. Women were not supposed to be outspoken activists and certainly not the kind of activist Edith became. They could be active in women-centered organizations such as the Garden Club and the Junior League, but not too conspicuously. Those organizations could be subtle forces for change. Yet, Edith made public her active support and sizable donations to the private Metairie Park Country Day School, various garden clubs, voter registration efforts, and a host of cultural organizations. She left town during the height of the school desegregation fight, but not before funding the major public campaign waged by the women of SOS (Save Our Schools), an organization fighting for school integration.

She had a willing partner in activism in her husband Edgar. When they married in 1921, Edgar was not yet a trailblazer and was far from a civil rights advocate. But Edith changed him, and his civic involvement and philanthropy became quite visible. Indeed, he became an informal liaison between the Black community and the political/social establishment.

Yet Edgar was never fully a part of that establishment. During business hours, he moved freely in the city's business circles. However, the doors of many of the exclusive men's clubs—not to mention the upper echelons where social antisemitism reigned supreme—were tightly closed to him. New Orleans's Carnival society was off-limits. Yet, because Edgar was a big wheel in the business world, he was invited to join the Boston Club, the premier private club. When he asked whether that invitation could include his best friend and daily lunch partner Monte Lemann, the answer was no. And so, Edgar refused to join the club.

The Sterns were Jewish in a predominantly Catholic city where only about 1 percent of the population was Jewish. Their Judaism was not primarily expressed in rituals observed at home or in the synagogue. Instead, their Jewishness was based on the moral teachings of the Torah and on the Jewish value of *tikkum olam* (literally, "to repair the world"), which is now understood as the pursuit of justice in all spheres of life.

Edgar was as public in his philanthropic pursuits as Edith was private, working behind the scenes. But together they formed an expansive partnership built on Edith's seemingly limitless fortune. Central to their shared life were their combined efforts to "repair" New Orleans. They forged new paths in education for Blacks and whites, built the first residential development in the country for the Black middle class, constructed a standout southern colonial mansion located outside the neighborhood where the social elite lived, and developed a high-quality hospital for Black people. Together they worked to renew the forlorn, deteriorating, and out-of-fashion French Quarter, helping it become the worldwide tourist magnet it now is. Edith, quietly and in hard-to-identify ways, bought and restored several houses in the historic district; Edgar, openly and with Edith's money and encouragement, rebuilt a major hotel in the Quarter, making it a hub of social activity. They bought a radio station for son Edgar Jr. to run and situated it in the Quarter; when WDSU became a TV station as well, it served as a beacon of integration in the early civil rights era. The only one of their children who remained in New Orleans, Edgar Jr. fashioned the station into one of the most innovative and progressive in the nation, winning a Peabody Award in the process. (The Peabody Award is for television the equivalent of the Pulitzer Prize for writing.)

Hovering over the story of this remarkable couple is Edith's father, Julius Rosenwald, the primary force behind the legendary retail giant Sears & Roebuck. In terms of wealth and business savvy, he was the Jeff Bezos of his day. Exploring Julius's life offers a window into his very strong influence on Edith. His philanthropy—especially his funding of 5,300 schoolhouses for Black students across the South, where no quality education was then being offered to Black children—provided a model for Edith's efforts. The impact of his friendships with Booker T. Washington, Jane Addams, Rabbi Emil Hirsch, and other philanthropists carried over to the next generation. His grants to individual Black artists, writers, and scientists were unprecedented. Healthcare institutions and YMCAs also benefited from the Rosenwald largesse.

Not only the objects but also the methods of his philanthropy resonated with Edith. In the school-building project, for example, Julius donated one-third of the cost of each, insisting that another one-third come from the local white community and one-third from the Black community. Black communities often made in-kind donations of supplies and time to cover their share. Many of Edith's donations were also contingent on matching gifts. In contrast to Edith's philanthropy, Julius's gifts, however, were widely publicized. He made them known so that others would follow his example, as did Jacob Schiff among others.

By ignoring racial restrictions and social conventions, Julius served as a role model for Edith. He brought Booker T. Washington to Chicago to meet the elite white business community at a luncheon he gave at the city's most prestigious hotel. Washington was also the guest of the Rosenwalds in their home for five days. This was quite a bold move. Even the local newspaper wrote about it. Augusta, Julius's wife, told her children about "the stir" in a letter, writing, "People will get over it." Bold, pathbreaking, unconcerned with what others would say—these were not common traits. Yet, Edith inherited them all. One cannot fully understand or appreciate the story of Edith without recognizing the path laid out by Julius.

When it came to unapologetic advocacy, Edgar Stern Jr. took the family prize. He learned well from his parents but applied their values boldly and in different arenas. He worked with his father to build the Royal Orleans Hotel, with the aim of catalyzing the revitalization of the Quarter, which in the 1950s was at its lowest point. It took nearly a decade to bring the project to fruition because of the lack of local and national interest in investing there. Edgar Sr. died in 1959, so Edgar Jr. continued the quest with great help from his father's chief assistant, Lester Kabacoff. Edgar Sr. had hired Kabacoff as his executive assistant because he was tired of sitting in on long-winded discussions of civic fundraising projects and political strategy sessions. He would tell people, "See Kabby," thereby avoiding endless meetings.

When the hotel opened in 1960, the staff was integrated, a first for New Orleans. Edgar Jr. ran on-air editorials, a new concept, on WDSU in favor of school integration when the state and city hierarchy were fighting against it tooth and nail. Then he financed probably the city's biggest public fight on any issue: stopping a Robert Moses–designed throughway that would run along the waterfront in the French Quarter and destroy a large part of that historic core. This fundamentally severed whatever thin ties he still had with the city's business and social community.

All the city's power brokers favored the highway. An energetic citizens' group, mostly historic preservationists, had been fighting the highway but making little headway until Edgar Jr. got involved. He hired two passionate local highway opponents, Bill Borah and Richard Baumbach, to lead the fight. In the end, Edgar's help, his Washington connections, and his credentials as a rich, successful New Orleans businessman made the difference. The expressway was stopped, and the French Quarter became one of the most popular tourist attractions in the country.

The story of the Sterns shines an interesting light on New Orleans, offering up insights and spotlighting personalities in new ways.

I

PONTCHARTRAIN PARK

As the story goes, the idea to build the first Black middle-class housing development in the United States backed by the FHA was born in the early 1950s at the dinner table of a most unusual couple in New Orleans. Edith and Edgar Stern were outliers in that socially regressive city where bloodlines reigned supreme. "It doesn't matter how much money you have; it's who your daddy was and who his daddy was" has always been the city's mantra, a New Orleanian once told me. However, Edith's "daddy" was not their kind; he was one of the richest men in the country, but he was also Jewish, liberal, and from Chicago. Edgar's father was perceived through a similar lens: even though he was a major cotton broker, he was also the son of German Jewish immigrants. In the New Orleans of the 1920s through the 1950s, improving life for Black citizens was no one's priority—except for Edith and, under her influence, for Edgar as well.

The home in which they dined was as much an outlier as the dining guests seated at the table there. A grand mansion set amidst formal gardens, planned by a leading female designer and filled with imported antiques, Longue Vue was as palatial as the most stunning homes in New Orleans. But it was not in one of the high-end neighborhoods where the elite of New Orleans lived. In fact, it was located on the last street within the city limits, across a canal from the suburb of Metairie, which at that time was only partially developed.

The dining table overlooked the Pan Garden, where a small sculpture of the god of nature was in full view. Atop a lace-edged linen cloth was a full service of fine bone china and delicate crystal. Edith and Edgar were a handsome couple. Edgar was tall and dapper and had dark features and a winning smile. Edith was slim and had short dark hair, delicate features, and an equally winning smile. She deferred to Edgar, as was expected in the decades after their 1921 marriage. She also knew that her wealth could be intimidating. Yet she used that wealth well and made sure her husband did the same.

Their dinner companions—the married couple Rosa Freeman and Chuck Keller—were similarly interesting and were also outliers but in a different way. Rosa, about ten years younger than Edith, sported short blonde hair set in the classic waves that were the fashion of the early 1950s. She had all the social credentials that Edith did not: she had been the Queen of Mardi Gras and was daughter of a former King of Mardi Gras. Chuck Keller was a mild-mannered, bespectacled man with a sharp chin and a receding forehead. He was Jewish and was born in Cleveland but grew up in Winnetka, a high-end early suburb outside Chicago. He graduated with an engineering degree from West Point, one of the few Jewish cadets there. Rosa and Chuck's marriage broke the social rules, but her credentials proved stronger than that transgression. After her marriage, those rules would never be her concern (see chapter 9).

After some chitchat among this foursome, the conversation gravitated toward a weightier subject: the development of the first middle-class Black community. It would be called Pontchartrain Park. This project was inspired by the personal experience of the Sterns' cook, Emma Brown. Emma was a treasured member of the staff who brought her children and grandchildren to play with the Stern children in the Playhouse. "The Sterns felt like family," remembered Emma's granddaughter Linda Aubert, a New Orleans singer and night-club performer. "I was comfortable there. I started playing the piano there. I could feel Mr. Stern's happiness at our being there, and that he wanted us included," she added. "He helped a lot of people."

Over dinner, Edgar reported with shock and outrage that Emma's downtown house had been lost in a fire. Across the country at this time, landlords in urban renewal neighborhoods, such as the one in which Emma lived, were setting homes on fire to collect the insurance proceeds. The powers that be had another agenda for her neighborhood, and the current residents stood in the way of achieving that. After the fire, Emma reported to Edgar that she could not find a decent, affordable place to live. Edgar found that hard to believe. So, he accompanied her on a housing search and discovered she was right.

At dinner, Edgar spoke about wanting to help Emma and her neighbors and talked about developing a Black middle-class community. The Kellers shared his outrage and liked Edgar's idea. The partnership was set. Unfortunately, the community that emerged from this conversation would not be built soon enough to solve Emma's housing problem.

As the dinner progressed, the foursome's enthusiasm and excitement grew. They knew this was the right thing to do. Rosa Freeman Keller recalled, "We went to see the mayor and developed a plan for a housing development with . . . sound housing, trees left where they were, nicely laid out streets."[1]

Even though the couples knew this project would raise eyebrows, the timing could not have been more appropriate. In the early 1950s, the economy was shifting from military to domestic production. Cars and the highways to drive them on were the new primary economic stimuli. Suburbs proliferated along the new byways, but many were not open to Black families. Model homes in the new suburban developments attracted crowds. Ranch and split-level homes, with a lawn and a carport or garage, were the favorite designs of choice.

Post–World War II America was changing fast but not for everyone. Black soldiers returned to the South after fighting in the war only to be treated as viciously as before they fought for their country. "Because of their military service, black veterans were seen as a particular threat to Jim Crow and racial subordination. Thousands of black veterans were assaulted, threatened, abused, or lynched following military service."[2] Sometimes, while still wearing the uniform of the US armed forces, they were killed for no reason. In New Orleans, two soldiers were reportedly beaten to death. Edwin Williams, a forty-three-year-old returning soldier who had served in the Navy, was stabbed to death with beer bottles while coming home from church with his wife and daughter in the West Bank neighborhood of Algiers; he had had the audacity to protest beer being thrown on him and his family by three drunk white men. Stories like this were rarely covered in the white newspapers, although the Black-owned *Louisiana Weekly* reported regularly on the frequent beatings that Black soldiers received. These senseless killings and beatings were happening to some extent around the country, as reported in the *Chicago Daily Defender* and the *Pittsburgh Courier*, but occurred more often in the South. Both Black newspapers frequently reported on New Orleans's incidents.

Even German prisoners of war were treated better than Black American soldiers. These POWs were held in several US sites, including for two years at Camp Claiborne outside Alexandria, Louisiana. German officers "could choose to work or to devote themselves to educational and recreational interests."[3] Imprisoned Black soldiers in the same camp had no such choice: they had to work.

Even though the daily insults meted out for being Black occurred as frequently as before the war, those Black soldiers who had served in Europe—particularly in France—had enjoyed rights and privileges that were unheard of anywhere in the United States, let alone in New Orleans. They had gotten a taste of a better life, and they wanted change when they returned home. They no longer felt resigned to second-class citizenship. They wanted fair employment opportunities, campaigned for the ballot, agitated for better public facilities, and protested police brutality. And they wanted access to decent housing.

World War II had not led to a loosening of segregation as Black soldiers hoped it would. Years later, their experience would invigorate the civil rights movement. But in the late 1940s and early 1950s, these men were just seeking opportunities and access to basic elements of daily life, including leisure-time activities.

For decades, Black New Orleanians had urged city government to create parks for Black citizens. In the rare case that the city responded, it provided only the land; the Black community had to raise money for equipment. Most of these parks did not last long because of white objections. And so Black residents embraced again a model of self-support and collective efforts that had before World War I led to the creation of Black banks, hospitals, and even towns.[4] It led, as well, to New Orleans's first Black school, library, and YMCA.

In 1949, Dr. Taylor Segue, a prominent Black dentist, wrote a letter to New Orleans Mayor deLesseps S. (Chep) Morrison, pointing out that Black golfers had no place to play in the city. He requested the meager privilege of playing on the city's public golf course in City Park one day a week. Ironically, the city's segregated golf course had been designed by the celebrated Black golf course designer, Joseph M. Bartholomew, Segue's brother-in-law. Bartholomew also designed the course at the Metairie Country Club and bought the land and designed a seven-hole course in Harahan, a nearby suburb, on which Black golfers were allowed to play. He also did landscape work for the Sterns.

Segue was born in either 1899 or 1900, his grandson told me, so was probably too young to serve in World War I and too old for World War II. He graduated from Howard University Dental School in 1922. Segue was also a friend of Governor Huey Long who, according to family lore, was an occasional dinner guest at the Segues' home. "My grandfather apparently told Long," the grandson said, "that he had an extensive patient list and he was convinced they would all vote for him [Long] if they only had the vote."

Segue's 1949 letter would help bring about a dramatic change in the lives of the Black middle class in New Orleans. The city agreed to create a golf course for Black players in a rapidly developing section of the city, and the Pontchartrain Park Homes were developed around it.

Although the mayor never actively supported the development of Pontchartrain Park, he took credit for it during his 1954 reelection campaign. As he said in a speech, one of his accomplishments was creating "a new city" of "8 to 10 square miles" in a former salt marsh near Lake Pontchartrain with 25,000 new suburban single-family homes, a golf course, and a park. This was Edgar's dream come to life.

To drive around Pontchartrain Park today is to feel like you have stepped back in time. Many of the houses look much as they did in the 1950s. Carports remain intact. Green lawns are neat with occasional modest flowerbeds. Few ranch-style house have been altered, and those that have retain recognizable elements of their original design. It remains a classic bedroom community.

Jeff Thomas, who grew up in "The Park," as it is known, and gave me a full tour of the community, told me that Edgar Stern "couldn't have anticipated the impact it had on the Black community and the city as a whole." As stage, film, and television actor Wendell Pierce, who grew up here, noted, "That's the thing about Pontchartrain Park. Its utterly ordinary, 1950s-style, cookie-cutter Americana appearance veiled what was in fact an extraordinary accomplishment for Black Americans: middle-class normalcy."[5] After Hurricane Katrina, which nearly leveled the community, Pierce became the voice for The Park, agitating for the same kind of recovery aid that was being directed at equally devastated white neighborhoods. His return encouraged others to move back and not give up.

What made the community unique to Terence Blanchard, trumpeter, opera composer, and movie score composer, was that "everybody was involved with everybody else's kids' lives." As he told Gwen Thompkins on her public radio program *Music Inside Out* a few years ago, "The future of the kids was what everyone cared about." Blanchard laughed at the idea that "we actually grew up around a golf course," surely a unique condition for a Black community. But there is an irony here: the course at Pontchartrain Park consistently drew more white golfers than Black golfers, and golf was not taught at the nearby public schools.

White Suburbia Next Door

Before The Park was developed, a substantial new white neighborhood—Gentilly Woods—was arising within the city's borders near Lake Pontchartrain. As would be true of Pontchartrain Park, the houses in Gentilly Woods were mostly bought by World War II veterans using their GI loans to buy their first homes. Few of the white homeowners personally knew any Black people, and when they learned about Pontchartrain Park, many were horrified.

During his first campaign and in his first years as mayor, Morrison avoided racial topics. Nor did he show any real concern for the local Black community or its long-neglected problems. Nevertheless, Morrison was, first and foremost, a political animal. He maintained relationships with a few Black leaders and managed, often under threat of lawsuits, to upgrade selected city services for the Black community. The late 1940s and early 1950s were unusually volatile in New Orleans. Pressures for racial change were coming on multiple fronts and had citywide impact. After the war, there were demands to hire Black policemen, to integrate the public bus system, to provide equal public facilities, and to equalize pay in civil service jobs.

In addition, the mayor received considerable pressure to improve conditions for Black citizens from his biggest supporters: Edgar and Edith Stern; Lester Kabacoff, a board member of the Urban League and primary assistant to Edgar; lawyer Monte Lemann and his wife, Nettie Hyman Lemann; the Kellers; and others. In memos and letters, Edgar warned Morrison that he must act on behalf of the Black population, or New Orleans could experience unrest like that occurring in other southern cities. Unrest in Florida, for example, over the issue of segregated recreation facilities led to integration of a golf course in Miami. Edgar warned Morrison that could happen in New Orleans if a way was not found—other than integration—to address Black needs. The goal was to improve the lives of Black citizens while not disturbing the segregation status quo.

The Community Lost

Emma Brown's downtown neighborhood had been a low- and middle-income Black community of modest shotgun and Creole cottages, some with driveways but all with a place to barbecue and picnic. The customary institutions, churches, small businesses, and gathering spots were spread throughout the area. Neighbors knew neighbors, watched each other's children, and took care of the elderly. Then, suddenly, houses were being torn down or set on fire, and tenants were evicted without cause—all because cleared center-city land had become a valuable commodity.

Across the country, economically and racially integrated urban neighborhoods like Emma's were being destroyed in the name of "slum clearance." In retrospect, experts acknowledge that "slum clearance" was a convenient label for targeted urban neighborhoods for which political leaders had another agenda. That agenda, which was usually unclear initially, could be to provide cleared space for a highway, cultural facility, transit station, sports venue, middle-class housing development, or public housing. The "slum" designation made urban renewal development possible.

The supply of affordable housing for Black residents of New Orleans was diminishing as each downtown urban renewal project evolved into a bus terminal, stadium, or highway. Even though several segregated public housing complexes were also being built, they contained fewer units than the neighborhoods being decimated. In addition, the small number of displaced families who were given public housing were never placed in a neighborhood comparable to the one that was bulldozed. Supportive social and family networks had been disrupted and dispersed. The damage to the well-being of Black citizens caused by the enormous loss of Black-owned businesses, housing, social institutions, churches, and more has only recently been acknowledged. The loss of Black wealth and the disruption of Black families germinated the seeds of social dysfunction.

The volatile years of the early 1950s and the Black community's demands for change could not have escaped the awareness of the Kellers or Sterns, who were already involved in various efforts on behalf of Black citizens. Nevertheless, Edith and Edgar found the lack of decent affordable housing for middle-class Black people particularly shocking and unacceptable. They wanted to do something about it, and the Kellers were willing partners.

It would take until 1955 for this pathbreaking housing development to be built. All manner of roadblocks stood in the way. Jacques Morial, son of Dutch Morial, New Orleans's first Black mayor, and brother of Marc, also a mayor of New Orleans, grew up in The Park. He told me that Edgar likely used his Washington, DC, connections to lobby the Federal Housing Authority (FHA) directly. "How else would this have happened?" Morial asked.

In his groundbreaking book, *The Color of Law: A Forgotten History of How Our Government Segregated America*, housing expert Richard Rothstein details how government policies, especially those of the FHA, systematically denied mortgage insurance and other governmental assistance to nearly every rental or homeowner development that permitted Blacks as tenants or homeowners. He further shows that white residents were incentivized to move from integrated cities to white suburbs where they could get FHA-insured mortgages that were not available in the cities. "White flight" of the 1950s and 1960s was spurred on in this way. Meanwhile, Black homeowners and businesses were denied any kind of government financing.

It follows that enlightened developers and organizations that wanted to build integrated communities were routinely denied FHA backing. It was a "rare occasion," Rothstein writes, when the FHA approved loans for segregated African American developments. Pontchartrain Park was the very first "rare occasion." In 1954, Mayor Morrison

> begged the FHA to insure a development for middle-class black professionals and promised the agency that no units would be sold to whites. The New Orleans NAACP chapter protested the creation of a segregated housing development. The agency ignored the protest, and the

development eventually consisted of one thousand homes for African-Americans only, surrounding a park and golf course and adjoining a similar FHA-insured development for whites only. In 1955 an FHA spokesman toured fifty cities where he addressed African American audiences, boasting of the New Orleans achievements and telling his listeners that such segregated projects were "the type of thing [the] FHA wanted."[6]

The FHA in the end seemed quite proud of its involvement in New Orleans, dispatching two of its officials to the groundbreaking. An April 5, 1955, photo of the "pile-driving ceremonies" at Pontchartrain Park Homes included Dr. George A. Snowden, assistant commissioner of the FHA; Gervais Favrot, general contractor for the homes; Edgar Stern, president of the development firm; Ralph Agate, head of the local FHA office; and Joseph Finley, VA loan guaranty officer.

Morrison's Bizarre Idea

Earlier, in August 1951, the *New Orleans States-Item* had reported that "the 184-acre Pontchartrain Park bought by the city for $173,963, to be used as a recreation ground for Negroes, has been cleared, Mayor Chep Morrison said today, but the city has no money to make any further improvements on the property." This was a repetition of the decades-long pattern in which the city occasionally purchased a property for a Black park, but the Black community was then responsible for buying all the equipment. But in this case, a sequence of appalling events preceded the park's creation.

The hurdles were many, but probably none were as big as just getting Morrison to support the project. He found ways to show concern for Blacks when prodded by his wealthy campaign supporters like the Sterns and the Kellers, but his private feelings were another matter. Insiders like the Sterns and Kellers were seeking fundamental change; Morrison was not. He was quite aware that most members of the population he cared most about, the white community, were not pushing for change—certainly not where the Black community was concerned.

Dr. Segue's letter requesting a "Negro golf course in the city" elicited a shockingly crass reaction from Morrison. On March 23, 1949, W. Ray

Scheuering, a top aide to Morrison, forwarded it to the mayor and asked how the mayor would like to respond. Scheuering wrote, "Since the proposed Negro recreation area in the vicinity of the Industrial Canal and the lakefront seems very remote, I am wondering if we have any other possible site in mind. If not, I will try to let them down easy with 'no money' reply."[7]

Interestingly, the mayor replied in two ways. First, he wrote "OK" in small letters below the "no money" reply suggestion. Then he handwrote this extended answer:

> There is an excellent piece of city property which is currently used as a public dump that could be made into a nice 9-hole course. It was one time, long ago in the days of the WPA made into an Algiers Park but has since fallen into neglect, until now it is an eyesore. It has water hazards, roadways, arched overpasses of concrete, etc., everything necessary to make it an ideal course for the [racial slur]. . . . Here are my reasons for recommending same: 1. It lies in a corner of Orleans Parish over in Algiers. 2. It is a mile away from the Westside Country Club (white) which has a 9 hole course. The westside club is a private affair and is not so exclusive as to cause a big howl from the gentry because of colored encroachments. 3. The Algiers Park is in a colored/poor (which section of Algiers along Behrman highway). 4. As a public golf course it would cause the [slur] to cross the river the same as the Algiers whites have to cross to the City Park and Audobon Park courses. . . . 5. Work of cleaning the place could begin . . . say in December for obvious (illegible) Federal . . . funds could be obtained.[8]

It is not known whether the mayor's suggestion to build a recreational area for the Black community in the former dump in Algiers was ever seriously considered.

This memo is not mentioned in the only published biography of Morrison, written by Edward F. Haas. Haas characterizes Morrison's reaction differently: "In the spring of 1949, determined protests from Black citizens who objected strenuously to the absence of a large municipal park and golf course for their own use caused Mayor Morrison to call a special meeting of his general advisory committee to discuss the matter."[9] Edgar Stern Sr. was the committee chairman. At a June 9, 1949, meeting of the all-white committee—

including representatives of Audubon Park and City Park, the New Orleans Recreation Department (NORD), and the planning commission—agreed that a sizable park should be established for Black residents "where there will be a minimum of neighborhood friction."

There was no place in New Orleans where friction would be "minimum." A representative of organizations in the Greater Gentilly Civic Improvement Association, for example, threatened to "bomb" the proposed residences.[10] The new, young white homeowners in Gentilly Woods were aghast at the prospect of five thousand Black residents living at their doorsteps. Eventually, a compromise was struck that limited the number of access roads to two and created a ditch to separate the two communities. Moving the housing development forward had its difficult moments.[11]

Intense Pressure from the Black Community

Meanwhile, pressure for equality was building elsewhere in the city. On September 27, 1949, attorney A. P. Tureaud, on behalf of the NAACP, filed a formal complaint protesting the segregation of City Park. The following year, he filed a lawsuit in federal court for the desegregation of the park under the Fourteenth Amendment's due process clause. If the city leaders did not move quickly, Morrison realized, the lawsuit could result in the desegregation of City Park. This was only one of the many lawsuits Tureaud filed that changed the racial structure of the city. By 1950, New Orleans still had no Black policemen, the only large city in the South without any.[12]

In 1952, Judge J. Skelly Wright delayed a decision on the desegregation of City Park and instead appointed a committee of six white and six Black citizens to work things out. The resulting plan was for Black residents to use the tennis courts and golf courses on Wednesdays and Fridays at City Park and Audubon Park. Eventually, in 1956, after the US Supreme Court ordered the desegregation of parks in Atlanta and Baltimore, Wright ruled that the same must happen in New Orleans.

During the early 1950s, Edgar's idea for a planned middle-class community for Black residents inched along until it became a full-fledged proposal. He was also exploring the possibility of creating a well-financed building and loan association specializing in Black residences and willing to extend second as well as first mortgages, as Julius Rosenwald had done in Chicago. However, it is not clear when the idea emerged of connecting the park and golf course to the residential development. Various documents in the Katrina-damaged Morrison files of the Louisiana Collection at Tulane University had been viewed years before by Jacques Morial. According to Morial, those papers revealed that Edgar urged Morrison to ease his fundamentally segregationist views without embracing integration, as described earlier. Edgar alerted the mayor to the vigorous Black protests in Miami that led to the full integration of that city's parks. He warned that this would happen in New Orleans if a Black golf course and park were not created.[13]

Surely, Edgar was not the only one aware of the great need for affordable housing for a growing workforce. Thousands of Black men and women were leaving rural Louisiana and Mississippi for low-wage, low-skill jobs in the port, transportation, light industrial, and service industries, which were desperately seeking workers. Surely civic leaders understood that New Orleans could not take full advantage of the postwar boom without a supply of cheap, low-skilled labor. These workers had to live somewhere near their jobs. Yet, it is difficult to determine who else among city leaders and businesspeople was trying to address this challenge. The personal predicament of the Sterns' cook seemed to activate Edgar's interest in developing housing for middle-income Black citizens. Edgar was head of the Mayor's Advisory Committee (i.e., his kitchen cabinet) from the start, so clearly he was in a position to make things happen.

Rosa Freeman Keller, in her recorded autobiography, noted that this was a tense time in the city and that Emma Brown's desperate situation was emblematic of the housing situation for most Black families. She stated that ongoing slum clearance activity had created citywide tensions. It was "a dangerous period for the whole community," she said. "Chep [Mayor Morrison] was scared . . . we were all scared."[14]

In response, Morrison instructed the Mayor's Advisory Committee and Edgar, its chair, to focus on public housing plans. The Desire Housing Project for low-income Black residents was then being built. A very large project—262 two-story brick buildings containing 1,860 apartments—it was built on 98.5 acres of swamp and a former housing dump. Yet it was considered a positive accomplishment, as were similar projects being built in cities all over the country. There was little recognition that these projects seemed to solidify segregation. Or perhaps, this total segregation, where none had yet existed, was recognized and, in fact, purposeful. The crumbling Desire Project was vacated and demolished in stages between 1995 and 1999.

The Black Community Is Divided

Edgar's idea to build a housing development for Black residents was controversial in the Black community. Some wanted to push for complete integration, but others would be satisfied with separate but truly equal housing. Most of those supporting the latter view were members of the Black middle class. At that time, New Orleans had a larger Black middle class than most southern cities, Jacques Morial explained to me, "because we always had a Black business class, and postwar, two Black colleges, in addition to K-12 teachers, longshoremen and entrepreneurs; [there was] more prosperity than in southern cities that were tied to mostly agricultural industries."

Morrison's commitment to maintain segregation was essential to his political success because both the long-standing and the newer middle-class white neighborhoods felt increasingly threatened by Black encroachment. "When Pontchartrain Park opened, Morrison boasted that he had preserved segregation by providing truly 'separate but equal' facilities that satisfied all but a handful of professional malcontents."[15]

Between 1947 and the opening of Pontchartrain Park Homes in 1955 and the park in 1956, Morrison tried to keep threats to segregation out of the public eye for fear of unleashing stronger white backlash than was already occurring. Hamilton Crawford of Baton Rouge, who was the contractor for the Gentilly Woods development just north of Pontchartrain Park, was brought on in the same role for Pontchartrain Park Homes. The Black community would have the same ranch-style homes that were on the other side of the "Dwyer Canal," the name given to the ditch creating a clear separation between the white and Black developments. It prevented the backyards of the white homes from touching the backyards of the Black homes, which was part of the compromise allowing construction to proceed on The Park.

A Gem of a Park Emerges Around a Cohesive Community

The 226-acre Pontchartrain Park housed a 2,500-seat Little League stadium, baseball diamond, picnic areas, lagoons, and more. Joseph Bartholemew was engaged to design the golf course, which would be the first eighteen-hole course that he could also play on. According to one work on Longue Vue House, "Bartholomew had also done site work for the Sterns when they were house building in the 1930s. In honor of Edgar, Bartholomew did not charge the city a fee for his design work."[16] After a 1979 renovation of the course, it was named for Bartholomew.

Morrison used public funds for the recreation area very strategically. About $200,000 from various city accounts were budgeted for recreation, but not in a lump sum through bonds or other means that would spark public discussion.[17] Morrison was clearly worried that breaking the precedent by paying for recreation equipment for the Black community would stir unrest in the white community.

The proposal to build a huge park for Black people with a golf course was clearly forced on Mayor Morrison. He had, after all, suggested using a former dump in Algiers for that purpose. At some point, what seems to be Edgar's idea of an adjacent subdivision for Black homeowners became part of the mix. Morrison also committed $600,000 in public funds for streets and other public utilities.

Groundbreaking for the Pontchartrain Park homes did not take place until 1955, but earlier advertisements displayed several types of model homes with such up-to-date amenities as drainage and central heating. Sales were quick, creating a backlog while construction was underway. Even though the Pontchartrain Park homes looked just like the ones constructed in Gentilly Woods by the same builder, they were smaller.

Edgar was not only committed to developing the community but also to energetically promoting it to potential buyers. On November 23, 1954, the *New Orleans Item* reported that Edgar organized and spoke to a group of Black leaders, explaining that houses, including lots, would range in cost from $9,800 to $25,000 with extras like air conditioning and laundry rooms available.

The variety of home design options was quite remarkable. There were thirty-five interior layouts with a choice of brick or cedar shakes on the exterior, mahogany-paneled doors, floor-to-ceiling cabinets, zoned heating, attic fans, and more. "Pontchartrain Park: Your Dream Home in a Dream Neighborhood with Paved Streets, City Sewerage and Drainage, Concrete Sidewalks and Driveways," read the newspaper ads that also included a map of The Park and testimonials from buyers, such as "a doctor, a school teacher." The availability of GI and FHA financing was noted in the ads. What a breakthrough! Nine model homes were opened, four of which were furnished by upscale stores including the Maison Blanche and Holmes department stores, Bradfords Inc., and Orleans Town Associates. Nearly 150 homes were sold in 45 days.

The GI Bill made it possible for most new Black homeowners in The Park to finance the purchase of their home, as was true across the country in the burgeoning white suburbs. Many of the Black buyers in The Park were tradesmen, and when it came time to upgrade, expand, or repair the houses, they mostly helped each other. Lionel Khaton, whose father was a carpenter, wrote, "When my dad built the addition to the house, he called on his friends to help; Mr. Williams was a concrete guy, Mr. Robert a tile man, Mr. Floyd was another carpenter, and so on. . . . These men would help for little or no charge because they knew my dad would be there to help them with their projects."[18]

The significance of the Pontchartrain Park homes cannot be overstated. The modern ranch-style design of the Crawford homes signified for Black residents of New Orleans their economic and social "arrival," as well as access to the American dream of equality, especially in an urban environment where historical and traditional residential designs signified white domination and separation. Brought to fruition by whites who could not be described as integrationists, Pontchartrain Park nonetheless represented an activist gesture that provided "a literal home base of self-respect for four generations of black New Orleanians."[19]

Pride of Place

Loyalty to one's neighborhood is common around the country, but the loyalty and pride felt by those who grew up in Pontchartrain Park were unusually fierce. Gwen Thompkins, a former NPR correspondent and editor who specializes in writing about New Orleans music and musicians, grew up there. "I remember complaining in the 1980s that *nothing* ever happened here," she told me, "but there was a lot going on that I didn't see. More than 90 percent of the people owned their own homes. Nearly every kid I knew went to college; the worst student in my class ended up becoming a jazz musician. One resident, Ernest Morial, went on to become the first Black mayor of New Orleans."

Actor Wendell Pierce put it this way: "Here's the key to understanding Pontchartrain Park, the secret of its success. It was a place in which nearly everybody owned their house, and each house had in it both a mother and a father. Our dads never had to talk about the responsibilities fathers had to kids; they demonstrated them by example. Our moms did not have to carry the burden of raising children by themselves. They did it with their husbands. That was the norm in Pontchartrain Park: single-family homes, each family headed by a mom and a dad, and everybody's mom and dad obliged to support the other in their common mission of raising up the next generation."[20]

"The Park is the most historically significant Black neighborhood in the U.S.," asserted Jeff Thomas, a longtime resident who, with two other former residents—Wendell Pierce and businessman Troy Henry—now owns the city's Black radio station WBOK. "The Park created the city's Black middle class." (Black Creoles in the Seventh Ward, a downtown neighborhood, were also members of the middle class.) A long list of judges, doctors, teachers, longshoremen, musicians, policemen, and City Council members, as well as two mayors, were residents. "The Park was a kind of test case nationally," Thomas added, "to see if Black people were able to maintain their homes and pay their mortgages. People took great pride in their homes." Interestingly, Thomas noted that the banks only grudgingly gave FHA-backed mortgages and at a higher rate than those given to residents of Gentilly Woods. Over time, property values in The Park failed to equal those in Gentilly Woods, where the homes were slightly larger. Gentilly Woods is now a mostly Black neighborhood.

Thomas waxed eloquent when describing the closeness among Park neighbors: "It was the first time we all had backyards and front yards. We had cookouts and seafood boils and games with all our parents actively involved. They were young. Divorce was rare." He continued, "For me, it all played out in sports." When the local Little League allowed Black teams to participate, "Pontchartrain Park started winning championships against all-white teams in football and basketball. We took the field knowing we could win, even though the white referees didn't treat us all equally. Whenever there was an opportunity, they would help the white team. We were taught to control our emotions, not to be suckered into a fight. All those lessons stayed with us." Nearly all the children living there attended the public elementary school in The Park, and a few went on to Isidore Newman, the highly regarded integrated private school, or Saint Augustine, the preeminent Black Catholic high school.

Pontchartrain Park is such an incredible success that it is hard to appreciate just how difficult it was to achieve. The period between 1949 and 1955 was still a time of staunch segregation. Separate but equal was the best possible standard to be hoped for. Just as with his dedication to the creation of the nearby Dillard University, it is not hard to understand why Edgar was so committed to making this park and neighborhood happen and why Edith was an enthusiastic supporter, both philosophically and financially. Edgar was clearly a political animal, and he had staked his reputation and financial support on Morrison and his anticorruption agenda. But Edgar exhibited a commitment that went above and beyond politics. The two projects—the park and the housing—were both very complex. But these were just the kind of challenges that Edith and Edgar were committed to tackle.

2

BEHIND THE MASQUE

Edgar's Hometown

There is a magic to New Orleans that rarely disappoints the expectant visitor. The historic French Quarter may be the most famous neighborhood in the country. Filled with centuries-old low-rise buildings not found elsewhere in the United States, the Quarter reflects French, Spanish, and Caribbean influences. Wrought-iron balconies, decorative ironwork, walled courtyards, and high-pitched roofs adorn vibrantly colored buildings. With its eighteenth-century ambience and mostly nineteenth-century buildings, the Quarter for most visitors feels like a foreign neighborhood.

Long filled with cultural delights, a special brand of jazz, and some of the best food imaginable, it has been a draw for all kinds of people seeking a respite from the sameness of everyday life. "And yet," as Gwen Thompkins has written, "in the nineteenth and twentieth centuries people also came to the city for the opera and shopping and theater . . . and a bevy of other delights."[1]

A favored image of New Orleans is the crescent, a reference to the inside curve of the Mississippi River where the original city—the French Quarter—was established. Thus, New Orleans is the Crescent City. This image explains the geography of the city: its crazy quilt of boundaries and mind-spinning grid of streets with no north–south or east–west logic. The street grid, spared the worst of urban renewal destruction, sits between the river and Lake Pontchartrain and is shaped by them. As author Frederick Starr, a veritable walking encyclopedia of New Orleans history and culture, wrote: "Because of the bend in the river, the entire grid is skewed. Hence, in a bizarre tribute to non-Euclidean geometry, parallel lines can meet in New Orleans. Which accounts for the fact that it is easy to become completely disoriented in the Crescent City, both literally and figuratively."[2] Even native New Orleanians can get lost after one wrong turn.

But there is another image, one that depicts the fundamental nature of New Orleans and confounds both natives and visitors. The image is the masque.

During Mardi Gras, masques are ubiquitous, decorating its balls, parties, parades, and even its parade watchers lining the streets. They obscure the personalities and even the gender of the individuals wearing them. Even the houses are masqued, with the exterior fronts often getting fresh paint while the side walls are left alone. So, too, is much of New Orleans hidden behind a masque, which is often colorful and beautiful but is most effective at hiding all that lies behind. The city's power centers, both social and political, are obscured. It is difficult to figure out who is pulling the strings, who is making certain actions happen. And even though the basic network of power brokers can be somewhat brought to light by scrutinizing the overlapping memberships of key political and quasi-governmental organizations, the innermost sanctum of power resides in the clubs: the Pickwick, Louisiana, and Boston. In New Orleans, it has been this way since long before Edgar's time.

Criteria for club membership are not made public, but one thing is certain. To repeat a comment told to me by a socially well-placed New Orleans architect years ago, "It's not how much money you have but who your daddy was and who his daddy was." In this respect, New Orleans is unusual. As Starr noted, "The impact of money there is moderated by the fact that New Orleans, unlike Houston or Dallas, was a major city even before the oil boom hit: its social hierarchies were already solidly in place."[3] As a consequence, the self-important oil money crowd was never able to take over and reign supreme.

As in an armed camp, the machinations among club members remain unknown to outsiders. The Boston Club is the pinnacle of power. Even though membership in the prominent Mardi Gras krewes means a lot socially, being in the right club means everything—socially, financially, and politically. Calvin Trillin noted in a *New Yorker* article that "exclusion from business-men's clubs means exclusion from most of the important decision-making in the city."[4]

There is never any doubt that within the clubs' walls are "the rooms where it happens," to quote from the hip-hop musical *Hamilton*. It was in those inner sanctums that the overturning of post–Civil War Reconstruction was planned in the late nineteenth century. "Secrecy was a key ingredient," wrote Marilee Eaves in *Singing Out Loud: A Memoir of an Ex-Mardi Gras Queen*, "symbolized by wearing of costumes and disguises, the hierarchy of invitations, the identity of kings, and the behind the scenes plotting that went on."[5]

By the twentieth century, according to author and historian John Barry:

> The only thing that had changed was the role of the Jews. The first Rex was Jewish. Jews belonged to the Country Club and the Southern Yacht Club, the second oldest in the country. The most socially prominent law firms and banks had Jewish partners and board members, and Jews and gentiles socialized.
>
> Yet Jews occupied a complex never-never land in New Orleans society. By the 1920s the clubs and Carnival excluded Jews, except for a few token members of Rex (but Jews were never in the royal court). The exclusion was gradual, beginning in the late 1800s and early 1900s as immigrants from eastern and southern Europe, including Hasidic Jews, seemed to threaten the nation's ethnic and racial identity. New Orleans, despite its Catholic heritage, showed a violent bias against Italian immigrants. Immigrant Jews were far more foreign; even native New Orleans Jews discriminated against them. Immigrant Sam Zemurray became president of the United Fruit Company and built one of the greatest mansions on St. Charles Avenue but was never accepted into the elite all-Jewish Harmony Club because, says the daughter of one of the city's oldest and wealthiest Jewish families, "he spoke with an accent."[6]

Perhaps in no other major American city was the social and economic price of standing up to the Establishment so high. The Uptown crowd took their status and social mores very seriously. If you were one of them, you knew what was permissible and expected, and you dared not venture off the clear path. Before he married Edith, Edgar showed no sign of wanting to do so.

The Immigrant Past

Edgar Bloom Stern was born in 1886, the middle of three children, into this socially stratified world. With his dark hair, dark eyes, and broad shoulders, the "handsome devil" Edgar was known for his good humor and skill at tennis. He favored spats and a walking cane. He enjoyed shopping for neckties and reportedly owned two hundred. He loved Cuban cigars and a martini before dinner. And even though the Jews of New Orleans had their own hierarchy, it did not compare in strength to that which made New Orleans stand out in the country. All Jews were outsiders. Socially, there was no place for them. The business world was a different story. Some Jews, like Edgar and his father before him, were so successful that they were accepted—up to a point.

In many ways, Edith and Edgar had similar backgrounds. The Stern family was originally from Bavaria and then moved to Liverpool. In fact, most of the German Jews who emigrated to New Orleans in the nineteenth century came originally from Bavaria and Alsace. Hasia Diner, who has written several books on the Jews of this period, noted, "Jewish population growth, urbanization and industrialization, and the pernicious spell of racially inflected nationalism, might have sufficed as forces to propel outward the migration of millions of Jews who emigrated from Europe . . . [but] positive forces pulled them to places where they thrived, and the aspirations of their migration became fulfilled."[7] Jews were not just fleeing the various tribulations of their home country but were also drawn to areas of the world that offered economic opportunity. For the Stern family, the United States and its sources of cotton defined that opportunity.[8]

In 1871, Edgar's father Maurice (pronounced "Morris") was sent at age sixteen from Liverpool to New Orleans, where he was to represent the Stern brothers who owned a shirt-making company in that English city.[9] Maurice, once he was established in New Orleans, was to broker bales of cotton coming down the Mississippi River from Memphis to send to Liverpool, where they would be processed and made into clothing. With the help of a third cousin, Bernard Newgas, he went to work for Lehman, Newgas & Company Cotton Brokers, which had been founded six years earlier. In 1882, after Newgas returned to England, Maurice purchased his shares of the business and became a formidable leader in the cotton business.

Maurice apparently learned English by attending services at Temple Sinai, a Reform synagogue where Rabbi James Koppel Gutheim delivered bilingual sermons, alternating between German and English. There he met Hannah Bloom (1859–1940), a New Orleans native. The Blooms had emigrated from

Bavaria to New Orleans before the Civil War and were active in synagogue, civic, and philanthropic life.

Financial Success and Social Advancement

"Maurice Stern's cotton business flourished at a time when New Orleans's commercial future was increasingly uncertain," historian Walter Stern, grandnephew of Edgar and Edith, wrote. "Tenant farmers and sharecroppers replaced enslaved Blacks as the South's agricultural labor force, and the rural country stores cut into the middleman role that New Orleans's cotton factors had traditionally played in supplying planters and selling their crops."[10] Yet Maurice's business remained strong. He seemed to be in the right place at the right time. Geographer and Tulane professor Richard Campanella wrote, "Nineteenth-century New Orleans was a city of middlemen. Here, financiers, agents, factors, traders, merchants and lawyers stewarded the flow of commodities between hinterland and foreland, and each profession had legions of supporters and enablers. Great wealth accumulated in the process, but so did risk—which created an opportunity for yet another profession: actuaries."[11]

The Sterns lived in an imposing 1880s Romanesque Revival house taking up half a city block on St. Charles Avenue in Uptown. Maurice's success brought him into the upper echelons of the city's business world: he became a director of the prominent Whitney Bank and of the New Orleans Cotton Exchange, as well as a member of multiple civic and business associations. He enjoyed memberships in the Harmony Club (Jewish) and Audubon Golf and Oakland Country Clubs. He also served in leadership positions in Jewish organizations—the Touro Infirmary (hospital), the American Jewish Committee, and Hebrew Union College (the Reform rabbinical seminary in Cincinnati)—and was president of Temple Sinai.

Much of the New Orleans German Jewish community of that generation belonged to Temple Sinai, along with the Sterns. The elder Sterns did not attend worship services frequently but were involved in other ways with the temple. Hannah Bloom Stern was one of two women to serve on the board of trustees, long before women commonly held such positions. She was also a board member of Kingsley House, a settlement house, and of the Sylvania

Williams Community Center serving the Black community.[12] She was active in the National Council of Jewish Women and the Red Cross and a major force in the founding of the Louisiana Symphony Orchestra. The pattern was set for their progeny—Solomon Walter, Edgar Bloom, and Sara May Lillian.

Edgar attended public schools in New Orleans and went to Tulane for his first year of college. He transferred to Harvard in 1903, following his best friend Montefiore (Monte) Mordecai Lemann, who would develop an estimable career in the law and would count among his friends Supreme Court Justices Felix Frankfurter and Edward Douglass White, as well as Judge Learned Hand. Edgar continued to do well at Harvard, as he had done at Tulane, and was inducted into Phi Beta Kappa. He wrote home almost daily, hoping his parents would keep the letters as his diary. In one businesslike letter that expressed his wish not "to be extravagant," he explained in detail his expenses to demonstrate why his monthly allowance of $1,000 needed to be increased to $1,300.[13]

Most letters breezily recounted his daily life, reporting regularly on the good grades he was earning. On one occasion, he included a sample swatch of the wallpaper he had chosen for his sitting room. Perhaps it was extravagant, he wrote, but he gave his mother complete credit for his good taste. He apparently had a series of girlfriends—including, reportedly, author Dorothy Parker, who in January 1920 sent him a note thanking him for a gift of perfume at New Year's. In fact, he received many such notes from women friends, thanking him for candy or flowers or "daring" him to come for a "cozy" dinner. He occasionally attended the theater, and apparently for one hour on one evening a week, he devoted himself to unspecified philanthropic interests.

In 1907, Edgar decided to compete for a spot as an undergraduate commencement speaker. He wrote home to report that he had submitted a talk billed as "a defense of the recent disenfranchising amendments to Southern state constitutions." These were the amendments that southern states were adopting during the 1890s that effectively nullified the US Constitution's Fifteenth Amendment giving Black men the right to vote after the Civil War. As Walter Stern, grandnephew of Edgar, noted:

> In his speech, Edgar presented the tortured, if not altogether original, argument that disenfranchising poor and illiterate blacks actually helped

> African Americans by encouraging them to work harder and become better educated in order to regain their voting rights. He argued that white Southerners had passed their disenfranchising amendments not out of "mere race prejudice" but in order "to emancipate themselves from [the] fraud and lawlessness" that they claimed was rampant during Reconstruction, when blacks both voted and held elective office. "This is not a movement of reaction," Edgar concluded, "it is a movement of progress."[14]

Such a view would have been totally in keeping with the New Orleans of Edgar's day. Racism was part of the city's DNA. Yet, twenty years later, Edgar would lead the herculean effort to establish Dillard University for Black students. He would also be soliciting support, as a trustee of the Rosenwald Fund, for schools of higher learning for Black students throughout the South.

Complicated Attitudes Toward Race

Race-related attitudes and actions in both the Rosenwald and Stern families were nuanced and sometimes inconsistent. As Walter Stern pointed out, Edgar took an early interest in Black education, read Booker T. Washington's *Up from Slavery* even before his future father-in-law Julius Rosenwald did, and embraced the idea that industrial education was appropriate for young Black people. Yet, even though Edgar called for increased public spending on Black education, rather than depending on charitable contributions, he did not seem to question or challenge the racial status quo.[15] After all, he was in the cotton trading business that historically was totally dependent first on slavery and then on sharecropping labor, as was the entire economy of the South. Many influences, however, would shape Edgar in the next twenty years that would dramatically draw him away from being a youthful apologist for segregation.

After graduating from Harvard, instead of going to law school as originally planned, Edgar joined his father's business, where his older brother already worked. By the time Edgar married Edith in 1921, he was, at age thirty-five, an eminently successful businessman and a well-established leader in the city's business community. He had become a member of the Orleans

Parish School Board and a director of Charity Hospital in 1912 and then a board member of the New Orleans Public Belt Railroad and the Community Chest (precursor of United Way), as well as a captain in the US Army during World War I. In 1917, he became a director of the Federal Reserve Bank of Atlanta and of the New Orleans branch of the Federal Reserve Bank. Prestigious affiliations like these were unusual for New Orleans Jews: Edgar was clearly considered a civic leader.

That Edgar was seen as a mover and shaker and had achieved some social standing was confirmed when he was invited to join the prestigious Boston Club, the most socially restricted club in the city. As mentioned earlier, he asked whether that offer could include his best friend, Monte Lemann. When the response was no, Edgar declined the invitation. Charles Stern, Edgar's grandnephew and Maurice's grandson, confirmed this. "My grandfather, Edgar and Monte had lunch together every single day," Charles said in a 2021 phone conversation. "There was no way that Edgar was going to give up that tradition for club membership."

At that time in New Orleans, during the workday Jews mingled or did business with non-Jews, many of whom were partners in their firms. But at lunchtime, everything changed. Non-Jews all went to their clubs; Jews went to restaurants. Often, they had a regular table. Dining at one of those historic eateries was an important New Orleans ritual. Edgar's unwillingness to give up his regular lunch partner to join the Boston Club made total sense.

Several of the high-end restaurants of that time still exist, with all their splendor and formality intact. Famous for its shrimp remoulade, grilled fresh fish with meunière sauce, and bread pudding, Galatoire's retains all its elegance at its original location on a seedy corner of Bourbon Street. Regulars have their own waiter who knows what they like, provides special service, and earns a Christmas gift each year. Having that special waiter separates the locals from the out-of-town visitor—and it matters. With its white tablecloths and elegant crystal, Galatoire's guarantees its guests the feeling of intimacy and importance. Other historic restaurants also remain, longtime favorites of both the local lunch and dinner crowds.

No matter the degree of Edgar's or other Jews' success and prominence, they remained outsiders when it came to the status markers that counted. Despite some friendships and business relationships between Jews and non-

Jews, there were clear social lines not to be crossed, particularly related to Carnival and everything that came with it—the parties, parade krewes, clubs, and balls. A commonly heard observation was that Jews left town during Mardi Gras to go skiing, so as not to embarrass their socially prominent non-Jewish friends who could not invite them to their balls and parties. Certainly, Edith and Edgar left, report family members, although not to go skiing.

The New Orleans Economy Still Strong—for a While

Despite its closed society, New Orleans after World War I had many strengths that helped it be successful. By the post–World War II era, these would be diminished in ways unique to this singular southern city.

With its deep French and Spanish influences, its commanding role as the birthplace of jazz, and its one-time position as the capital of King Cotton, New Orleans possessed a character unlike that of any other American city. The state's preeminence in sugar, cotton, rice, coffee, timber, and a growing oil industry dominated by Standard Oil was holding strong. This was a carryover from the days before the Civil War when New Orleans was the richest city in the country and before the new Erie Canal in New York began drawing away trade business. In the 1920s, when Edith first arrived, it was still the wealthiest city in the South. The strength of its banks and other financial businesses far exceeded those of Dallas, its closest competitor. It was more prosperous than Houston, Atlanta, Memphis, or Birmingham. And its Cotton Exchange remained one of the three most important in the world.

The port was second only to New York. Good wages helped both Black and white families inch toward prosperity. The banana import business was dominant, but all manner of raw materials passed through, only to be manufactured elsewhere into an array of products. Yet the word "elsewhere" is key to understanding New Orleans's subsequent economic decline. As one observer noted, "The industrialization in the country of the 1920s passed New Orleans by." Coffee and some southern spices were processed locally, but little else. New Orleans did not "make" things or add value to goods that passed through its port in any competitive way; its primary business activity was in the management of wealth and in loaning and controlling money. One most consequential exception was Higgins Boats, which manufactured the landing craft used extensively in World War II, particularly in the Normandy invasion. The Higgins Boat was promoted as "the boat that won the war."

Louisiana was still predominantly rural. Poverty and illiteracy were extensive, both conditions that the state has yet to fully confront. But the entrenched ruling hierarchy, rooted in New Orleans, remained "smug and self-satisfied" with this "feudal state," writes T. Harry Williams.[16] In 2025, the state still clings to a shameful minimum hourly wage of $7.25 and retains its fiercely anti-union, right-to-work commitment. No wonder Louisiana remains one of the poorest states in the nation. There has been little commitment to create the kind of opportunities for advancement, entrepreneurship, or self-sufficiency for its poor and Black populations. It seems as if New Orleans is satisfied with educating its children to serve as low-paid service workers in the tourist industry. This failure of government underscores, as we will see, the value and importance of what Edith and Edgar Stern and both the Rosenwald and Stern Funds accomplished during critical decades of the twentieth century. They provided all manner of resources and opportunities for Black citizens that the government was unwilling to give.

The Era of Huey Long and Sam Zemurray

Two formidable personalities had a major impact on New Orleans and beyond during the 1920s and 1930s. One was Huey Long, a Louisiana-born renowned demagogue who rose to become Louisiana's governor and then US senator; the other was Samuel Zemurray, a poor, Russian-born Jewish immigrant. The Sterns consistently opposed Long, the populist and sometimes vilified politician, who had presidential aspirations. Zemurray, dubbed the "Banana Man," transformed the banana from a throwaway item to a desired fruit by building a global company for its import and sales. That company dominated the New Orleans port and changed the geography and politics of Central America. A ruthless businessman who became one of the richest men in the United States, Zemurray was one of the largest donors to Tulane University when Edgar was on its board but was not in the Sterns' social circle.

Huey Long rose to power as a champion of the poor while ruling in a corrupt and dictatorial manner. "He excited people and he excited emotions, arousing in his relatively short but explosive career every feeling in the political spectrum—amazement and admiration, disbelief and disgust, love and hatred, and, with many individuals, cold apprehension," noted T. Harry Williams in his biography *Huey Long.*[17] The poor and working middle class loved the free textbooks, paved roads, and new bridges that he provided. The elites did not; their control of the state had been unchallenged until 1924, when Long emerged on the scene. "Crude, coarse and common," Long raged against the moneyed class, aimed to seize control from big corporations, and used all sorts of mechanisms to weaken the deep-rooted control of the mostly New Orleans–based elite.

With Long's election, the state's power center shifted away from New Orleans. According to Liva Baker, "The fundamentalist rural Protestant north, overwhelmingly segregationist, had seized control from the French-flavored, mellower Catholic south, urban and more racially tolerant, and race had replaced economics as the major political issue. This last trend persisted in Louisiana politics through the 1960s, 1970s, and 1980s."[18]

Long vilified the business and political establishment centered in New Orleans, and the elite hated him back. To this day, members of the New Orleans establishment roll their eyes at the mention of his name. They oppose anything that might derive from, be the result of, or is similar to a Huey Long initiative from decades ago. And yet without Huey Long there would have been no Charity Hospital, a vital healthcare resource for Black and white residents of New Orleans, and no social services for the poor of the state. He may have been crude, but he was not always wrong: he represented the best and worst of populism.

Zemurray's influence in many ways went beyond his transformative impact on Central America. A lifelong outsider, he was an Ashkenazic Jew from Eastern Europe with a heavy accent; he had none of the refined, "fitting in" personality of the dominant members of the New Orleans Jewish community, who came from Western Europe. He was looked down on as crass and rough around the edges.

Many East European Jewish immigrants arrived with an attachment to traditional religious customs and the Yiddish language. A small observant community grew up around South Rampart and Dryades Streets, where there were Jewish-owned general stores and a kosher bakery, butcher, and delicatessen. In contrast, most of New Orleans's Jews had long ago left behind traditional rituals, foods, and social attitudes.

At that time, the Jewish community in the city was small, totaling perhaps eight thousand or 1 percent of the population.[19] But more than most Jewish communities around the country, Jews in New Orleans had turned assimilation into a high art, bringing with it substantial numbers of intermarriages. For many, it was about "fitting in," and if that meant turning one's back on their Jewish heritage, so be it. "Earlier arriving German Jews, who had already successfully assimilated, did not want hordes of their more traditional coreligionists to jeopardize the gains the older group had achieved."[20] The Reform denomination thrived in New Orleans: "In no other major American city was Reform Judaism so dominant as in New Orleans. Comprised of old-line families, mainly German and French, who had long since adapted to the city's mores, this outward-looking community cared less for preserving a separate Jewish identity than achieving social acceptance in the wider world."[21]

Assimilation had worked well for the community, especially for the men who, like Edgar, had achieved high levels of success in the business community. Acceptance into Mardi Gras society still eluded them for the most part, but their standing was secure in the public and private business worlds. Owning large downtown department stores and brokerage businesses, serving in high positions in prestigious law firms, being members of business societies, and holding coveted seats on hospital and university boards, this community was not about to let the East European and Russian Jews like Zemurray muddy the social status waters. Rich Cohen, who wrote a biography of Zemurray, notes, "Erudite and refined, assimilated to the point of being unrecognizable, they formed a closed society that traced its roots in the city back a hundred years or more. These men were protective of their position, which, many feared, would be jeopardized by men like Zemurray. In this way, Zemurray was doubly rejected: turned away from the clubs of the German Jews just as decisively as he was turned away from the clubs of the Catholics and Protestants."[22]

The influx of refugees from the ravages of pogroms in Eastern Europe would change the face of many American Jewish communities. New Orleans Jews perhaps understood well the sentiment of the wealthy New York banker

Jacob Schiff, who saw the refugees flooding his city and said "enough." At one point, he engineered the diversion of these immigrants from New York City to Galveston; from there, scores of Polish and Russian Jews set out to settle in western cities. It is important to note, however, that Schiff's city of New York had already welcomed thousands of those refugees.

Few people today in New Orleans speak of Zemurray's philanthropy, but in his later years, his quiet generosity helped fund the birth of the State of Israel. In the 1920s he had met Chaim Weizmann, an early Zionist leader and later the first president of Israel, and they became friends. Zemurray's donations were used to buy land for early settlements, support the Zionist pioneers, plant farms, and secure boats to transport refugees from Europe to what was then Palestine. His contributions rescued thousands of those Jewish Holocaust survivors after the war who were stranded in displaced camps, enabling them to sneak into Palestine while nearly every country was denying them entry. Zemurray was one of the funders of the *Exodus,* the storied ship that took Jewish refugees from displaced camps to Palestine, landing there despite the British blockade. He even persuaded the oppressive dictator General Rafael Trujillo to accept a few hundred survivors in the Dominican Republic.

Zemurray also helped engineer approval of the 1948 UN resolution calling for the creation of the State of Israel. Because of his banana ventures, Zemurray wielded great power in Central America. He reportedly persuaded enough countries to approve that UN resolution to carry the vote.[23]

His philanthropy also benefited the New Orleans community. His contribution of more than $1 million to Tulane launched the university's Latin America Studies program, funded construction of several campus buildings bearing the names of members of his family, and endowed professorships. He also funded the establishment of a clinic for troubled children in New Orleans and the city's first hospital for Black women; when Zemurray died on November 30, 1961, he left half his estimated $30 million fortune to Touro Infirmary. He also created a Radcliffe professorship for women and funded the first school for the advanced study of agriculture in Central America.

Interestingly and somewhat inexplicably, reports Peter Chapman, "No reference books on Jewry in the US South mentioned him and his role in US entrepreneurship. Maybe he preferred it this way. He wore 'no conspicuous prominence on his sleeve,' the rabbi of the New Orleans synagogue he attended later recalled."[24]

One did not need the opposition to Huey Long's tenure to recognize that the ruling hierarchy was resistant to the kind of gradual reform found elsewhere in the country. Rule by the elite was a long tradition in New Orleans, often attributed to its French and Spanish roots. A high tolerance for corruption in the state and the city has been attributed to that tradition as well. Reconstruction saw the first meaningful challenge to this social structure, as "carpetbaggers" came down from the North and had the audacity to cooperate with Black citizens. Reconstruction was an outrage to the ruling class for many reasons, but seeing Black men exert power and serve in the state legislature may have been the most enraging.

The Supreme Court Enforces Segregation

For Black citizens, everything took a dramatic turn for the worse with the Supreme Court's *Plessy v. Ferguson* decision in 1896 upholding the constitutionality of racial segregation laws for public facilities and, most importantly, for schools. As long as facilities were "separate but equal," racial segregation was permissible, according to the Court decision. Homer Plessy was a light-skinned Creole; the term "Creole" has multiple meanings but in this sense refers to those of mixed African and European ancestry. Plessy had been asked to challenge the separate train car rule by the group bringing the court case, the Citizens' Committee to Test the Constitutionality of the Separate Car Law. He refused the conductor's order to move to the car for Black riders and was thrown off the train. According to one scholar, "The railroads had agreed to participate in the ruse, eager to settle the constitutional question before spending a lot of money on extra cars."[25]

Although Plessy's action was intended to challenge the constitutionality of segregration, the Supreme Court decision had the opposite effect. It legitimized and extended Jim Crow laws and customs. Literacy tests, poll taxes, proof of land ownership, and other methods of intimidation guaranteed a precipitous drop in the number of Black voters. The Plessy decision was in effect until overturned by the 1954 Supreme Court decision, *Brown v. Board of Education.*

In the late nineteenth and early twentieth centuries, as Adam Fairclough writes in his definitive book on the history of civil rights in Louisiana, *Race and Democracy*, "Lynching was a fact of everyday life and the edifice of white supremacy [was] impregnable. To protest meant risking life and limb."[26] By 1920 white supremacy was at its height, and the Ku Klux Klan was reorganizing and growing.

The KKK had been formed right after the Civil War, led by Major General Nathanial Bedford Forrest, to intimidate southern Blacks from voting and exercising other civil rights. South Louisiana—New Orleans in particular—was a Catholic stronghold in the predominantly Protestant South. The Catholic Church's stiff opposition to the KKK somewhat moderated its activities. There were somewhat fewer lynchings in Louisiana, and the KKK "never attained the degree of political influence in Louisiana as in other states. . . . Race relations were harsh but not as [bad] as Alabama and Mississippi," notes Fairclough.[27] From 1882 to 1938, Fairclough writes, an estimated 4,673 lynchings took place across the United States. Of that number, at least 389 occurred in Louisiana, of which 333 were committed against African Americans; only Georgia, Mississippi, and Texas witnessed more lynchings during that time.

It was not until the 1920s and 1930s that Black protests began in earnest. Court actions were brought primarily by A. P. Tureaud, a Black Creole lawyer who headed the New Orleans office of the NAACP and worked with future Supreme Court Justice Thurgood Marshall, who was based at the NAACP main office in New York. Because Black citizens had no political leverage, the courts were their only recourse. Tureaud successfully fought the city's segregated housing ordinance. The city nevertheless became increasingly segregated with the building of public housing projects in the 1930s, some designated for whites and some for Blacks.

As Fairclough notes, "NAACP's pioneering work in the courts eventually [became] the backbone of the more celebrated phase of the civil rights struggle."[28] With its advocacy efforts bearing fruit—getting Black police officers hired; equalizing Black and white teacher salaries; integrating state colleges, buses, and parks; and registering Black voters—the NAACP was moving the needle toward public school integration in small increments: it was pushing the limits of the time's possibilities. The decades of the 1920s and 1930s were the "prehistory" of the civil rights movement, what the Black leader Bayard Rustin called the "classical period" of the later movement. It was a time when Black activists and white sympathizers were beginning to work together. Edgar and Edith must have been aware of the actions of white segregationists and the KKK; all manner of racist and antisemitic epitaphs were scrawled on the entrance gates of Longue Vue. They were neither immune to nor intimidated by the inescapable hatred.

Unplanned Integration in a Segregated City

Even though segregation was entrenched at this time, New Orleans had its own form of modest integration: one might call it "relaxed segregation." Fairclough writes:

> The Crescent City was a world unto itself, and its lazy, hedonistic culture seemed to discourage extreme racism. During the annual ritual of Carnival, for example, both races abandoned themselves to good-natured exhibitionism; white and black spectators crowded the sidewalks together, yelling "Throw me something, mister!" with equal demented fervor to the masked figures on the passing floats. The city also had a relatively low level of housing segregation: most blacks and whites lived in mixed neighborhoods, sometimes in adjacent sides of "double shotgun" houses. Many white families, moreover, employed black cooks and nurses, who inhabited small wooden "shotguns" located on side streets close by the prestigious avenues and boulevards.[29]

Each city's neighborhood had its own social identity, even if some working-class Black families were found scattered throughout. Downriver from the French Quarter were the older neighborhoods of the Marigny and Bywater, their modest shotgun cottages—erected by Creole builders—lined tightly one next to the other. Ablaze in bright blues, sharp greens, and yellows, many with three-color paint jobs, the shotguns and Creole cottages were direct imports from the Caribbean. In those homes in the 1920s lived working-class whites and Blacks employed at the port, the sugar and timber mills, and slaughterhouses. In fact, there were integrated workforces in various sectors of port activity.

Uptown above Canal Street, neighborhoods evolved along the Mississippi River, gaining in wealth and status as they moved upriver until reaching the wealthy enclave of the Garden District. Classic white mansions with galleries, gables, gardens, and occasional turrets were situated on oak tree–lined streets. Bordered by the river on one side and St. Charles Avenue on the other, this was the neighborhood inhabited by the city's elite. The feeling of exclusivity was everywhere and was simply part of Edgar's world.

St. Charles Avenue Reflects the Difference

Everything about New Orleans was and is different from every other American city, which made every difference about Edith stand out more. Even its grand avenue, St. Charles Avenue, where Edgar grew up and Edith and Edgar first lived, has a different character than those that define other cities such as Fifth Avenue in Manhattan, Euclid in Cleveland, or Michigan Avenue in Chicago. The first streetcar line in the United States ran along St. Charles Avenue, and it is one of the handful of surviving trolley lines today.[30]

In many ways, St. Charles has come to define the residential character of New Orleans just as the French Quarter defines its entertainment side. And even though its four miles of stately homes mixed in with occasional churches, synagogues, schools, civic structures, and broad-limbed live oak trees became—mostly in the upper end—a "showcase for the affluent," the size and grandeur of those homes did not match the extravagance found on other grand avenues, and the street had more of a mix of uses than similar ones in other cities.

St. Charles Avenue's identity is predominantly that of the high design of classic New Orleans mansions, with their porches, columns, balconies, and individualized windows. Yet, no officially imposed standards defined its streetscape; no guidelines shaped its architecture. In fact, the mostly Black craftsmen who built the houses had as much influence on their shape and appeal as any architect. And yet it feels like an overall harmonious streetscape.

According to one book on the subject, "St. Charles's character was created not by governmental action from above but through the direct action of its wealthy citizens, many of them Jews, who followed one another up the avenue as the New Orleans and national economy expanded in the late nineteenth century."[31] This was the era of economic expansion in which early Sephardic and German Jews participated and coexisted without apparent tension. The two leading synagogues—Temple Sinai and Touro Synagogue—were located on St. Charles, along with the homes of prosperous Jews, such as the Lemanns, Hernsheims, Godchauxs, and Isaacs. Also present on the avenue are such educational institutions as Tulane and Loyola Universities and the Catholic girls' school, Academy of the Sacred Heart. St. Charles was where Edith and Edgar lived in a rental house after they wed. But Edith never felt she belonged there, and they did not stay very long.

New Orleans was and remains a complicated city to get to know. As in many cities, different groups dominate different neighborhoods. But New Orleans is almost like two cities: the Vieux Carré or French Quarter, and everywhere else. Uptown along St. Charles Avenue, the Garden District was the favored neighborhood of the moneyed class. In the 1950s, when some wealthy women moved from Uptown into the Quarter, their message was loud and clear: the French Quarter was as historic as any neighborhood in America, and its architectural treasures were not to be messed with. This occurred in an early phase of the historic preservation movement.

However, in the 1920s, when Edgar first brought Edith to this unique city, the Quarter was a decaying neighborhood. Upscale families had moved out and up along nearby Esplanade Avenue. Working-class families and new, mostly Italian immigrants took their place. It was also a Bohemian refuge characterized by cheap rents, unbridled fun, and coffeehouse gathering spots. The French Quarter represented the world of jazz, nightlife, and culture and was the storied home of artists and writers such as William Faulkner, Sherwood Anderson, and Oliver La Farge. Mixed in with the bawdy and the bars were elegant restaurants including Galatoire's, Antoine's, Arnaud's, and Broussard's.[32] In contrast, Uptown was the world of social distinctions and Mardi Gras balls, or of exclusion from them, and where societal mores were taken seriously. Uptown houses had ballrooms, walls of art, and glittering chandeliers.

Most significantly, Downtown had jazz, first emerging from Congo Square on the edge of the Quarter where both free people of color and enslaved Blacks drummed their inherited African beats. The enslaved were given Sundays off, and Congo Square was where they gathered. The emerging music spread through the adjacent Storyville and South Rampart areas. Where live music played, nightclubs and gaming establishments—and brothels—sprang up. Jazz also was being played in other parts of town, including at the West End on Lake Pontchartrain and in all manner of Creole and Black society clubs in Tremé, located back of the French Quarter. Louis Armstrong grew up nearby and got his musical education in the streets, later becoming the national representative of New Orleans jazz. Yet, with all the city's variations, neighborhood distinctions, and blending of varied groups, its social and political life had long been in the hands of that cabal of insiders for whom Edith was as alien as one could be.

A Failed City?

One can start a vigorous debate today in New Orleans over why the city lost its economic luster and standing above other southern metropolitan areas and whether its social stratification had something to do with it. The debate was not popular in Edgar's day, but it emerged as the city started falling behind economically. As Eli Evans wrote in *The Provincials,* a history of southern Jewry:

> The amount of civic energy and money drained off every year from more meaningful pursuits by such a back-breaking planning and financial effort [Mardi Gras] has left the field open to the Jewish community to lead and contribute to the civic organizations that run everything else in town—charities, the opera guild, the symphony, the museums, and organizations like the League of Women Voters. And they have taken up the slack to such an extent that Jews have won the *Times-Picayune* Loving Cup [given by the daily newspaper] for "unselfish service in New Orleans" more than one-third of the number of times since the award was established in 1901.[33]

One of the most articulate expressions of the viewpoint that New Orleans's stratification had everything to do with its descent from the glory days of the 1920s through World War II was given by former City Councilman Frank Friedler Jr., who was Jewish, in a speech delivered in the 1990s at the Wyvern Club and excerpted here:

> I contend that though the prosperous Americans choose to live in the Garden District, they were absorbed into a societal philosophy where parentage was more important than ability. Our society became one of exclusion, not inclusion. Its symbols became memberships in exclusive clubs and of course, Mardi Gras organizations, where the bluest of blue bloods would at least be king for a day. In contra-distinction to this sort of societal growth, the remaining America developed in a meritocracy, where the strongest, the brightest, the hardest workers, became the community leaders—and these values raised the quality of those they picked as political leaders. New Orleans developed a society of exclusion; New America developed a society of inclusion. And the choice has proven to be a very expensive mistake for all of us in this room.[34]

Friedler argued that some individuals were able to escape the impact of these exclusionary policies. Even though the excluded included "'out of town strangers,' Jews, Italians, [and] Blacks," some people—like him and, of course, Edith and Edgar—could still succeed very well. But, unfortunately for the fate of the city, this exclusionary policy in the 1950s–1970s was directed at the executives sent to New Orleans to run major oil and other corporations. They were the ones who decided whether corporate headquarters stayed in New Orleans or went elsewhere. Despite their decision-making power, they were not, Friedler argued, "treated royally," as they should have been. In any other city, they would have been invited into the inner sanctum of the social upper crust. Instead, they were given the cold shoulder, and so they picked up their marbles and moved their operations elsewhere.

This exclusion hindered the development of a broad-based business community, causing New Orleans to lag behind Atlanta, Houston, and Dallas—and even Memphis, Nashville, and Birmingham—in economic development. Added Friedler, "The pie is just smaller here. So, you see, the macro-impact of this policy now threatens the whole community—even the economic security of the 'included.'"

Many local New Orleanians, even though they may recognize the cause, are happy to leave things as they are as the rest of the world moves forward. As one insider said to me, "Thank God we're a failed city." This can be taken in two ways: (1) We like the way the social system does not change, or (2) the slow pace of change has been one of the best ways of protecting the city's historic architecture and cultural differences.

This is the world of New Orleans that Edgar was used to; however, Edith, who grew up in Chicago, had no reservations about disrupting it. Edith and Edgar represented two strains of reform at a time when the status quo remained rigidly entrenched. He was more conservative but was moved to the left, pulled along by her liberal and Progressive-era instincts, both politically and socially. Their relationship was both a marriage and an alliance. Was it possible for two remarkable people to move the city's dial, one with access and one without? How these two Jews together navigated the hot-button issues of the time and moved the dial of reform is the heart of a story that sheds light on the twentieth-century history of New Orleans.

It is difficult to determine in which area of New Orleans life Edith and Edgar had the greatest impact, but surely education was one of them. Indeed, education was the focus of Edith and Edgar's Stern Fund when it was created in 1936. And before the Sterns made their mark, the Rosenwald Fund was already changing the educational landscape for Black students in the South. Clearly, Rosenwald's influence on both Edith and Edgar—his view of philanthropy, his attitude toward Black people, his willingness to break rules—was immense. By the late 1930s Edgar had evolved into a progressive of sorts who still favored maintaining the strict social separation of the races while advancing opportunities for Black people. Edith had moved ahead of him, supporting integration but quietly and inconspicuously.

3

FITTING IN

In sentiment and action, Edith Rosenwald Stern was unmistakably her father's daughter—independent, determined, and unafraid to go where others did not. Julius Rosenwald had a great influence on her, but her actions were all the bolder because she was an activist and philanthropist at a time when women enjoyed few means to act outside the domestic sphere. Women were not even allowed then to open a bank account or take out a mortgage without their father's or husband's signature.

Edith was born in 1895, the same year in which her father first invested in Sears. The middle child of five, she lived with her family in the suburb of Highland Park, just outside Chicago. It took some time before Julius (known within the family as JR) was able to accumulate substantial wealth and all the trappings of affluence became part of her daily life. During her early years, the family was still living modestly, and both parents spent a lot of time at home. That meant that she and her older sister Adele (b. 1892) and brother Lessing (b. 1891) experienced a very different youth from their considerably younger sister Marion (b. 1902) and brother William (b. 1903). Her mother Augusta had more time to spend with the oldest three children. Marion observed—maybe with an edge of resentment—that she had to teach Edith and Adele how to cook and sew—even though by the time she came along, a hired cook and a governess were on staff.[1]

Based on interviews with all five children, Leon Harris's 1979 book, *Merchant Princes,* showed that family life did change with the increase in wealth—except, according to Adele, for her parents' "insistent training in the virtues of thrift." JR often took the streetcar to work, and when they traveled by train, he took a berth rather than the more expensive drawing room, avoiding anything that "smacked of indulgence." Marion recalled:

> That thrift business *was* awful. They were so terribly stingy with us that we had the smallest allowances in our crowd and our friends got sick of treating us. I think it was insane and why we all ended up on the [therapist's] couch. . . . Mother kept a closet full of scraps and old clothes and odds and ends of fur and made our clothes at home from that junk. On my wedding trip I looked appalling in those homemade dresses. But the older children fought for us. Dellie and Edith would say, "Don't do this dress over again," and . . . "if she goes to college give her decent clothes." My parents didn't, so Edith did. She bought me the first pretty clothes I ever owned.[2]

Yet Marion also said this of her father: "Except about thrift, he was easygoing."

As their wealth increased, the family built and moved into a bigger house in Highland Park, "on one of the largest lots in Chicago."[3] (At roughly the same time, Edgar's family moved Uptown on St. Charles Avenue to a Richardsonian Romanesque Revival house built in 1889 and occupying half a city block.) Built in the Prairie style that Chicago is known for, the sizable Rosenwald house had twenty-one rooms, including a ballroom. The grounds spanned two acres, with sunken gardens and flowerbeds, which formed one of the largest private gardens in the Chicago area.

Early on, Edith took an interest in flowers and gardening, something she shared with her mother. Augusta took advantage of the time that hired help and childcare afforded her by taking a class on Shakespearean sonnets, joining a book club, taking music lessons, socializing with women friends, and enjoying opera and theater. She loved books, reading often to her children and serving as a library volunteer. She was also an active suffragette, which must have inspired her daughters.

With extreme wealth came more social engagements, galas, and fundraisers for the parents and less attention paid to the children. Marion, the youngest daughter, noted that it was really Ede' (Edith's nickname) and Adele who raised the younger two. There was, of course, a governess, but according to Marion, JR thought that having one just for Marion and Bill was too extravagant. So, he organized a kindergarten in their ballroom with a teacher and fourteen other children. The group included the Black chauffeur's son, named Renault after one of the Rosenwalds' cars. And there was a butler, but because Augusta had been "put off by the English butlers" of their rich New York friends and did not want her Chicago friends to have a similar reaction, they hired a Japanese butler; she was sure that none of her friends "could find a Japanese forbidding."[4]

Summers were partly spent in the Rosenwalds' bucolic country home in Ravinia, an area thirty-six miles from Chicago. "Ravinia was Paradise—so much freedom, such a beautiful big beach, the ravines to explore," recalled Marion.[5] Ravinia is now known for its summer music festival.

All the children considered their parents to be lively and fun at times. According to Marion, Edith was a serious woman but enjoyed being teased by the children, and Edgar loved jokes. Marion felt that Edith was more like her father than her mother Augusta, who was "a woman of great executive ability" and had "a great interest in philanthropic work and good deeds." Augusta felt very strongly that the children should never flaunt their wealth, as Marion shared with Harris:

> I think that one thing we children each learned from our parents was the importance of the example we set. And I don't mean a snobbish sort of fashion setting like the Warburgs or the Lehmans—just the opposite in fact.
>
> My mother never ceased telling us with pride about the calluses she wore on her hands as a child scrubbing floors and helping to raise her sisters and brothers. And after my father made so much money and they went east, where they were entertained at the feudal estates of the Schiffs and the Strauses outside New York, my mother was more than ever resolved never to become like that, never if she had a country place to have statues or anything else she considered pompous or stiff. Mother was very naïve, but she was a very great lady—very sensitive, in the good sense of being sensitive to the feelings of others and not just her own. And when she built Ravinia, she insisted that it be kept natural, using the ravines and local flowers and only tanbark trails and gravel roads—nothing forbidding.[6]

Summers also meant frequent trips to Europe, not uncommon for moneyed families of that era, even before JR became very wealthy. Nor was it unusual to send a teenage girl to finishing school in Europe. It apparently was not Edith's choice, but she did spend her senior year in high school at a school in Dresden, pining for her fun-filled life at home. "She loathed the drab environment, the regimentation and the unbending, unsmiling teachers in their stiff clothes. She even found the meals monotonous and unimaginative."[7]

Childhood Antics

Awareness of the rapid economic, social, and cultural changes in Chicago permeated the Rosenwald household. "I met the world at my parents' home," Edith remarked. As Marion recalled:

> Sunday dinner was a time for the whole family and anyone who was in Chicago. [It was] a collection of usually very interesting people. I think my parents felt, this was part of our education, and I think they were right. I remember once when a man from Israel [Shmaryahu Levin, a noted Jewish author and Zionist leader] was sitting at the end [of the table] with my parents. The kids were at the other end. For some reason, my sister [Edith] began to imitate the gestures of this gentleman from Israel who spoke with his hands and so she was doing it, silently. All of a sudden, he stopped and his hands were out and so were hers. I'm afraid he looked down the table and saw her and that was a little embarrassing and funny.[8]

Edith was sent to her room. Her gift of mimicry was not always appreciated.

Such dinners were served with all the elegance one would expect at the time; formal table settings, silver ice buckets, and fine linen were on display. But Marion recalled, "What do you suppose these great roasts and fine filets were washed down with? Grape juice! Can you imagine anything more awful! You see father was a teetotaler—no liquor allowed in the house at all. We never questioned what seemed to us a puritanical attitude, but we did manage to tease him about it unmercifully."[9]

Certainly, Julius and Augusta had some quirks that were remembered very clearly by the five children. But as in so many families, the children's memories did not always align. This is not surprising in a family where the two sets of children were so far apart in age.

Activist Women

In the 1920s, women had just gotten the right to vote, were raising their hemlines, and were beginning to find interests outside the home. In Chicago, active women's clubs focused on uplifting the lives of the poor and the immigrant, bringing culture, book clubs, and art museum tours to deprived residents. This was the heyday of the pathbreaking work of Jane Addams, founder of Hull House, which set a pattern for settlement houses everywhere.[10]

Addams, who was also from Illinois, had a privileged upbringing not unlike that of the Rosenwald children. Her father was both a banker and mill owner. It was the cheerless lives of his impoverished mill workers and of their uneducated and unhealthy children that inspired her to embark on a life of helping the poor and deprived. Rosenwald, like other philanthropists of the day, was a big supporter of Addams, and she was apparently a frequent dinner guest at the Rosenwald home. "The adolescent [Rosenwald] girls were riveted to this fascinating visitor, listening as her tales unfolded."[11] But there were a host of other famous guests, including Mrs. Vincent Astor, Theodore Roosevelt, and Pearl Buck.

Edith grew up in a notable era of social activism and political reform. Yet, racism, pervasive and deep, defined Chicago during and after World War I when the Great Migration of southern Black people swelled its Black population. The large numbers of new Black residents were a great shock, and Chicagoans responded with their own version of racial discrimination. There were fewer "For Whites Only" signs than in the South, and some public spaces, like parks, were not off-limits—but discrimination was still oppressive. "Chicago was New Orleans without signs, which itself added to the problem."[12]

Yet, Chicago was still the "Promised Land" to thousands of Black men and women fleeing the South on the Illinois Central Railroad that ran through New Orleans. They were ready to go anywhere the train would take them as long as it was "up north" and far away from southern racism. Louis Armstrong, a native of New Orleans, began his musical innovations there but was unable to perform in an integrated band as he wanted to do. He fled to Chicago in the 1920s for better opportunities; indeed, he first gained national prominence there. Mahalia Jackson, the renowned gospel singer and another New Orleans native, left as well.[13] The South Side of Chicago was primarily populated by emigrés from southern Louisiana.

Chicago was as industrial as any city in the United States, with all the ills that came with it. The golden age of investigative journalism—the muckrakers—was in full swing. Upton Sinclair was writing about inhuman conditions in the meatpacking industry centered in Chicago. Investigative journalist Ida Tarbell exposed the unethical maneuvers of John D. Rockefeller and his Standard Oil Company, as well as the underhanded style of the monopolistic trusts. Ironically, around this time, his son John D. Rockefeller Jr. launched his philanthropy geared to advancing educational opportunities.

The First Marriage

Edith returned from her senior year in Dresden restless and unsettled but as spirited as ever. She quickly married, which may have been a rebellious act.

The "tall, attractive man" who pursued her was Germon F. Sulzberger, whose family owned a substantial meat-packing firm. The Rosenwalds apparently did not approve of him. Yet Edith prevailed, and in 1913, at age eighteen, she got married. The couple set up house in an apartment in New York and went off on a European honeymoon during which, apparently, Edith already felt the first pangs of doubt.

Returning from abroad, Edith studied shorthand and typing so she could be of help as her husband's secretary. It soon became clear, however, that the marriage was doomed, and with great trepidation, she reported this to her parents. Even though divorce was something that just was not done at that time, her parents supported her decision to leave the marriage. They were very concerned, however, about the reaction of JR's mother Gussie, with whom Edith was extremely close. She surprised them all by declaring, "This is the best bad news I ever had."[14] In the unpublished typescript "Autobiography of a House," Edith wrote, "This had a tragic ending. After a few years, he [Germon] finally had to be put in an asylum. At twenty-three she [Edith] started her first girlhood. No Merry Widow had a better time."[15]

Edith happily gave up the New York husband but not the New York life, and a few years later she met a dark, good-looking, and charming Jewish man there. A friend who was staying with her had a date with Edgar but was a little nervous about having him pick her up at Edith's apartment; she had a feeling that he and Edith would connect. She was right. He came, they met, and the attraction between them was immediate and striking. How the friend knew they were right for each other is hard to say. But they were both very attractive, fun-loving, and often the most popular person in the room at any party.

Edith described this incident in "Autobiography of a House," found in the Longue Vue Archives: "He had come for a Harvard-Yale game, inviting a Philadelphia girl who was staying in Edith's apartment. . . . [The girl] invited him up for a drink, although she had sworn she would never let [Edith and Edgar] meet, because she sensed they were made for each other. My, he was handsome as he walked into that room with his most gallant Southern manner."[16]

Their courtship was swift, and one day in April 1921, they took a ride up the Hudson River for a leisurely day in the country. They stopped at a restaurant called Longue Vue. Edgar proposed. Edith said yes. And they knew what to name their future New Orleans residence.

They were anxious to marry, but Edith's divorce had not been finalized long enough for them to get an Illinois marriage license, which was needed so they could be married at the Rosenwalds' Ravinia country home. They had a deadline, however: they had reservations for a honeymoon voyage to Europe soon after. So, JR engaged a private train car going east from Chicago. There were thirty-five guests. When they arrived in Indiana, the car was sidetracked, and the marriage ceremony was performed. Then the train car returned to Ravinia, where the celebration proceeded.

Cracking the Masque

The 1920s were a particularly challenging time for a socially conscious newcomer like Edith to move to New Orleans. Even though they had just gotten the right to vote, women in the city did not seem to be as liberated as Edith was determined to be. Yet New Orleans was not just a sharp contrast to Chicago; it was a sharp contrast to all other American cities. Across the board,

New Orleans remained a closed society, true to its history. And only the "in" people shared that history, whether it was personal, social, political, or even financial. In New Orleans, the "right people" made all the decisions. Their judgments, their observations, their instincts meant everything. Class distinctions were rigidly in place. As a true-blue New Orleanian told me some time ago, "Bloodlines, club affiliation, Mardi Gras Carnival krewe membership, where one attended school (high school, not college), and home address were defining social identifiers." They shaped the city's politics and economy. And in New Orleans, the rules of segregation held firm.

That cabal of insiders had never met anyone like Edith Stern. They had never had to deal with her family's and her determination to advance social values, aid the underserved, and work toward a just world. She was a woman in a city where everything—even the details of the Carnival season—was planned by men. New Orleans was an enigma for Edith that she would have to explore and understand and then both overcome and change.

The Newcomer

Edith Rosenwald Stern had none of the requisite social identifiers. She was a "northerner," an epithet often uttered with the curl of a lip. She came from Chicago, having absorbed and claimed as her own the liberal values that surrounded her. Edith was involved in her father's philanthropic efforts, and she shared his passion for social justice. "I was made aware of the human rights struggle from an early age. The Rosenwalds were always known for their war against segregation," she told New Orleans artist Dawn DeDeaux in a 1978 interview for *Arts Quarterly,* the magazine of the New Orleans Museum of Art (NOMA). Edith was a major funder of NOMA's new wing and auditorium, and played a significant role in the museum's development. She was clearly a liberal, not a common political identity in this longstanding conservative city where many were still licking the wounds of the Civil War—often referred to locally as the "War of Northern Aggression."

Demanding and tough as nails when she wanted to be, Edith was called "The General" by granddaughter Anne Hess and described as "fearless and formidable" by her secretary of thirty years, Vilma Schexnayder.[17] "When she set her mind to something, she couldn't be talked out of it," noted grandson Bill Hess. Bill lived for some years in the guest house at Longue Vue and now lives nearby. And "if she was in a bad mood," says a longtime associate, "get out of her way." As an older woman, she stomped her cane when angry.

According to grandchildren Anne and Bill, Edith was "hyper-critical of family"; "she would say, 'Helen [Anne's birth name] dear, you're not smiling, don't walk that way, you're slouching or you're talking too loud.' These [criticisms] often grated on me and, I suspect, also on my cousins." Bill added, "She was merciless to the girls and my mother. Sitting up straight mattered to her." She also was "merciless" to those who would join the family through marriage. "She checked out Susan [Bill's wife] with everyone who knew her." However, Susan told me, "once we were engaged, she was wonderful to my son. She would take him to the toy store and ask him what he wanted. She was a magical great-grandma."

Yet, in many ways, Edith was as properly social as befitted the upper crust. She was always modestly dressed, with her dark hair well coifed. Edith's notions on how one should behave were rooted in the first half of the century. Anne added, "In society, all agree, she was deferential."

Probably the richest woman in New Orleans, Edith was both extraordinarily generous and tightfisted at the same time. She argued with her longtime secretary about a raise but gave a limousine, a Lincoln Town Car, to her chauffeur Isaac toward the end of her life. She also paid for Emma Brown, her cook, to go on a church's tour to Jerusalem, Rome, Egypt, Syria, and Jordan.

She lived for six decades in this southern city, placing herself in the thick of city politics, school desegregation, and cultural life during a time of entrenched racial segregation. In those six decades, Edith Stern helped transform her adopted city. Although often quiet with her philanthropy, she was fierce in her pursuit of social justice. For example, when she escorted her Black staff—twenty or more—in a rented schoolbus to register to vote, people were outraged. Bomb threats and vicious phone calls followed, but she was undaunted. Determination should have been her middle name.

"Formidable" seems to be another description often offered about Edith. She was "intimidating" to others. For Nicholas Lemann—*New Yorker* staff writer, Columbia School of Journalism professor and emeritus dean, and the grandson of Edgar's best friend Monte Lemann—the Sterns "were part of our lives forever." He knew Edith well but not Edgar, who died when Lemann was a young boy. To young Lemann, "Edith was terrifying," he told me in conversation. "So elegant and stylish and she knew everybody. She was so rich, beautifully dressed and she lived in a mansion. New Orleans didn't have anyone as rich as them. They were in a category of one." Lemann recalled Edith's impact on New Orleans culture and the arts; she sustained the survival of the symphonic orchestra and made major donations to NOMA.

Jewishness Through a Social Action Lens

What Lemann did not recall were Edith and Edgar's Jewish-related involvements. Records show their financial contributions supporting the settlement of Palestine and various Jewish organizations, but there is no evidence of their active participation in those organizations. The Sterns, however, were members of Temple Sinai, founded in 1870 in Uptown as the first Reform synagogue in New Orleans; most of its members were German Jews.[18] The family was supportive financially and participated in its various activities, but Temple Sinai was not a major presence in their busy lives. Grandson Bill recalls going to K&B Drugstore every Saturday for ice cream, while their cousins "were dragged to synagogue every week."

The only sign that Longue Vue was a Jewish home was the small mezuzah nailed to the side of the first entry door. A mezuzah, which contains a parchment scroll inscribed with verses from the Torah, is found on the doorways of Jewish homes; it fulfills the biblical commandment to "write the words of God on the gates and doorposts of your house." The Sterns' mezuzah had a decorative silver case inscribed with the initials of Edgar's parents, Maurice and Hannah Stern.

Edith was not only uninterested in religious observance but also seemed to have a limited knowledge of Jewish rituals. Leon Harris described her attitude as "mildly mocking about Jewishness." Edith told him in a 1977 interview, "My father insisted when we were children that we go down to the ghetto in Chicago and serve food to the Jewish orphans. I once raised a great furor there because I 'unkoshered' the kitchen by serving soup and sausage in cups and saucers reserved for milk and cocoa or vice versa, and a rabbi had to be called to 'rekosher' the china. I thought at first I would be punished severely but when I got home, Father laughed about it."[19] Yet Edith's interest in Jewish-related issues and causes was awakened when the family took a trip to Europe and Palestine in 1936 to celebrate their fifteenth wedding anniversary and Edgar's fiftieth birthday. The family traveled together until arriving in Switzerland, where the children were enrolled in boarding school. A house was rented nearby for their governess, Miss Grant. While the children were in school, Edgar and Edith visited family in Austria and Germany, traveled to Poland and Czechoslovakia, and then went on to Palestine.

In Europe, they saw firsthand the early stages of virulent antisemitism and recognized the danger that lay ahead for European Jewry. Edgar kept a detailed diary that he published in a limited edition after returning home. The year before, the Rosenwald siblings had begun to arrange for some of their European relatives to emigrate to the United States, which was still allowed for those who had immediate family members in this country. The siblings reportedly arranged for more than three hundred European Jews to emigrate to America.

Both Edgar and Edith were extremely impressed when they arrived in Palestine and saw the transformation of the land from desert to orchards. They marveled at the gardens in the kibbutzim. Mostly, they were impressed by the dedicated work of the relocated German and East European Jews. These were the "new Jews," as Bill Hess described them.

Before Edith and Edgar became major philanthropists with a focus on New Orleans, they were very generous in supporting the nascent settlement in Palestine. Such support was by no means universal among Jews at the time, religious or not. Edith's brother Lessing, for example, was very involved in the American Council of Judaism that was opposed to the establishment of a Jewish state. Some Jews feared that support of a Jewish state might bring resentment and accusations of dual loyalty.[20]

Years later, in 1973, when Bill was about to marry Susan Okun Aschaffenburg from New York City, he casually mentioned to Edith, "I'm sure we'll find a judge somewhere." Edith reacted forcefully, saying, "If there's no rabbi, I'm not coming." So, Bill and Susan were married in New York City at the St. Regis Hotel by Rabbi Ronald Sobel of Temple Emanu-El, as "Establishment" a Reform rabbi as one could find in Manhattan. It was a small wedding with about twenty guests.

"Jews from New Orleans Are Just Different"

The Sterns' lack of interest in religious observance was shared by many southern Jews—and, for that matter, by some Reform Jews elsewhere in the country, especially in the first half of the twentieth century. But southern Reform Jews were even less traditional than other US Reform Jews. As historian Melissa Fay Greene noted, "Simply, quietly, in a world ruled by Anglo-Saxon Protestants, Southern Jews had laid aside their yarmulkes; forgotten their Hebrew letters; cultivated a taste for shellfish, baked ham, and pork roast; and celebrated Christmas and Easter with their children. Many of the age-old traditions of Judaism had become virtually indecipherable to them."[21]

In the 1960s, a prominent Atlanta rabbi, Dr. David Marx, described how southern Jews should conduct themselves: "We as Jews of the American South, must make a home for ourselves here, in one of the Diaspora's hinterlands. Let us not, therefore, go out of our way to cling to religious anachronisms, thereby making ourselves strange to our neighbors. Let us release our grip on Judaic antiquities, while preserving in our lives, and for our children, the distilled and relevant core of the Jewish faith. Let us make religion a private matter and adapt our public personae to the demands of our region and country."[22] Many southern Jews followed Dr. Marx's advice.

Yet New Orleans Jews have long been considered even less observant than other southern Jews. For example, a Jewish friend of mine from New Orleans told me about one Passover seder held in her mother's home in the 1960s. That year, her mother could not find a shank bone for the traditional seder plate that sits in the middle of the table. The shank bone represents the lamb that was the special sacrifice on the eve of the exodus from Egypt. The blood of the lamb was put on the doorposts of Jewish homes to indicate that they were Jews and were to be spared the plague of killing the firstborn. But no shank bone was to be found, so her mother used a *hambone*. Then at the end of the seder when kids are tasked with finding the hidden matzah and are customarily rewarded with a small prize, her mother instead gave them chocolate *Easter* bunnies.

Bill Hess, who broke with Stern family tradition by becoming more observant, is very involved in national Jewish organizations. When asked to explain how New Orleans Jews are different, Hess, like most Jews interviewed for this book, gave the usual shrug: "All I can tell you is that I often hear at organizational meetings I go to away from New Orleans, 'Jews from New Orleans are just different.'" But then he added, "Look, draw a line of 500 miles around New Orleans and there is just nothing, except maybe Texas, so of course they're on their own and different."

FOOD IS EVERYTHING

An interesting analysis of why New Orleans Jews are different comes from Marcie Cohen Ferris, whose book, *Matzoh Ball Gumbo: Culinary Tales of the Jewish South*, offers fascinating stories of Jewish families throughout the South. Of New Orleans Jews, she notes that they simply cared more about fitting into New Orleans's unique local culture than maintaining their Jewish traditions. It is, after all, difficult to maintain a kosher kitchen in the land of oysters, crawfish, shrimp. and pork.

Food is central to New Orleans culture for every New Orleanian, no matter their background. It is also important to note that only New Orleans saw such a predominant influx in the mid-nineteenth century of French and German Jews from the regions of Alsace and Lorraine and Bavaria, followed by Russian and East European Jews in the late nineteenth century. Add the Acadian, or Cajun, influences, and you have a culture different from other southern cultures. Ferris notes, "Through the foods they ate Jews sought to blend into society, to support business interests in one of the richest economies of the world, and to demonstrate loyalty to the white Creole culture that surrounded them. They avoided associations with Old World religion in their synagogues and at their tables, and as they embraced slavery and other Southern institutions, New Orleans Jews affirmed their allegiance to race, class and place."[23]

A WORLD OF ITS OWN

Peter Wolf was born and raised in New Orleans, moved north for college, and stayed. Many decades later, he moved back. In 2013 he published, *My New Orleans, Gone Away: A Memoir of Loss and Renewal*, which gives an interesting account of growing up Jewish in New Orleans. One of two Jewish kids at Metairie Park Country Day School (class of 1953), Wolf calls New

Orleans Judaism "a particular brand of liberal Judaism." He reluctantly attended confirmation class at Temple Sinai but was not confirmed. He "never disguised his Jewish identity" but said that most Reform New Orleans Jews are really "indifferent to their Jewish roots. The Southern variety of Reform Judaism is a blend, simultaneously assimilated and Jewish." His family did not celebrate Hannukah, but Wolf describes a Christmas party, replete with a well-decorated tree, given by his parents, as being huge, lavish, and attended mostly by Jews, including the Temple Sinai rabbi. "All I knew about Judaism was what I had picked up at two family Passover seders . . . at my aunt's house."[24]

New Husband, New City

Before their marriage, Edgar may have been considered progressive by New Orleans standards. After marrying Edith, his progressivism deepened but never quite matched hers. He joked that he was in the business of giving away his wife's money—the "son-in-law business," he called it. He recognized that he would never have been able to contribute as generously without Edith's fortune. After their marriage, Edgar became a board member of Sears & Roebuck and was put on the Rosenwald Fund Board (Edith was not). He was closely involved in the Stern Fund that he and Edith established in 1936. In fact, it was first called the Edgar B. Stern Fund, despite its corpus being mostly Edith's money from her Sears & Roebuck stock, and Edgar was its president. Eventually it became the Stern Family Fund, with Edith as president.

Together and with a varying group of family members, Edgar and Edith's impact on the city over five decades was transformative. They were the only couple to have both received the prestigious Loving Cup award, given annually by the *New Orleans Times-Picayune* for noteworthy civic contributions, until 1995 when Anne Milling received it, followed in 2008 by her husband, King Milling. Edgar Jr. carried on the tradition of generosity and, after Edgar Sr.'s death in 1959, partnered with Edith particularly on civil rights matters.

As Edith told Leon Harris in a 1977 interview:

> We tried to set a pattern here, Edgar and I. We hoped to change the local way of life, but I think we failed. Among New Orleans men, there

> was simply no tradition of generous giving. Jews usually, but not always, gave more than others, but no one gave seriously. And women gave nothing at all. Southern women are brought up to be decorative not forceful, modest not vital. I must have seemed a monster to them, but if that pattern has been broken here, it's we out-of-town women who have done it.
>
> The focus of the rich here is on Carnival. They're entirely absorbed in Mardi Gras. And Jews are excluded from that, so those who can afford to, find reasons to leave town at Carnival time.[25]
>
> Whatever we've achieved here, we had to do ourselves. When the New Orleans Country Club was organized, we and the Godchauxs and a few other Jews were charter members (unless the Godchauxs are considered Episcopalian rather than Jewish), but the membership never again opened for Jews.[26]

Everyone I interviewed for this book commented on how Edgar and Edith adored each other. Longtime secretary Vilma Schexnayder was scheduled to be interviewed for this book but died days before we could meet. After Vilma's death, her daughter, author Karen Essex, shared Vilma's recollections. "Edith played the traditional wife," Karen said. "She adored Edgar, but Vilma had the impression that Edith was the smarter of the two but that she publicly let him take the lead and the credit."

Early on, Edith seemed to defer to Edgar in various ways, much as she had promised in a letter she wrote to him days before their wedding in effusively romantic language: "I remember once saying what a perfect background I would make for some real man's career, and I feel now I know this real man and nothing can make me happier than to take second place and back him up with all that is in me. And it will be *moral* support this time, Edgar dearest. I am so very proud of you, and if you could only be a woman for five minutes, you would realize that we ask no more of marriage."[27]

Standing Out

As much as the Sterns and New Orleans Jews were different from other southern Jews, Edgar and Edith differed from other New Orleans Jews as well.

In fact, they were also different from most New Orleanians. They had the trappings of New Orleans wealth with their big three-story white mansion situated on eight acres.[28] However, its location, some distance away from any of the upscale neighborhoods of the city, seemed to shout independence from everyone. The sprawling house itself was unlike any other in the city. It was designed so that each side looked like the front of the house with a distinctive design and overlooked a garden. Inside, an eclectic assortment of antique furnishings was placed alongside charming Woolworth knickknacks. Mixing the refined with the kitsch was an Edith specialty.

Edith had a passion for Woolworth; as she told Edgar on their honeymoon, she wished she were a Woolworth heiress, rather than a Sears one. For their honeymoon, Edgar and Edith took a voyage to Europe on a grand, luxurious ocean liner on which were held extravagant balls and formal dinners. One night, they were formally dressed and ready to go to dinner, when Edith shocked Edgar by tossing what he thought was a valuable string of pearls out the cabin window. She laughed and explained they were from Woolworth. "Ede adored Woolworth's," noted her friend Margie Blumenthal. "She wore jewelry, pantyhose, shoes, and God knows what else from the good ol' five-and-dime. It wasn't that she was cheap; she simply loved to roam the aisles, and more often than not turn up with a useful and attractive product."[29]

Yet Edith did appreciate expensive jewelry. Stephen Moses, a second-generation fine antiques dealer in the French Quarter, told me that Edith came in one day and said, "I've got to go to a fancy ball." She borrowed a tiara. Instead of returning it, she bought it, saying, "It was too pretty to return." Moses marveled at her seeming contradictions: "Edith had $5,000 embossed table linens but served coffee mugs from Woolworth's. To mix and match like that you have to be very secure. She also had silver holders with three cigarettes and matches on tables throughout the house." Edith liked to talk about antiques, Moses said, but also often asked for donations to her favorite causes. "She was so well-established," he added, that "she was an easy person to talk to." Edgar Sr. and Jr. shopped there as well, he said. Edgar Sr. often came in to find a gift for some occasion.

Granddaughter Sandra MacIver, daughter of son Edgar Jr. and wife Polly, remembers the special Woolworth shoes—and how many pairs her grandmother owned. Edith once asked her father whether Sears could make this particularly colorful shoe that she liked. He told her no, so she bought many pairs from Woolworth.

Sandra, whose family lived a two-minute walk away from her grandparents, spent a lot of time with Edith at Longue Vue. Her parents often visited Aspen, Colorado, and when they were away, Sandra stayed with Edith. "I loathed Aspen winters," she said in a phone interview from her home in Bainbridge Island, Washington. While at Longue Vue, Sandra explored every room, all of which had toys in them. She dressed up in Edith's vast designer clothes collection. After Edgar's death in 1959, Sandra "became her shadow," constantly staying at Edith's side and even "helping her write thank-yous to all the condolence notes."

Edith, Sandra remembers, was a heavy smoker, keeping a bowl of sugar candies nearby to mask the smell on her breath. She had a heavy cough and carried around cough syrup, although some wondered whether it was *really* medicinal. She even went to an Elizabeth Arden spa with a chain-smoking friend when she was trying to stop smoking. If she was going to stop smoking, she reasoned, she might as well get a beauty treatment to make her feel better. It worked for the friend but not for Edith.

Sandra recalled in our phone conversation:

> She would read story after story to us, Winnie the Pooh, Dr. Seuss, with us sitting by her side. She would take the limo to her Voters Service office everyday, a cinderblock room with a desk [in the basement of city hall]. She took a lunch box. Then she would come home, get into a caftan, nap, dress to the nines for dinner even after Edgar died. I'd sit next to her in her dressing room as she picked out jewelry from drawers filled with it. She had long, red fingernails. First, she'd put cold cream on her face and [then] deep-red lipstick. Then a watch, a brooch, two rings and a bracelet or two. And always the Woolworth shoes.

Edith would luxuriate in the mornings as well. Anne Hess recalls, "Edith slept in, eased her way into the day with breakfast in bed, wearing a bed jacket." Luxury was something Edith was perfectly comfortable enjoying. It was demonstrated by the dinner parties she loved to host in her elegantly furnished dining room, to say nothing of extravagant New Year's parties. It was demonstrated in the toys she continually gave to the children and the parties she held for them.

Anne remembers Longue Vue as being a magical place with all its goings on and trinkets placed under her pillow. Her nearby cousins, as Sandra also recalled, were always around. "We all even had mumps together," Anne laughs.

A Special Aide

Edith had a personal maid named Natalie Forcia, who was as much a companion as a maid. Her grandson is Dr. Michael White, the clarinetist, bandleader, composer, jazz historian with a doctorate in Spanish, educator, and much-loved member of New Orleans musician royalty. Born in 1954, he remembered Edith well. "My grandmother was Edith's personal maid," he told me over coffee, "but she was also a personal confidante, sewed and ironed her clothes, and traveled with her to Mexico and other trips." Dr. White's fondest memories are of the Christmas parties he spent with the Stern family, playing with the Stern children and the children of other employees in the Longue Vue Playhouse in the early 1960s.[30] "They had the largest Christmas tree I ever saw," he said, recalling his feeling of awe. Although Dr. White does not remember this, there was a Black Santa Claus at the party. The Sterns apparently hired the same one every year. "I found a pair of school shoes, Stride Rite, under the tree," he said with a warm smile. "I was disappointed. I wanted toys."

Dr. White also recalled how Edith "leaned down to talk to me. She seemed happy that I was there. . . . She had a majestic presence, an aura. She seemed like Queen Elizabeth." He added, "It was a racially turbulent and hostile time everywhere else. I vividly remember seeing the protesters [to school integration]. The times I played with the Stern kids in the Playhouse was the first time I experienced Blacks and whites treated as equals. It was different everywhere else. I thought all white people were evil. The Sterns were the exception. It helped balance me."

In the 1960s world outside Longue Vue, Dr. White experienced the worst of New Orleans racism. He, his parents, and sister initially lived in the Ninth Ward, a predominantly Black neighborhood. Eventually, the family moved

Uptown to Dante Street in the Carrollton neighborhood to live with his grandmother Natalie Forcia. "There were Italian groceries everywhere. Grandma would send me to buy sugar and syrup. It was terrifying." Wherever he went, he said, "White kids taunted us, waved bats and threw rocks, toilet paper, dried eggs. They called us names. Monkey." He stiffened as these painful memories surged back.

Why sugar and syrup? Natalie Forcia had something of a second career. Explained Dr. White, "She worked for every major caterer in the region, Italian, Jewish, Black. She did private parties and weddings. She made spun-sugar roses and rose petals for cakes, some topped with doves. She made dolls for wedding cakes too." A photograph in the Longue Vue Archives shows an elaborate decoration for the top of a wedding cake. It was shaped almost like a basket, with a sizable bell hanging from its handle and extraordinarily intricate white flowers climbing up the sides. One local woman whom I spoke to remembered being sent to Forcia's house to pick up spun-sugar flowers and petals that her mother would use to decorate her party table. Children would pick up the loose petals scattered on the table and eat them like candy.

The Sterns helped publicize Natalie Forcia's baking talents. Dr. White recalled, "They put her on WDSU-TV. She was written up in the *New Yorker* and *Ebony*. She shipped candy to distant buyers." Her financial success paved the way for better things for the whole family. Raised Catholic, he, his parents, and his sister all went to private Catholic elementary schools and Xavier University of Louisiana. His uncle, Dr. Clarence Forcia, graduated from Howard University Medical School and became one of the few Black doctors in Alexandria, Louisiana, until he died suddenly in 1960 in his thirties. White's aunt, also named Natalie, played the clarinet and bought him one. "I loved the sound," he told me. His destiny was set.

At one point, Natalie Forcia and Emma Brown, the Sterns' longtime cook, lived a few doors from each other on Liberty Street. Dr. White said, "It was a coincidence that they both owned houses on the same street at a time when few Black people owned their own home. The Sterns might have helped both of them in some way."

Linda Aubert, Emma Brown's granddaughter, knows that is true. Not only did the Sterns send Emma to cooking school, but they also helped her in many other ways. They bought Emma's house for $6,000, and her grandmother paid the Sterns back monthly. At the time of this writing, Linda is still living in that double shotgun. Emma apparently learned to read and write at a reading program the Sterns sent her to. Grandson David Stern, Philip's son, grew up playing with Emma's children in much the same way as White did. David's attachment to Emma was strong enough to inspire him to fund a reading program in her honor.

Linda also recalled the Christmas parties in the Playhouse. Her visits there began in the 1950s, so she remembered Edgar, who died in 1959. Edgar was "a big robust man who loved to sing 'God Bless America' with my grandmother." "It was such a big tree," she recalled. "Edith was elegant and enunciated each word." She also remembered that the Sterns had a leg of lamb every two weeks and often had "veal birds; it was the way they tied up the meat."

Complicated Relationships

The Sterns' involvement with their own children and grandchildren was sometimes complicated, particularly when it came to their Jewishness. Edith, for example, planned granddaughter Sandra's wedding to David Steiner (her first husband) in ten days' time at Longue Vue in 1968. A Unitarian minister, Rev. Alberto D'Orlando, husband of Sandra's favorite Metairie Park Country Day School art teacher, officiated; he was the choice of the marrying couple.

Religion had never been important to Sandra and her parents, Edgar Jr. and Polly. "But it was to Edith in her own way," she notes, "so she made a chuppah [Jewish wedding canopy], generously decorated with lilies of the valley, all her doing." That was Edith's one concession to Jewish ritual. But after thinking about the chuppah, Sandra added, "I think she purposely may have kept the chuppah small, almost like an awning projecting from the house [instead of a larger, traditional freestanding tent-like structure]. It was so low-key." "Judaism was always important to her," she continued, "but she didn't talk about it. That was the way to survive in an antisemitic world. She had a Christmas tree but only for the staff in the Playhouse."

Yet, Leon Harris reported that "when daughter Audrey planned to marry the *New York Times* art critic Tom Hess in a lay ceremony in 1944, Edith absolutely insisted that the public ceremony had to be performed by a rabbi, and it was. But when the rabbi naturally proposed there be the symbolic breaking of a wineglass, which is traditional at Jewish weddings, Mrs. Stern was again outraged and refused. Jewish, yes—too Jewish, no!"[31]

It seems that the family's level of Jewishness depended on which family member was involved. Granddaughter Eve Stern, daughter of Philip, told me that she and Edith were very close and she learned a lot from her, but that "Edith—like everyone else in the family except grandson Bill Hess—had no interest really in Judaism." As a teenager, Eve decided that she really wanted to be Jewish, even though her mother, then the wife of Philip, was not—and as the daughter of a non-Jewish mother, Eve would not be considered Jewish. Eve learned Hebrew and studied hard to fulfill the requirements for conversion. "For a while my father studied with me, I think, just to do something with me," she recalled in a telephone conversation from her home in Tucson.

At that time, Eve and her family lived in Washington, DC, and Eve went to Sidwell Friends School, a Quaker school. "When I wanted to study Judaism seriously," she added, "my father wanted nothing to do with it. But my mother, who was not Jewish, said if you're serious, I'll take you." She had a conversion ceremony, including immersing in a mikvah, the ritual bath. At age thirteen, Eve became a Bat Mitzvah. She and Edith were very close, and Eve persuaded Edith to say a prayer in Hebrew at the ceremony. "She used to call me to recite it over the phone to check that she had learned the Hebrew right," Eve remembered with a laugh. Eventually, Eve embraced elements of other religions as well, such as Buddhism and Quakerism.

Members of any large family are often very different from one another. The Sterns and the Rosenwalds were no exception. They each were shaped by both family and place. For the New Orleans family, place had its own specific impact on each member.

To say that New Orleans in 1921 when Edith arrived was for her an alien world is to just touch the surface of the reality she faced. How she melded progressive politics and Jewish marginalization with her enormous wealth makes for a fascinating story. The Rosenwald financial legacy, combined with her liberal Chicago upbringing, shaped Edith and, in turn, deeply influenced her marriage, her children, and her larger New Orleans life. But New Orleans was Edgar's town, and she would have to adjust to it.

Adjust yes, but on her terms. And as with her father before her, her impact would be immeasurable.

4

LIKE FATHER, LIKE DAUGHTER

In 1932, Edith Stern invited Marian Anderson to give a private performance in the Playhouse at Longue Vue. That event, held eleven years after the Sterns' marriage and Edith's arrival in New Orleans, was both an act of defiance and a reflection of Edith's deep interest in the arts. Anderson, a tall, impressive woman with short, cropped hair and high cheekbones, would later be world famous; in 1943, Anderson would astound the world as she sang the national anthem at Constitution Hall in Washington, DC.[1] But in the early 1930s, she was still largely unknown, although the Sterns recognized her extraordinary talent.

That night, the audience of seventy-five friends listened in awe as Anderson sang Mendelssohn's *Elijah.* Her contralto voice boomed beyond the four walls of this modest structure built for intimate performances and parties. And the private event made history in New Orleans, as Edith observed:

> In 1932, it was a bold gesture for a Southerner to host a black female. What if she appeared in that decollete gown: where would she be fed; and how would she be accepted on a social level? What useless, unnecessary anxiety. Marian Anderson, a great artist and a great woman, took over. Few there will ever forget the ecru chiffon long "Shirtwaist dress" with exquisite matching lace cuffs and collar. . . . It was her decision to be served in the dressing room that had been arranged. Later she made her appearance, gracious, dignified, and accepted modestly the enthusiastic kudos.[2]

Edith and Edgar had first heard Anderson sing in a small Black church. Their cook Emma Brown had told them that a fabulous singer was coming to give a benefit performance at First African Baptist. The Sterns bought five tickets at ten cents each. Dr. Will Alexander, head of the Commission on Interracial Cooperation (1919–30), happened to be visiting from Atlanta and was a dinner guest at their home.[3] The three attended. Edith wrote in "Autobiography of a House," "Only three whites entered the fallen down, pathetically poor church with perhaps 50 others of the congregation, witnessed this glorious Amazon, in a sapphire blue sequined evening dress."[4]

Edith then decided she had to have a dinner party so people could hear this extraordinary voice. Edgar admonished her, saying, "You know my dear, that is not done here."[5] Edith was aware of the social norms of strictly segregated New Orleans, but she hardly intended to be constrained by them. She had lived there eleven years; she knew what she needed to do, and she did it.

This dinner and performance were early strikes for social justice in New Orleans. That private event not only defied every provision of the city's code of conduct but was even illegal: socializing between the races was prohibited. Remember that this occurred in 1932 when department stores, parks, and theaters were either off-limits to Blacks or of limited access to them. A performance by a Black entertainer at a non-Black-only venue was similarly illegal. "It shows how strong her commitment was," the late Sybil Morial, wife of Dutch Morial, told me in a phone conversation in 2022.[6]

Supporting Black artists financially was not on any local philanthropic agenda. But ignoring convention was the mark of Edith's life since arriving in New Orleans, and it would be so consistently until her death in 1980. This was part of her family history. She was the daughter of iconoclast Julius Rosenwald, owner of Sears & Roebuck and philanthropist, who was not afraid to defy social conventions in support of Black people, especially in the South. Edith continued this tradition of defiance in New Orleans, where such behavior was perhaps even more heretical. She was following a pattern set by her father.

Edith's Role Model

In 1912, Julius Rosenwald brought Booker T. Washington to meet forty-five of Chicago's most prominent and influential men—all white—with the hope that they would join him in financially supporting Tuskegee, the Black university that Washington founded in Alabama. By then, Washington was a nationally known Black educator. Rosenwald had the confidence of a man whose success in reaching the top of the business and social world had been earned with smarts and tenacity.

Washington was then one of the country's best-known Black authors, having written *Up from Slavery* in 1901 about his remarkable path from enslaved to educator. Rosenwald hosted Washington and the forty-five men for lunch at the fashionable white-only Blackstone Hotel, the city's finest, overlooking Lake Michigan. The elegant site was famously known as the hotel of presidents, from Teddy Roosevelt to Jimmy Carter, as well as of Hollywood stars and the Astors, Rockefellers, and Vanderbilts. Washington was the hotel's first Black guest.

Rosenwald's white chauffeur at first resisted driving a car with a Black passenger. He later changed his mind, figuring if it was okay for JR, it would be okay for him.[7] The event caused quite a stir. Even more eyebrow-raising, Rosenwald invited Washington to stay in his home for the five-day visit; the *Chicago-Examiner* then ran a story with the headline, "Noted Negro Educator Will Stay at Home of Philanthropist While Here." JR's wife Augusta, known in the family as Gussie, wrote to daughter Adele: "This week we shall entertain rather simply and informally for Booker T. . . . Of course, his stopping here has caused a great many comments, but we don't mind. People will get over it."[8]

On its own, the story of the Julius Rosenwald Fund is an extraordinary one; his impact on others, particularly Edith and Edgar, multiplies its importance.[9] Nothing that Edith and Edgar did as philanthropists can be understood without knowing the Rosenwald story. Their attitudes and philanthropic strategies were directly influenced by JR's efforts. Today, JR's story is becoming better known, respected, and emulated across the country. Many consider Rosenwald one of the preeminent philanthropists of the early twentieth century. His philanthropic efforts often overlapped with those of John Rockefeller, who once said "he would donate to anything Rosenwald did because he trusted his philanthropy."[10]

"Julius Rosenwald was the most courageous, bravest, fiercest, first social justice philanthropist," former Ford Foundation president Darren Walker told me in a phone conversation in 2022. "He argued back then that the root causes of our social problems were white racism, prejudice and bias, fifty years before the Kerner Commission. After the riots in the '60s, I came to the same conclusion. He was my hero. He upset all the powers in the South."[11] Walker added that the Rosenwald Fund was ahead of every other foundation, including the Rockefeller, Russell Sage, and Carnegie Foundations, in identifying race as "the singular role at the heart of the problem."

As the visionary head of Sears & Roebuck, JR brought the famous mail-order catalog to unprecedented heights of success; in the process, he helped create a national consumer culture. In many ways, the Sears catalog—and for a while the Montgomery Ward catalog too—had an enormous impact on US society that is hard to imagine today. Historian Daniel Boorstin wrote a trilogy titled *The Americans* that celebrated cultural, social, and technological developments in American history; the first book in the trilogy centered on the "colonial" experience, the second on the "national" experience, and the third on the "democratic" experience. In that third book, Boorstin asserted that the two most influential books in American history, and the ones that unified and perhaps democratized the nation as a society, were the Bible and the Sears or Montgomery Ward catalog.[12] One unified the country via the commonality of the Christian religion, and the other by making possible the commonality of every conceivable tangible aspect of daily living. The catalogs became readily available to all classes and races across the nation through an expanding rail system and the extension of mail order and the postal service to rural America. It was a time of great social and economic changes as industrialization and urbanization swept the country, while railways and the telegraph were shrinking the country and waves of immigrants were filling urban neighborhoods.

Rosenwald became a philanthropic powerhouse. Yet he has not gotten the same attention in the history books as his contemporary mogul-philanthropists Rockefeller, Carnegie, and Mellon. His business achievements were surely comparable; his wealth was in the same category. Perhaps one reason that he is barely remembered today is the time limit he put on his foundation. Or perhaps it is that Rosenwald was in retail, whereas the others were in oil, railroads, and heavy industry. Or, perhaps, it is that Rosenwald was Jewish. Walker agreed with these reasons: "He is unknown, in part, because he is Jewish, and he spent down his fortune unlike the others, who left foundations with their name on them. He designed his philanthropy without ego, so his name does not live on."

His civic importance, however, was certainly broad based and of national scope. JR was also a ready and willing resource when asked to serve by national leaders. President Woodrow Wilson tapped Rosenwald to be on the Council of National Defense, "which was to lay plans for what would become, after the country entered the war [World War I], the virtual government takeover of the production and distribution of economic resources." Rosenwald was one of four Jews among the seven nongovernment appointees; the other three were Supreme Court Justice Louis Brandeis, financier Bernard Baruch, and union leader Samuel Gompers. "All this marked the first significant representation of Jews in the government," according to John Barry.[13] Rosenwald also traveled and gave pep talks to the troops during World War I, introducing himself as "General Merchandise."

In 1914, Julius and Augusta visited Palestine and were moved by the young pioneering Jews who were rebuilding their lives. More than three-quarters of a million Jews had fled the pogroms of Russia, and 300,000 similarly fled Galicia in Eastern Europe to Vienna. No country was willing to take these refugees. Rosenwald donated millions to their resettlement in Palestine and was celebrated by both Jewish and American leaders. As mentioned, Edith also supported settlement in Palestine and was especially interested in tree planting, a means to transform the land from desert to green space. A special tree, a thank-you gift from Israel, was later planted at Longue Vue.

Despite his support, JR refused to back the Zionist cause, which he felt would open American Jews to accusations of dual loyalty. This concern was shared by many Jews then and would be felt for decades. He also believed Palestine would never be self-sufficient.

Early Concern for Improving Black Lives

Rosenwald's philanthropic focus on the needs of the Black community was unique in several ways. He had the single greatest impact on the education of Black children in the South; without him, there would not have been schools, teachers, or libraries for many Black youth. The "Rosenwald Schools" that are still standing are often treasured in their southern communities.[14] In 2015, Aviva Kempner produced a compelling documentary, *Rosenwald: The Remarkable Story of a Jewish Partnership with African American Communities.* It created a new interest in Rosenwald's philanthropy.

The Rosenwald Fund reflected the personal vision of a first-generation Chicago Jew shaped by the Jewish values of tzedakah (charity and justice) and tikkun olam (repairing the world).[15] Rosenwald reportedly said that he wished to earn $15,000 a year—$5,000 to live on, $5,000 to save, and $5,000 to give away—an extraordinary formula for a life well lived. He developed a strong propensity to help the downtrodden partly because of his own experience with antisemitism in Chicago.

Rosenwald himself was unsure whether his passion for helping others grew "because I belong to a people who have known centuries of persecution, or whether it is because I am naturally inclined to sympathize with the oppressed."[16] Rosenwald also noted, "As a Jew I would naturally have greater sympathy for a persecuted race, and this is probably what has brought to my mind the injustice, to and the helplessness of, the colored man."[17]

Born in 1862 to German immigrants in Springfield, Illinois, JR spent most of his youth in Chicago. His father Samuel had emigrated from Westphalia in 1854 to Baltimore with $20 in his pocket. Like so many immigrant Jews of the mid-nineteenth century, he was fleeing revolutions and a depression. Once in the United States, Samuel, again like so many fellow Jews, became a peddler, selling an assortment of goods from thread to watches. Those peddlers sold to Black and white, free and enslaved, without distinction, establishing a bond that would last for decades. After two years, Samuel went to work for a family that had achieved success in retail clothing. Within a decade of their arrival in Baltimore from Germany, the Hammerslough brothers owned several stores that Samuel helped manage. "Managing a dry goods store was another prototypical job for a nineteenth-century Jewish immigrant, a post that many a peddler ardently desired."[18]

In 1853, the Hammerslough brothers were joined in Baltimore by their twenty-year-old sister, Augusta.[19] Four years later, Samuel and Augusta were married. For a few years, they moved about the country managing branch stores for the family, before settling down in Springfield to work in the Hammerslough store there. They lived in a house a block away from the home of

Abraham Lincoln, who was already known to have declared a "high regard for the Jews."[20]

Julius Hammerslough, Augusta's brother, had moved to Springfield from Baltimore around 1855 and is generally acknowledged as its first Jewish resident. He served as the first president of the Springfield Hebrew Congregation, a forerunner of the present Temple B'rith Sholom. He ran Hammerslough Brothers Clothiers for about a decade before moving to New York. Several accounts indicate that Hammerslough was present at Lincoln's "House Divided" speech in 1858. He certainly attended Lincoln's first presidential inauguration. And he was a frequent visitor to the capital, once escorting the sister of Mary Todd Lincoln to a state dinner. After Lincoln's assassination in 1865, Hammerslough accompanied the president's remains from Chicago to Springfield. He was a leading proponent for building the Lincoln Memorial in the nation's capital.

Springfield was dominated by Lutherans, who had also emigrated from Germany. As the capital of Illinois, it became a political and financial center of Union support during the Civil War. With new industries emerging and railroad service growing, Springfield offered good prospects for the family's retail business. Julius Rosenwald was born soon after the Rosenwalds moved to Springfield, the same year Lincoln left to go to Washington, DC, as president. Five siblings followed, one of whom died. In 1868, Samuel bought the store from the Hammerslough family and renamed it S. Rosenwald & Co. The store did a land-office business in Civil War uniforms for the Union Army throughout the war.

In the tradition of a whole host of German Jews—Gimbel, Guggenheim, Straus, Mack, Goldwater, Flexner, Filene, Rich, and Kuhn—Samuel was a very successful shopkeeper. Julius helped in the store from a young age. He never finished high school; instead, following his father's path, Julius moved to New York City in 1879 to work for the Hammersloughs. They had become prominent men's clothing manufacturers. Later, Julius decided to move to Chicago to manufacture summer clothing with a partner. His business was a great success, and this was a great time to be in Chicago. In 1890, JR met Augusta "Gussie" Nussbaum, one of seven daughters and a son of another German immigrant in the clothing business. They were married that same year.

Chicago Gains New Status

Chicago had suffered a devastating fire in 1871 that destroyed 18,000 buildings and left 100,000 homeless. Yet it had not only recovered from that disaster but also was booming by the time JR moved there. While the country was emerging from a recession, Chicago was growing rapidly, using a new architectural style to produce the first modern skyscrapers with steel-frame construction, plate glass, and terra cotta. Louis Sullivan, Dankmar Adler, John Wellborn Root, and Daniel Burnham were the star architects of the tall buildings. At the same time, a new residential design, the Prairie style, emerged from the drawing board of Frank Lloyd Wright. The stockyards were also full. Pullman was building his famous sleeping cars in a planned community just outside the city. Chicago was one of the country's major rail hubs. Prosperity provided an atmosphere of possibilities.

Edith's birth in 1895 coincided with the sparkling afterglow of the 1893 Columbian Exposition (Chicago World's Fair). The fair had effectively put Chicago on the map as the shining star of American cities. Chicago's leading citizens shared a deep fear of being considered second class to New York. Its business leaders were sharp and successful, but the upper echelons of society worried that, with all their financial success, they may have neglected to cultivate the niceties of proper social standing. The exposition was a giant white banner waved in the face of Mrs. Astor, the doyenne of Gilded Age society in New York City. It was Chicago's way of declaring its social status.

Urban Pride

With Chicago's new national standing came a sense of pride among the city's business leaders like JR. A new can-do spirit permeated the city, and Chicago became known for innovation and forward thinking, qualities reflected in everything JR was doing. With the exposition came horse-drawn streetcars, bright gas and electric lights, the first large-scale test of AC (alternating current), elevators, safer drinking water, and portable Kodak cameras. The visitors to the exposition and the country were dazzled.

Before the fair, Chicago was already second to New York in population but was considered a hog-slaughtering backwater, given that its stockyards were the city's primary source of employment. The old Chicago of filth, coal smoke, vice, violence, and questionable drinking water took pride, despite its shortcomings, in how fast it had rebuilt itself after the Great Fire. Chicago had clearly risen from the ashes. But with the exposition, it had also produced a grand show. With its staggeringly large Ferris wheel—holding thirty-six cars and two thousand passengers—the fair provided the stature the city craved to compete with the impact of the Paris Exposition of 1889 and its Eiffel Tower. Chicago's social problems, economic ills, rampant corruption, and other negative trends were momentarily obscured by the hoopla of the exposition, although they were never far from JR's consciousness.

The Columbian Exposition propelled the Chicago school of architecture to the head of the class and inaugurated the City Beautiful movement's model of city planning—characterized by wide boulevards; monumental classical buildings with Roman columns, pediments, decorative cornices, and eye-catching white paint; commemorative statues; and expansive landscapes. In the masterful hands of Frederick Law Olmsted, landscape architecture became recognized as a critical design form. The transformative potential of grand architectural projects, showcased by the exposition, took root in urban development thinking that would lock the country into big ideas and top-down planning for the next century. Architect Daniel Burnham, in charge of the exposition's overall design, summed everything up with his oft-quoted remark: "Make no little plans; they have no magic to stir men's blood." This is the most common version of his famous remark. The full quote is "Make big plans; aim high in hope and work, remembering that a noble, logical diagram once recorded will not die. Make no little plans. They have no magic to stir men's blood and probably will not themselves be realized." Chicago's leading residents took this advice seriously. Rosenwald's accomplishments surely reflected his belief in the possibility of transformative change.

The Columbian Exposition's greatest and most lasting impact was how it changed the way Americans perceived their cities and their architects. Architectural design was no longer just the purview of the rich. Suddenly architects and, by extension, urban planners gained new standing, for better or worse. Suddenly, the idea took hold that cities could be transformed from dirty, unsafe places to attractive places to live. The City Beautiful movement was transcendent.

Chicago has remained a city unusually focused on architecture. It is no surprise that Edith, more than her father, would be interested in architecture. This would become apparent when she and Edgar were building their homes Longue Vue I and II.

The Hidden City

Chicago was indeed refashioned physically and culturally. Beneath the glitz and glamour of the exposition and the Gilded Age, however, poverty was increasing; the social ills and inequities that Rosenwald would seek to redress were becoming more apparent. Conditions continued to worsen after the turn of the century, but in 1900, racial animosity was still at a minimum. The influx of white European immigrants did not have the same impact that the arrival of Blacks during the Great Migration would have.

America's "Second City" was unprepared for these Black men and women. At the turn of the century, only about 1 percent of the population was Black.[21] As the number of Black residents increased, so did segregation and discrimination. Immigrants and then Black families fleeing harsh conditions in the South filled the poorly constructed housing built for visitors to the exposition along avenues leading to its location in Jackson Park; these homes were designed to be temporary, not built to last. "After the war was declared in 1917, the influx of Southern Blacks to Chicago was overwhelming—to the point that Blacks constituted 20 percent of the workers in the meat-packing industry in 1918, compared to 3 percent in 1909. . . . The trains could not bring Blacks to the North fast enough to fill the job vacancies left by 350,000 Illinois men who had either enlisted or been drafted into the 1917–18 European conflict."[22] In 1919, race riots lasted for days.

In the 1920s, the immigration laws tightened. Fewer new immigrants filled the places vacated by the upwardly mobile Eastern European immigrants. As the settled immigrants moved up and out, Black workers took their blue-collar jobs. The population shift had a dramatic effect on the city. "The Black migration was one of the largest and most rapid mass internal movements of people in history—perhaps the greatest not caused by the immediate threat of execution or starvation," noted Nicholas Lemann.[23]

Many of those southern migrants settled on the city's West Side. Unscrupulous people eager for a quick buck engaged in blockbusting that was soon followed by rapid urban decline. "The sad drama of neighborhood transition played out faster there than anywhere else in Chicago. Sleazy realtors known locally as 'panic peddlers' would move a black family into a neighborhood . . . (and then) go around to the white families and warn them that they'd better move out before it was too late, thereby obtaining their houses at rock-bottom prices."[24]

Those conditions did not escape Rosenwald's awareness (nor of Edith and her siblings), even as he concentrated on expanding the Sears business. He had to have witnessed the worst decline as he drove through Black neighborhoods every day on his way to work. The large red-brick headquarters of Sears & Roebuck—covering five full city blocks—was on the West Side. Other factories, such as Western Electric and International Harvester, were located there too.

Chicago's West Side had little to offer other than inexpensive housing. As Lemann notes, "The South Side had plenty of slums—the worst slums in Chicago physically—but it was the seat of civilization, the home of the great black institutions and of the middle class. Like Harlem, it was a place whose name connected pride and possibility of success all over black America. The West Side, for blacks, was always predominantly poor, with a weak institutional structure, and it had an especially depressing history."[25]

Sears & Roebuck Would Never Be the Same

It was a complicated road from clothing manufacturer to partner in Sears & Roebuck. Sears was a fledgling mail-order house when JR invested $37,500 in it in 1895, as Chicago was just emerging from the depression of 1893. Richard Sears was a brilliant marketer, but organizational and management skills were not his strong points; they were Rosenwald's. JR soon became the dominant partner, and his leadership transformed that mail-order firm into the largest retail company in the country. In ill health, Roebuck sold out in 1895 to Rosenwald and his brother-in-law, Aaron Nussbaum. Then Nussbaum sold out to Rosenwald in 1901 for $1,250,000. The company was already thriving before JR headed it, but he made it a runaway success. In one of the fastest expansions in the history of American business, Rosenwald pushed Sears ahead of Montgomery Ward and Company in sales by 1900. The war of the catalogs was on.

Aaron Montgomery Ward had invented the catalog in 1871. Together, Ward and Sears expanded the retail business into mail order, instead of store only. Like Walmart and Amazon decades later, they drove thousands of small stores out of business. Farmers no longer needed the country store when they could order from the catalog. Rosenwald expanded the Sears catalog—the "Wish Book," as it was popularly called—to offer a wide variety of items, including whole houses to be assembled on site: it became the IKEA of housing. Those wishing to raise chickens could purchase live chicks from the catalog. Stoves, pianos, and even buggies were offered.

In 1905, Rosenwald's friend Henry Goldman, head of the banking firm Goldman Sachs, suggested that JR take the company public. It was clear that Sears was "a real powerhouse in the merchandising business . . . [but] not many mercantile establishments up to that time had been transformed into public companies. Railroads, oil companies, and steel companies had done so, but not stores."[26] Taking Sears public was what really made JR rich. Eventually, Sears became the largest retailer in the world.[27] By 1912, he was one of the richest men in the country with an estimated worth of $23 million.

At the company, Rosenwald introduced amenities for Sears workers: rooftop parks, landscaped open spaces, a hospital, a cafeteria, an athletic field, and a library. He was chided, however, for generally paying low wages. Yet, the company had a liberal approach to management, embodied in an unusual profit-sharing program for its employees, apparently one of the first and one of the most generous. The company donated 5 percent of its net earnings to the profit-sharing program. And during the depression, JR aided his employees in need. But when Rosenwald tried to hire Black employees, white workers resisted fiercely. He pulled back, looking for other ways to address racial inequities. Yet even his attempt to hire Black workers was unusual.

Edwin Embree, president of the Rosenwald Fund from 1928 to 1948 (when it was closed), once observed, "Mr. Rosenwald was saddened by his inability to change the discriminatory practices in his own firm and in the Chicago office building he owned. His associates, employees, and tenants would not agree to giving Negroes wider opportunities for employment, and fearing that he might create antagonism against the very people he was trying to help, he did not unduly press these efforts."[28]

Confronting Antisemitism

Perhaps Rosenwald was reluctant to push too hard on racial matters in Sears because of his being Jewish in a fundamentally unfriendly world. Julius's father had written to relatives in Germany, "Although there is not much anti-Semitism here, yet we are not on the same level with the Christians. . . . In business one hardly ever hears anything like that, but the children often hear about it, and that is unpleasant enough."[29]

JR was not known to have said much about antisemitism, but he was sensitive to it. Nearly every American Jew was aware of the Leo Frank trial in 1913 and Frank's subsequent lynching in 1915 in Atlanta; JR contributed to Frank's legal defense fund. Frank, from a respectable German Jewish family, was accused of killing a young female worker at the factory he managed. After a heated trial, he was convicted on dubious evidence. Antisemitism raged throughout the South, but the governor reversed the conviction and acquitted Frank. Tragically, Frank was then lynched by an enraged mob.

Rosenwald was himself the target of verbal antisemitic attacks by Henry Ford. Ford was perhaps the greatest single contributor to the spread and legitimizing of antisemitism in the United States, at a time when the Ku Klux Klan flourished and its membership greatly increased. Harris characterized JR's reaction as a "measured, even timid response to anti-Semitism."[30] He continued:

> Ford, the quintessential American hero, attacked Rosenwald in his virulent newspaper, the Dearborn *Independent*. But Rosenwald opposed a Jewish boycott of Ford products because "revenge is never justifiable." And when Ford, after five years of flooding the country with anti-Semitism finally apologized under severe pressure, Rosenwald said: "I congratulate Mr. Ford that he has at last seen the light. He will find that the spirit of forgiveness is not entirely a Christian virtue, but is equally a Jewish virtue."[31]

JR's distaste for Ford did not stop him from making a calculated business decision in 1924. He hired a known antisemite, Robert Elkington Wood, as vice president in charge of the company's factories and retail stores. Wood soon became the public face of the company. A West Point graduate, Wood made his reputation working on the Panama Canal and then at Montgomery Ward, where he opened retail stores to unload inventory that had built up during World War I. He opened the first Sears retail store in 1925, and the number of stores soon surpassed those of Montgomery Ward. But he did not hire Jews as buyers or for any executive positions until 1954. These big retail stores later became the target of intense hatred because they were blamed for causing the closure of so many small businesses. So, it may have been shrewd thinking on Rosenwald's part to hire Wood and so keep Jews out of high-target positions.

Rosenwald's Philanthropy Sets a New Pattern

Julius Rosenwald's story is remarkable on several levels, only one of which is his extraordinary business success. His business acumen seemed to have developed in the classic way of many of the heroic self-made American businessmen of the eighteenth to twentieth centuries. Yet, that was only the first chapter of his unique life. His innovations in philanthropy were what propelled him beyond the typical success story. It is worthwhile to consider the influences that shaped Rosenwald and his philanthropy, given the direct impact JR had on his descendants.

The impact of the city of Chicago itself must be acknowledged first. One would have to have been insensitive to life itself to be unmoved by the deprivation and struggles of the city's impoverished residents. Rosenwald responded not only in a big way but also in an innovative manner. The city and the harsh conditions in which so many people lived would have had an impact on Edith as well. Her sense of injustice was born in response to the conditions she witnessed.

Even when he had only modest means in the early 1900s, Rosenwald's charitable instincts were evident. He gave mostly to local Jewish causes, just as his parents had done despite their financial limitations. A Reform Jew, JR was heavily influenced by his rabbi, Emil G. Hirsch, an immigrant from Luxembourg and the charismatic leader of Chicago's Temple Sinai, one of the oldest synagogues in the Midwest. Hirsch, himself the son of a rabbi, was known for his sermons on the social ills of the day, which were so popular that they often attracted the press.

The "special brand" of Judaism that the Rosenwalds practiced seemed to predict the Sterns' Jewishness, even though the Rosenwalds attended synagogue more frequently than their children would. Marion, Edith's younger sister, recalled, "I would not say that our household was overly Jewish-oriented, but it certainly was a Jewish household. My father always went to Temple on Rosh Hashanah, on Yom Kippur and on most Sundays—the day the Reform prayer service was held. We girls did not. But we were imbued with the feeling that Jewish families are known for their closeness, for respecting each other, and for family loyalty."[32]

Reform Judaism and Social Justice

In the late nineteenth and early twentieth centuries, the number of Reform synagogues was growing around the country. Reform Judaism encouraged Sunday services, instead of or in addition to Saturday, to accommodate store owners who had to stay open on Saturday for their businesses to survive. Inspired by the German Enlightenment around the turn of the eighteenth century, Reform Judaism dispensed with the wearing of head coverings and prayer shawls, services in Hebrew, separate seating for men and women, and the prohibition against music on Shabbat.

Temple Sinai under Rabbi Emil Hirsch's leadership became "one of the most influential Reform congregations in the country."[33] The message of social justice was central to all his sermons. But he even went further: "Property entails duties, which establishes its rights. Charity is not a voluntary concession on the part of the well-situated. It is a right to which the less fortunate are entitled in justice."[34] JR completely bought into this idea of moral obligation. Years later, Edith and her siblings did so as well.

Clearly, Hirsch was the first and major inspiration for JR's philosophy. His sermons likely drew Julius to attend Sunday services, which were often filled to capacity; non-Jews attended as well. The 2,000-seat synagogue was designed by the leading architects Louis Sullivan and Dankmar Adler. Rabbi Hirsch not only used his powerful oratory on behalf of social justice but also was a man of action: he started the first vocational school for Jewish immigrants. "It was largely Rabbi Hirsch who set Julius Rosenwald on the road to becoming one of the preeminent philanthropists of the early twentieth century."[35]

One of JR's first donations and apparently "the most meaningful—and sacrificial—gift of his career [was made] on behalf of the Jews of Russia."[36] He attended a meeting where a report was given about the horrors of the pogroms of Russia and pledged $2,500, which at the time was more than he would earn in a year. By 1908, Rosenwald, already a multimillionaire, was broadening his philanthropy, giving $8,000 to the Illinois Industrial School for Girls and to Jewish organizations helping new immigrants, farmers, and the poor. The size of the Chicago Jewish community had grown dramatically, from 10,000 people in 1880 to 300,000 by 1920, and many were poor.

Up until that time, JR had remained cloistered in the white upper-class, mostly Jewish world, with little awareness of the Black population other than that introduced to him by Rabbi Hirsch—but that must have been quite a consequential introduction. Hirsch was one of the founders of the local NAACP, along with social reformer Jane Addams.

Rosenwald gave his first donation of $250 to the NAACP for legal work in 1911. The next year, after an appeal from Oswald Garrison Villard, cofounder of the NAACP and grandson of abolitionist William Lloyd Garrison Jr., he gave $2,000. John D. Rockefeller Jr. and Madame C. J. Walker, the Black cosmetics entrepreneur and reportedly the first female self-made millionaire, also were generous donors. In 1912, the relatively new activist organization held a conference in Chicago at Temple Sinai at Rabbi Hirsch's invitation and established the local chapter of the NAACP. Rosenwald agreed to serve on its board.

By 1912, JR was one of the richest men in Chicago.[37] Before the Rosenwald Fund was created in 1917, Rosenwald was funding Black elementary schools in the South and Black YMCAs. Yet, like most white Chicagoans of the period, he was not sensitive to race on a personal level. He was still using words like "darkies" and "n——s" in correspondence but apparently dropped those terms soon thereafter.[38]

The first major focus of JR's philanthropy was Black YMCAs. He considered YMCAs to be a great community resource because of their effectiveness in bringing people together and enriching their lives. He came to see them as fulfilling an important need for Black men who moved to cities looking for work, but where there were few, if any, places where they could stay, eat, or socialize. In 1910, he made his first major donation outside the Jewish community, giving $350,000 to build Black YMCAs.[39] This gift united two of his interests: YMCAs and the welfare of Black people. In a speech announcing his donation, Rosenwald said, "The man who hates a black man because he is black has the same spirit as he who hates a poor man because he is poor. It is the spirit of caste. I am the inferior of any man whose rights I trample under my feet. Men are not superior by accident of race or color; they are superior who have the best heart, the best mind. Superiority is born of honesty, of virtue, of charity, and above all, of the love of liberty."[40]

As he became more interested in Black-related projects, JR came up with the idea of issuing challenge grants that changed the face of YMCAs across the country. He offered any location $25,000 if it could raise another $75,000 locally to build a Black YMCA.[41] Twenty-six YMCAs and YWCAs took on his challenge. JR made these contributions, and he encouraged other wealthy Jews to contribute as well, even while knowing that "no Jew was allowed to serve on the national or local boards of any" YMCAs.[42]

The Social Reforms of the Jane Addams Era

JR, already sympathetic to the social reform movement of the day, had become friends with a group of progressive activists interested in improving the lives of those in need. Primary among them was Jane Addams, a fellow NAACP board member, who bought an old mansion in 1889. There, she began helping new immigrants to learn English, enjoy the arts, and seek the help they needed to adjust to their new country. She named it Hull House after the original owner of the mansion. This was during the Progressive era (1900–29), when waves of new immigrants came primarily from Southern and Eastern Europe, especially Italy, Poland, and Russia. They suffered under horrific working conditions in factories. Rosenwald made his first donation to Hull House in 1902 and joined its board, serving for twenty years.

Jane Addams was a major figure in the Chicago of her day and undoubtedly was a major influence on JR and an important role model for young, impressionable Edith. Addams was the consummate social reformer, concerned first and foremost with people trapped in poverty and cut off from education and culture. Intentionally, Addams and her partner Ellen Starr located Hull House in the poor neighborhood of the near West Side, which was packed with mostly East European immigrants. By 1911, Hull House had expanded to 13 buildings. "Until 1950 the West Side was mostly white and represented the remarkable progress made by the children of poor immigrants from Eastern Europe," noted Nicholas Lemann.[43] As mentioned, this neighborhood was also the site of the hulking red-brick headquarters of Sears Roebuck, which provided many jobs for nearby workers.

Over time, Addams became more and more a political activist, increasingly leaving the management of Hull House to her founding partner. She became one of the best-known activists in Chicago, and her reform mission spread elsewhere around the country.

Interestingly, Hull House attracted volunteers from a new and growing population of well-educated women—many of whom were college graduates—who were financially secure but were without a job or any real sense of purpose. They experienced a sense of "uselessness and frustration" and were "dying from inaction and restlessness."[44] They were drawn to volunteer work that propelled many into the workforce or other volunteer positions. "From the beginning there was a dual purpose in the experiment [of Hull House]. [The founders] were interested in providing an outlet for the talent and energy of college-educated young people, but they also sincerely wanted to help those trapped by poverty. They felt a sense of adventure and mission, a feeling of getting back to the basic elements of life. But at the same time, they both betrayed a sense of paternalism, a feeling of *noblesse oblige* as they viewed the crowded slums."[45]

Nevertheless, that two well-educated young women of means went to live in the slums to help the poor was a good story, and Hull House became one of the most famous settlement houses in the country. Establishing Hull House was Addams and Starr's sure way to break out of the traditional women's role "as wife, mother, or teacher, as pious, submissive, frail lady" in which they had no interest.[46] Given that Addams was an occasional dinner guest at the Rosenwald home, one can assume that her model of the independent, activist woman held appeal for young Edith. "The adolescent girls were riveted to this fascinating visitor, listening as her tales unfolded."[47] Yet, there is no indication that Edith felt compelled to volunteer in any Hull House activities during her teenage years. It was not until she moved to New Orleans that her social activist side become evident. Gussie Rosenwald made her own financial contribution to Hull House, but it is unknown whether she volunteered there.

Rosenwald had other philanthropic interests, including the new University of Chicago Laboratory School headed by John Dewey, which practiced an entirely new way of educating students; the Juvenile Court Committee, which dealt with "at risk" youth; Russian Jews affected by the Russian Revolution; and the Chicago Hebrew Institute, which helped East European immigrants learn English.

A New Interest for JR

Addams attracted a diverse group of friends and supporters. Some became Rosenwald's friends too. One of the friends from that group, Paul J. Sachs, financial partner of Henry Goldman of Goldman Sachs, gave JR two books to read. One of these books, Booker T. Washington's *Up from Slavery*, is often cited as having an outsized influence on JR. The fact that Washington was criticized for not advocating on behalf of Black voting rights or social integration did not seem to bother JR. But of equal and perhaps even greater influence was *An American Citizen: The Life of William H. Baldwin Jr.* (1910) by John Graham Brooks, a former Lutheran minister, reformer, and sociologist. Baldwin was the general manager of the Southern Railway and head of the General Education Board (GEB) of the Rockefeller Foundation established in 1902. John Rockefeller started the GEB to provide aid to public education (mostly for teacher training) for southern Blacks and whites; its primary aim was to establish public education systems where there were none, but it also focused on higher education and medical schools in the South. From 1940 until it closed in 1960, the GEB supported many of the same efforts as Rosenwald. Baldwin, wealthy and philanthropic, was also a friend and associate of Booker T. Washington. He served on the board of Tuskegee Institute, founded by Washington primarily to train teachers.

Baldwin both contributed and fundraised on behalf of several Black causes, particularly Tuskegee. This combination of actions appealed to JR. He wrote an enthusiastic letter to daughters Adele and Edith about Baldwin. He said, in part, that Baldwin was a "man who really *led* a life to my liking and whom I shall endeavor to imitate or follow as nearly as I can. I never read of a more interesting character."[48] Clearly impressed by Washington but greatly inspired by Baldwin, JR followed him onto the national stage, moving beyond Chicago to address the issues of Black health, education, and accessibility.

In 1911, before he even thought about establishing a philanthropic foundation, Rosenwald gave $2,000 a year to fund ten scholarships annually to Hampton Institute, one of the oldest Black colleges in the country and Washington's alma mater. He followed that up with grants to Tuskegee, Fisk, and other Black colleges, all of which he did on a challenge basis, a concept he learned from John D. Rockefeller Jr. This is when he discovered how successful "challenge fundraising" could be—he would donate one-third of the funds, but only if the other two-thirds could be found from others. Edith would adopt this same approach to her philanthropy.

That same year, JR hired a Pullman car and took the family—a trip that Edith refers to years later—as well as Rabbi Hirsch and others, to Nashville to visit various schools and medical institutions and then to Tuskegee. "I was astonished at the progressiveness of the schools," he told a reporter. "I don't believe there is a white industrial school in America or anywhere that compares to Mr. Washington at Tuskegee."[49] These family trips to Tuskegee became annual events.

Interestingly, JR's first and second contributions to Tuskegee were of 1,260 men and women's remaindered shoes and hats from Sears. Washington, apparently surprised by the nonfinancial nature of the gift, required all the students to pay a small amount for the shoes and hats so they would not get into the habit of taking handouts. Rosenwald gave similar gifts for years thereafter but soon also gave generous financial support and served on Tuskegee's board.

It was with Washington that JR developed the program to build one-room schoolhouses for Black children throughout the South even before he formally established the Rosenwald Fund. The schools taught the "three Rs" and useful trades, such as building arts, dressmaking, and gardening, though some criticized that work as menial. The buildings were designed by Robert Taylor, a Tuskegee architect who had been the first Black student at MIT, earning his architectural degree in 1892.

"Establishing the principle that Blacks have a right to a public education was a radical act," noted Darren Walker in a phone conversation with me. "He had to argue [for] that. It was pioneering." JR devised the matching challenge in 1912, saying, "I have found by investigation that many people who cannot give money, would give a half day or day's work and others would give material in the way of nails, brick, lime, etc."[50] Years later, Edwin Embree, then director of the Rosenwald Fund, noted that Black communities "always" gave more than they could afford.[51] And because the white community also had to contribute funds for each school, JR was challenging the white South in a way no one had ever done.

Directing attention to the South and expanding that focus over the coming years, Rosenwald made a major pivot from funding Tuskegee and higher education to funding primary education. He displayed a strong interest in the education of the whole person from childhood to adulthood, understanding the importance of early education to subsequent development.

In 1917, Rosenwald was asked to serve on the Rockefeller Foundation Board. As noted, Rosenwald's and Rockefeller's donor activities overlapped in several ways. Yet, it is too simple to assume that JR was trying to compete with or win the respect of the super-rich, well-known Gentile philanthropists—the upper crust of society who rarely, if ever, welcomed Jews. There is no indication that he sought to socialize with the big and famous wealthy donors; it seems to have worked the other way around. The financier Jacob Schiff declared, "I believe there is no one who has done so much to make the name of a Jew respected, to raise it, not only in the eyes of our countrymen, but everywhere, as Julius Rosenwald."[52]

Rosenwald wrote several magazine articles, such as "The Trend Away from Perpetuities," published in the *Atlantic*, trying to persuade other foundations to put a time limit to their existence. Harris observed:

> Rosenwald influenced a number of rich men and their lawyers to be careful that their foundations should not be too limited in purpose. But in terms of self-liquidation, he was far less successful. Influenced by Rosen-

wald, John D. Rockefeller Sr. released for current expenditure funds he had given to the University of Chicago, and Andrew Carnegie released some to Tuskegee. Although non-Jewish millionaires including the Rockefellers and Pierre S. Du Pont, publicly praised Rosenwald's self-liquidating idea and his professionalism in philanthropy, appointed him to the boards of their funds . . . and even gave substantial sums to Jewish causes in his honor, very few followed his example of spending principal.[53]

Changing Education in the South

Rosenwald was already making donations to Black hospitals, Black colleges, Black YMCAs, the National Urban League, NAACP, and the Boy Scouts of America before he established the Rosenwald Fund in 1917. He was also supporting *The Crisis*, a publication started in 1910 by W. E. B. Du Bois to cover news of interest to Black communities. As Du Bois put it, its mission was to "set forth those facts and arguments which show the danger of race prejudice, particularly as manifested today toward colored people." Although JR socialized with Black people, neither he nor the Fund advocated for integration.[54]

JR is best known for making possible through his challenge grants the construction of 5,357 one-room schoolhouses, which educated 663,615 students, and shops, libraries, and teachers' homes in 883 counties in fifteen southern states from 1913 to 1932; 372 of these schools were in rural Louisiana.[55] "By 1932, one-third of all black children in the South were attending Rosenwald schools."[56]

Rosenwald would provide one-third of the cost of each facility only if the local white community contributed one-third and the local Black community contributed another third in kind or in dollars. The Rosenwald Fund and state taxes combined paid only 70 percent of the cost of new schools; Black communities raised the rest by contributing money, materials, land, and labor.[57] As part of the process, these communities would hold "arousement meetings" to stimulate local interest. According to one witness, "You would have been over-awed with emotion if you could have seen those poor people walking up to the table, emptying their pockets for a school."[58] Rosenwald himself always thought the generosity of the local Black community was more significant than his own, considering how little money they had.

"More significant than the schools themselves," wrote Rosenwald Fund trustee Alfred Perkins, "was the fact that, as a result of Rosenwald's cooperation with state agencies in the construction effort, the South had come to recognize its obligation to provide education for all its citizens." By using challenge grants and involving other public agencies and citizen groups, the Fund achieved "larger purposes than originally envisioned."[59]

The Rosenwald Fund also provided money to train Black teachers and stock the libraries with books by both Black and white authors to help break down racial divisions. It invested in curriculum development and provided fellowships for Black principals and other leaders. There were even "Rosenwald Days," held annually to "re-arouse community interest in schools, to clean up and beautify the school buildings and grounds. It was often an occasion to raise collections for needed repairs or additions to equipment."[60]

The genius of the Rosenwald School program lay not only in its innovative funding arrangement, which ensured buy-in by both the white and Black communities, but also in the holistic education philosophy that guided the curricula of the schools. Edith later would introduce to New Orleans a new pedagogical philosophy that would change education in that city and beyond.

The school program also had an impact beyond the Black community. "The Rosenwald Fund gave its school design plans free of charge to anyone who asked for them, and they were used for more than 15,000 white schools," many of these in communities outraged by the idea of Black students having better facilities than white students.[61]

Their increased access to elementary education had a profound effect on Black Louisianans. Between 1920 and 1930, the rate of illiteracy among the Black population declined from 38 to 23 percent. Equally important, the school-building program mobilized local Black communities in a collective effort that enhanced their solidarity and gave them a tangible stake in the education of their children. Edith and Edgar must have been aware of this impact. It undoubtedly helped shape their giving goals.

Rosenwald's impact on the education of Black southerners was immeasurable. Although he gave to Black colleges, he understood that the path to get there had to begin with access to a primary education. As 1959 Pulitzer Prize winner and *Atlanta Journal-Constitution* editor Ralph McGill wrote, " It is my studied judgment, expressed many times in recent years, that the human and spiritual values created by the Fund have been among the major reasons why so much of the South managed to begin acceptance of the United States Supreme Court's school desegregation decision without violence, and why, when defiance did appear, there were Southerners ready and willing to combat and help defeat it."[62]

Blazing a New Trail

Both before and for a decade after the creation of the Rosenwald Fund, JR ran the show himself, just as Edith and Edgar would do with their family fund. It was only when the value of its corpus of Sears Roebuck stock swelled during the 1920s that JR sought help in managing the Rosenwald Fund. In 1927, he hired Edwin Rogers Embree, who was then on the Rockefeller Foundation staff and who had been raised by a passionate and outspoken abolitionist, his grandfather John G. Fee. Fee was instrumental in founding a racially integrated town—Berea, Kentucky—where young Embree grew up in a truly integrated neighborhood, with Black and white families occupying alternating houses on the block. He left there to attend Yale University.

Rosenwald and Embree could not have been more in sync; Embree was the perfect staff partner. Much of the innovative and path-setting work of the Fund from the early 1930s until it shut down in 1948 was clearly due to Embree's leadership as president. After all, Rosenwald died in 1932, and according to his instructions, the Fund had to be closed within twenty-five years of his death. As Embree wrote years later, "Activities in behalf of Negroes have consumed twice as much of our money and of our thought as all other programs."[63]

Under Embree's leadership the Fund became even more aggressively activist, embarking on an unprecedented path to place progressive individuals in government positions wherever possible. Embree was determined to change government policies, but he knew that policies were made and executed by program staff. He devised a program to underwrite positions within the Roosevelt administration to advance the interests of the Black population.[64]

For example, in 1933, Embree placed a high-level advocate for the nation's Black citizens in the office of Interior Secretary Harold Ickes (a fellow Chicagoan). Clark Foreman, who was from Georgia, was a civil rights activist and the first Rosenwald Fund staff member hired after Embree took it over. Foreman served as an adviser on race problems in Ickes's office. In 1935, Ickes appointed Foreman director of the Power Division of the Public Works Administration and five years later as director of defense housing for the Federal Works Agency. Foreman was succeeded in Ickes's office by PhD economist Robert C. Weaver, who went on to become the first head of the Department of Housing and Urban Development, appointed by President Lyndon B. Johnson. Other Black professionals were appointed to government agencies, and their salaries were paid by the Rosenwald Foundation; they came to be known as FDR's "Black Cabinet."

Embree had reorganized the Fund and with JR's enthusiastic support brought on its first Black trustee, the sociologist Charles S. Johnson, who served as the first Black president of Fisk University. This was decades before other philanthropies appointed Black trustees. In the early 1940s, eminent Washington, DC, lawyer Charles H. Houston, a leader in the NAACP legal assault on school segregation, also became a Fund trustee.[65] Houston's presence probably accounted for the Rosenwald Fund's covering one-third of the cost of the *Brown v. Board of Education* lawsuit.

The Fund staff was integrated as well. Black Chicago YMCA executive George R. Arthur joined the staff to focus on an expanded college-building program; he was "probably the first person of African descent to work for any foundation in a professional capacity."[66] Also in the mid-1930s, M. O. Bousfield, a doctor active in the National Medical Association, was hired to focus on Black health, and George I. Sanchez, of Hispanic descent, came on board to focus on research. The Fund also employed women of Japanese descent: "During the Second World War, in spite of great anti-Japanese sentiment throughout the country, the philanthropy employed on its clerical staff at least three women of Japanese ancestry, one of whom was Embree's own secretary. In making such appointments, Embree made clear that the fund not only opposed workplace discrimination rhetorically, but rejected it conspicuously in practice."[67]

Before Rosenwald's death, the schoolhouse program was ended "lest . . . the southern states might come to rely too heavily on outside aid for Negro schools and so be delayed in assuming full responsibilities for the schools of this section of the population as a regular and integral part of the public provisions for the education of all the people."[68] For his efforts, JR was demonized by powerful southern politicians such as Georgia's governor Eugene Talmadge, a staunch white supremacist. He was also criticized by some scholars and activists for upholding the status quo of white supremacy and racial segregation.

Booker T. Washington and W. E. B. Du Bois

Whether to accept or resist the status quo of segregation was at the heart of the philosophical divide between Booker T. Washington and W. E. B. Du Bois that shaped much of the public discourse. Washington (1856–1915) had established the Tuskegee Institute to train young Black men as teachers and in useful trades and skills so they could "live by the production of hands . . . to dignify and glorify common labor and put brains and skill into the common occupations of life."[69] This training would enable them to survive in the Jim Crow world. But at the same time, Washington made clear that "in our humble way . . . in all things that are purely social we can be as separate as the fingers." That did not sit well with many people, both white and Black. There were plenty of racists at that time for whom even Washington's benign message was too extreme. And to say his message rankled Blacks looking for real equality was to put it mildly.

Du Bois (1868–1963) represented the opposite point of view, arguing fiercely and eloquently for equality across the board. He was the white supremacist's worse nightmare: he was brilliant, articulate, the first Black PhD graduate of Harvard in 1895, an eloquent writer, sociologist, historian, and civil rights activist who helped establish the NAACP. His challenge to the values and methods of Washington was comprehensive:

> So far as Mr. Washington preaches Thrift, Patience, and Industrial Training for the masses, we must hold up his hands and strive with him, rejoicing in his honors and glorying in the strength of this Joshua called of God and of man to lead the headless host. But so far as Mr. Washington apologizes for injustice, North or South, does not rightly value the privilege and duty of working, belittles the emasculating effects of caste distinctions, and opposes the higher training and ambition of our brighter

minds,—so far as he, the South or the Nation, does this—we must increasingly and firmly oppose them.[70]

It may seem inconsistent that Rosenwald supported the projects of men who held contrasting racial philosophies that were also dividing the Black community. "JR was not the only white or Jewish philanthropist to support both Washington's Tuskegee and Du Bois's NAACP; Jacob Schiff did the same thing. In JR's case his support was based on the belief that Blacks deserved both legal rights and the right to a decent education,"[71]

It is noteworthy that JR earned the undying respect of both Black antagonists. In an editorial for the NAACP magazine *Crisis,* Du Bois wrote, "The death of Julius Rosenwald brings to an end a career remarkable especially for its significance to American Negroes. As a Jew, Julius Rosenwald did not have to be initiated into the methods of race prejudice, and his philanthropic work was a crushing arraignment of the American white Christians." He singled out JR's support of Black YMCAs. And in an angry tone, Du Bois railed about the racism that required an individual to step in and do what the state should have done. Du Bois referred to the schoolhouse program, noting, "The South accepted this gift effusively, and never even to this day has apparently grasped the failure of democracy which permitted an individual of a despised race to do for the sovereign states of a great nation that which they had neither the decency nor justice to do for themselves." Then citing Rosenwald's building of hospitals, public libraries, and the establishment of a foundation to continue his work, Du Bois said, "He was a great man. But he was no mere philanthropist. He was, rather, the subtle stinging critic of our racial democracy."[72]

The sharp division between the attitudes of Washington and Du Bois can still engender strong debates. There are no references in any of JR's public or private remarks, nor those of Embree or any of the Fund trustees, to these polarized attitudes on the future rights, education, or status of Black people. Yet, clearly, the Fund adopted an accommodationist strategy, seeing it as the only one that enabled schoolhouses to be built. Racists, in fact, burned down at least one schoolhouse before it could open, but it was then rebuilt. The Rosenwald Fund had to work through the existing white segregated system.

Maya Angelou, John Lewis, and Julian Bond were among the many Black children educated in a Rosenwald School. Lewis, the legendary civil rights leader, was one of the original thirteen Freedom Riders, chairman of the Student Nonviolent Coordinating Committee, and a Georgia congressman from 1987 until his death in 2020. He was interviewed for the Ciesla Foundation's film on the Rosenwald Schools. In part, Lewis said:

> I grew up in rural Alabama about 50 miles from Montgomery. During those years segregation was real. You could feel it, you could see it with your naked eye. . . . It was very hard and very difficult for an African American to get a first-class education. We had then broken-down school buses to ride, the overcrowded shacks to attend school. . . . We had hand-me-down books. I wanted to get an education as a child. My mother, my father, my grandparents, my great-grandparents told us over and over again to get an education. . . . During my early days in elementary school, it was a little school a short distance from our home, walking distance. White, beautiful little building was the Rosenwald School. My mother, her sister, some of her brothers had attended the school. It was the only school we had. It was supported by the community. When it came time for repairs, to buy a heater, the people came together to buy a heater. You may call it a stove because it burned wood. And later they were able to buy coal to put in the stove to keep this potbelly heater hot for us during the winter.[73]

More Innovations

JR had other varied interests, but there was nothing that so commanded his attention as the Chicago Museum of Science and Industry, which is housed in the Palace of Fine Arts, the only building that remains standing from the 1893 Columbian Exposition. JR had been impressed by industrial museums that he visited years earlier in Munich, Vienna, Paris, and London. He observed how thrilled his son William was by those museums' exhibits. When the idea to create a science museum in Chicago was floated, JR pledged $1 million and helped make it happen. However, he resisted strong attempts to name it after him. It opened in 1933 during the Century of Progress Exposition. Given

JR's interest, it is not surprising to see Edith's passion for museums emerge after Edgar's death.

JR was also greatly concerned by the diminishing availability of decent affordable housing, especially after the Great Migration. He was haunted by the dire housing conditions he saw as he went to work, passing blocks and blocks of decades-old structures that were in miserable condition. Later, Edith and Edgar were similarly distressed by the lack of good, affordable housing, which led to their development of Pontchartrain Park. JR tried different solutions to the housing crisis. First, he established a low-interest-loan bank and then a private housing effort. Neither succeeded. He was interested in finding ways to invest in efforts that today would be called "program-related investments."

Around the turn of the twentieth century, a new form of housing was evolving that JR thought might ameliorate the housing shortage. Rosenwald had first seen this appealing building form in Vienna. This low-rise housing, containing five floors of apartments, added density without its residents losing their connection to nature; the buildings could also be designed to incorporate aesthetic elements. These courtyard apartments, so named because many were built around a central courtyard opening onto the street, came in several configurations. The first apartments of this type appeared in Chicago in the early 1890s; their architectural elements were established over the next fifteen to twenty years, and they continued to be built until the Great Depression.[74]

In 1929–30, with his grandson Alfred K. Stern in charge of construction, Rosenwald built the Michigan Boulevard Garden Apartments in Chicago.[75] They were five stories high, of brick with terra-cotta embellishment, and had a courtyard, fountain, 421 apartments, and street-level shops. The street-front businesses included a Sears store, an A&P grocery, a bank, and several Black-owned businesses, such as a candy store and a millinery shop.

JR wanted the complex to be racially integrated, but he discovered that was just not possible at the time.[76] Built in the then-thriving Black neighborhood of Bronzeville near to theaters, music spots, and stores, the rents were kept reasonably affordable for the middle class. The investor return was set at 5.59 percent.

A year after its completion and occupancy, Rosenwald, in a letter to the building's board of directors, declared the Michigan Boulevard Garden

Apartments a great success. "The feeling of satisfaction which is mine," he wrote, "is due to the splendid results of our great vision." The net income, he noted, was actually 6 percent. More importantly, the project had demonstrated that "modern housing facilities for Negroes can be provided on a strictly business basis." And the occupants "have proved that the Negro is a law-abiding citizen and desirable tenant."[77] This note of condescension was probably emblematic of the period. JR's hope was that other similar projects would follow, but the stock market crash and Great Depression killed those efforts.

According to architectural historian Daniel Bluestone:

> Rosenwald took the courtyard apartment form to a new level—drawing upon the extraordinary tradition of juxtaposing increased residential density with the humane incorporation of exactly the opposite—gardens, landscape, trees, and shrubbery. . . . It is notable that "garden" was even incorporated into the name. . . . Earlier Chicago efforts starting in the 1890s [were designed] to bring garden and landscape into the frame of apartment living, as a reform of tenement housing conditions. . . . Rosenwald's wealth permitted him to work at a scale that had generally not been previously achieved in Chicago, with over 400 units in a single development.[78]

After Rosenwald's death, the financial drain of upkeep was too much for the investors; government help was needed. The apartment complex was then turned over to the Chicago Housing Authority, which unfortunately did not use its resources to maintain it. The apartment building suffered the same disinvestment and decay as the neighborhood and was abandoned. For several decades "the Rosenwald," as it was popularly called, was left to deteriorate until a group of historic preservationists fought to bring attention to both the historic and bricks-and-mortar value of the complex. In 2002, Landmarks Illinois put the apartments on its Most Endangered Historic Places list. Later, the National Trust put it on its Most Endangered list. Finally renovated and renamed, the Rosenwald Court Apartments reopened in 2016, with the developers obtaining the kind of multilayered financing and tax credits that were used to restore historic buildings for low-income residents across the country.

Pioneering Support for the Arts

When the Rosenwald Fund was reorganized in 1927, not only did Embree become its president but the board was also expanded beyond Julius, his wife Gussie, and Lessing, their oldest son, to include other family members and non-family members. Gussie resigned, and three new family members came on: daughter Adele Rosenwald Levy; grandson Alfred K. Stern, son of Marion Rosenwald Stern; and Edgar B. Stern. Each was supposed to serve for one term, but when Edith was asked to join, she suggested that Edgar remain in her place. In fact, Edgar stayed on the board until the Fund closed in 1948. For a non-integrationist, serving on this board must have been an eye-opening experience for Edgar. A shifting array of non-family board members were mostly friends or former associates of Embree, although Eleanor Roosevelt served a term as trustee in the later years.

As mentioned, Embree had worked at the Rockefeller Foundation, where he observed the success of its grant program for teachers of education and liberal arts and had supervised a similar program for doctors, nurses, and scientific researchers. Soon after he arrived at the Fund, he initiated the Fellowship Program for "individuals of exceptional promise" in the creative arts who would bring recognition "to the Negro race as a whole." It would demonstrate that Blacks were "capable of contributions equal to those of the members of any other race."[79] Rosenwald was an enthusiastic supporter of the program, telling Embree, "Be daring, discover new talent, let them succeed." Darren Walker told me that "other foundations all took lessons from Rosenwald in supporting the arts. He supported the arts earlier and more than Rockefeller, Carnegie, and Mellon. They didn't start until the '30s."

Daniel Shulman notes that the Fellowship Program, which began in 1928, was "the largest and most influential single patron of African American art in the twentieth century, perhaps ever."[80] From 1928 to 1948, the program spent $1.65 million ($22 million in 2026 dollars) to provide from one- to three-year fellowships for 587 Black individuals and 278 white southerners in the fields of education, public health, agriculture, sociology, economics, the humanities, and the sciences, as well as in creative writing, visual art, music, drama, and dance.

The list of recipients is remarkable and included the noted writers Zora

Neale Hurston, James Weldon Johnson, Langston Hughes, Ralph Ellison, and James Baldwin; historian John Hope Franklin; civil rights activist W. E. B. Du Bois; dancer and choreographer Katherine Dunham; and artists Charles White and Richmond Barthé. Aided by these fellowships, which often came at a critical time in their development, they went on have successful careers and even fame.[81]

The artistic achievements were staggering. Jacob Lawrence's *Migration Series* is one of the great works of twentieth-century American art; Gordon Parks's photographs of African American life had broad impact; Elizabeth Catlett's wood-block print series, *The Negro Woman*, including both historical and ordinary women, has some of the same power that Lawrence's series has; and Augusta Savage's sensitive sculptural depictions of African Americans (in 1929, she was the first to receive an art fellowship) broke new ground. The selection of Catlett and Savage indicated that the Rosenwald Fund was not overlooking the accomplishments of women artists.

In other fields, there was Charles Drew, who needed help to finish medical school and went on to discover a way to store blood plasma. A grant to future Nobel Prize winner and undersecretary general of the UN Ralph Bunche allowed him to make his first trip outside the United States. Grants went to future university presidents Max Bond and his brother Horace Mann Bond, biologist E. E. Just, and psychologist and educator Kenneth B. Clark.

There were white recipients too, who were either southerners advancing racial change or artists and writers who were depicting the South in new ways. Kentucky-born novelist Elizabeth Hardwick was a "fiery critic" for the *Partisan Review*. Future editor of the *Atlanta Journal-Constitution*, Ralph McGill received the Pulitzer Prize for editorials condemning racism in the South. Eighth-generation Virginian Robert Gwathmey went north for art school and discovered the contrast between living conditions for Black northerners and Black southerners. With the funds provided by his fellowship, he returned to the South to depict racial oppression and economic inequality. He took pride in being called the "white Jacob Lawrence."

These fellowships changed the lives of their recipients, enabling them to pursue their passions and their crafts. Without them, the sensitive depiction of Black culture would have certainly been short-changed. Edith followed her father's example by providing funds to a young Black opera singer, Annabelle Bernard. Without Edith's help, Bernard, like the Rosenwald grantees, might never have made it onto the world stage.

In 1928, the same year the Rosenwald Fellowship program began, Embree traveled throughout the South, seeing firsthand the needs and challenges faced by southern Blacks. He and other foundation leaders, encouraged by Du Bois and other Black leaders, recognized the need to strengthen higher education for Black students in the South. Embree's first action was to secure agreement from the General Education Board of the Rockefeller Foundation to be a partner in the effort.

Embree then devised a broad strategy to fund Black higher education in three cities of the South—Atlanta, Nashville, New Orleans—as well as Washington, DC, providing grants for fourteen additional private Black colleges, seven state Black colleges, industrial high schools in five cities, and a dozen hospitals scattered throughout the country.[82] It is difficult to imagine what Black higher education in the South would have looked like if this funding had not been provided. Soon after Embree developed this strategy, opportunity struck in New Orleans from which Dillard University would emerge, with Edgar playing the key role.

5

A PLACE TO LIVE AND A PLACE TO LEARN

Years later Edith would be knee-deep in politics, organizing voter registration drives aimed at African Americans, rescuing the Louisiana Symphony from bankruptcy, and helping the New Orleans Museum of Art grow its collection and its building in City Park.[1] But for the first two decades of her life in New Orleans, Edith focused on hearth and home. She built a distinguished mansion, Longue Vue, which is now a historic house and garden museum, and founded two schools embracing an educational philosophy new to the South.

Undoubtedly, Edith felt a great sense of achievement in having established two pioneering schools: Newcomb Nursery School, the city's first Montessori school and first preschool, and Metairie Park Country Day School, a progressive private operation. But Edith was most passionate about the creation of Longue Vue, in its two versions. This is where she applied the creative juices that made her—and, in large part, Edgar—a designer or, at least, a collaborator with the cast of professionals they employed. Edith did such a spectacular job that decades later, Walter Isaacson, who wrote the foreword to *Longue Vue House and Gardens,* remembered that when the house and gardens were opened as a museum, "Everyone went to see them not merely because the gardens were so beautiful but also because the estate had been the home of the most respected family in the city."[2] In a remembrance delivered at Edith Stern's funeral, her son Philip said this of Longue Vue: "It symbolized her personality; everything was perfection and beauty. You felt that in every nook and cranny, around every corner, you could expect to find something that was special and exciting and beautiful."

Twice Edith chose to tell the story of the house: first, in a twenty-three-page, single-spaced document she lovingly dictated and treated as if it were a lengthy book; and second, in ten double-spaced pages that she dictated to a friend, Mrs. Lee Schlesinger, when she was living in the Pontchartrain Hotel the year before she died in 1980.[3] Edith had a lot to say about this house and for good reason: Longue Vue is both incredibly personal and publicly important in its design, construction, craftsmanship, unique furnishings, and distinctive use.

Undoubtedly, it is no coincidence that Metairie Park Country Day School was built less than a mile from Longue Vue. Longue Vue was located very near the border dividing New Orleans from the emerging suburb of Metairie, and Country Day was built at the edge of the suburb. Garden Lane, where Longue Vue would be constructed, branched off a new street being built by the city. The parcel of land Edith and Edgar bought to build on was nowhere near any upscale neighborhood, but it had advantages that secured its exclusivity.

The New Orleans Country Club (Jews were not welcome, but the Sterns were a rare exception) on Longue Vue's east side protected their site from further development. In addition, two canals—the 17th Street Canal on the west and the Palmetto Canal on the south—provided both drainage and additional seclusion. Over the years, they kept adding land to reach a total of eight acres of grounds surrounding the house.

When the final parcel was purchased, it preserved the seclusion that the Sterns sought, which had recently come under threat, as Edith wrote in "Autobiography of a House":

> The truly rude awakening came when a very real subdivision threatened all the property on the west side of Garden Lane. Imagine forty kitchen doors facing onto one's front yard; forty radios blasting the silence of erstwhile rural peace. [The additional parcel] made it possible for the lane to be closed off, and the "Estately Entrance" from Bamboo Road was a dream that would come true in 1940. One can visualize the miniscule size of the Live Oaks when that number could be planted in those few feet. That allee of oaks trumpeted the birth pangs of the existing Longue Vue.[4]

Longue Vue I and II

The first house was five thousand square feet and was designed by Edgar's architect friend, Moise H. Goldstein, in a colonial or classical revival style popular in New Orleans at the time. It was built soon after the couple were married in 1921. Edith was an enthusiastic gardener and clearly wanted to make the most of the grounds around the house. She was an active member of the local garden clubs, having inherited a strong interest in flowers from her mother. The garden club movement had been growing since early in the twentieth century.

In 1934, Edith helped finance the publication of *Wild Flowers of Louisiana* by Caroline Dormon and in 1947 would hire her to advise on flower plantings in the gardens.[5] Dormon became a celebrated spokeswoman for conservation, educating the public about the importance of saving and maintaining native plants, a passion Edith shared.

Edith's desire for expansive gardens was served by a house at the edge of the city limits, where there was little development. Edith designed the gardens around their first house, where she and Edgar lived and raised their three children for sixteen years. The couple met landscape architect Ellen Biddle Shipman in 1934 or 1935 and began to commission new gardens from her. The striking result of Shipman's designs, combined with inspiration gained during an extended family trip abroad in 1936, led to a decision to build a new house to better match the new gardens. Longue Vue I was moved in 1939, its furniture included, down Garden Lane. A crew of mules spent several weeks pulling the house on logs, moving it just a short distance each day. Meanwhile, the site for Longue Vue II was cleared and ready for construction. This time, integration of the house and gardens was of paramount importance. Achieving that goal was essential to the beauty and charm of Longue Vue II. Over the next decades, Shipman would become the adviser most relied on for every design element both outside and inside the house.

The Critically Consequential Designer

Ellen Biddle Shipman (1869–1950) was born in Philadelphia into a conventional middle-class family. At an early age, she exhibited a love for the outdoors and an interest in plants. Daughter of a career soldier, she spent many years exploring the outdoors with her father after the family moved to Nevada. From her father, she learned a lot about the natural world.

Landscape design was one of the few career pursuits open to women early in the twentieth century. Studying and working in the design professions had become acceptable areas of employment for young women, along with medicine and teaching. By the 1890s, arenas for working women expanded to include sports, performing, settlement houses, factories, offices, stores, and, of course, suffrage efforts.

Shipman attended Radcliffe, then known as the Harvard Annex, and was enrolled there for one year. At Radcliffe, she became involved in suffragette activities and met fellow student Louis Shipman, who was active in the intellectual and artistic circles of Cambridge. Ellen soon married Shipman, and the pair moved to the growing arts community in Cornish, New Hampshire. Augustus Saint-Gaudens, a Beaux Arts sculptor, had founded the colony and was a key figure in it.

There, Shipman developed a strong interest in flowers as a critical part of a landscape. She also met her eventual mentor, Charles A. Platt, one of the leading architects of the day and known for designing grand country estates befitting the Country Place Era.[6] He had studied landscape design early on. Platt's innovation was designing house and gardens at the same time, making them a single, interdependent unit.

Eventually, Shipman established her own firm, which had a female-only staff. Her work was "defined by a formal design that she developed over a lifetime, often articulated by rows of trees and/or hedges; she cultivated abundant garden beds bursting with flowers and foliage."[7] One recognizes this style today at Longue Vue with its sixteen garden areas, or what Shipman called "garden rooms." In 1934, *House & Garden* dubbed Shipman the "dean of American women landscape architects." In fact, Shipman transformed landscaping into a new art form and set the style for the country.

Shipman started working at Longue Vue in 1935. It did not take long for the Sterns to greatly appreciate her work and follow her instincts. The first garden at the new house was designed for Edgar, who was passionate about gardens. At his request, Shipman created a reading garden by the Goldfish Pond, a modest little hideaway complete with a bench. He reportedly spent time there for years to come.

Once the Sterns decided to totally replace the existing house, they spoke with a number of architects before landing on Shipman's recommendation: William and Geoffrey Platt, the sons of her mentor, the architect Charles Platt. All three were nationally famous for their classical revival designs. William became the primary architect for Longue Vue, while Geoffrey focused more on historic preservation.

The Platts, Shipman, and the Sterns "had the happiest relationship over the years," Edith said in a 1978 interview. The five of them spent a lot of time scouting important houses in the New Orleans area. Edith recalled, "What fun were those trips studying the various uses of Greek Revival. So many of these basic principles have been adopted. . . . Someone else had braved breaking an architectural unwritten law. Why not again?"[8]

The house is a composite of several residences in this region, with elements selected from different styles—classical Palladian, Greek Revival, Georgian, and Creole. The architecture of Longue Vue may have been the only arena in which Edith accepted the norms of the local aristocracy; yet even while accepting them, she created her own version. Through Longue Vue, she was determined to fit into her adopted city but on her own terms.

Driving into Longue Vue is an experience in itself. Its graceful extended entry driveway is framed by great live oaks, their branches wired to grow up, rather than sideways and down. The Doric columns on the second-story front wall of Longue Vue II reflect its Palladian influences. The overall design is a modification of Greek Revival style, as Edith explained: "The usual plan of the main house with two repeated small houses at either end, called 'Garconnieres,' was translated here into a garage to the north and the Whim House, a guest house, to the south. Just beyond the garage is the double-height Playhouse designed to have the feeling of a barn with its rough-hewn timber trusses. A balcony in the Playhouse was created to accommodate musicians and singers. If acoustics are unpredictable, Bill Platt hit the Jack Pot in the Playroom. The double height, vaulted ceiling; the cypress wood paneling seems ideal. The vernissage of that is unforgettable."[9]

Each façade of the house is different, and each opens to a specially designed garden. Of course, there is a first-floor breezeway, so important in southern homes during the hot months. A circular vestibule contains niches for flowers. Just inside the primary entrance are both a cloakroom and a small reception room, where the bathroom windows are etched with patterns copied from the room's rose-filled wallpaper to avoid needing curtains.

The Novelties Seemed Endless

What is most striking about Longue Vue, however, is not its grandeur or design details but its livability. It is filled with appealing architectural elements, fascinating pieces of furniture, and occasional Woolworth collectibles. Edgar was a big fan of the newest gadgets, so the house has many technological advancements. It was one of the first in Louisiana to have built-in air conditioning and a house-wide electric clock system. Longue Vue clearly reflects its owners' passions. There is a room just for wrapping presents; there is one just for arranging flowers, with four sinks of different depths. In the ceiling above the central circular stair is a glass dome.

Yes, Longue Vue has all those elements and more, but mostly it just feels comfortable. One can easily find a niche in the library to curl up and read a book. One can imagine enjoying a birthday party or a game in the family sitting room, called the Blue Room. This was Edith's favorite room, where a Kandinsky painting hung over the fireplace (her first purchase of contemporary art) and where she liked to work on her needlepoint and talk to her grandchildren. It was a family gathering spot to read, converse, listen to the radio, and later watch TV. It was also where birthday parties were celebrated. There was a special chair for the birthday celebrant, whether a member of the family or household staff. All the staff were given elaborate birthday parties, much like what was done in the Rosenwald household when Edith was growing up. Gifts were wrapped in colors taken from the Kandinsky painting.

Just beyond the Blue Room is what was originally an open porch overlooking the golf course. William Platt enclosed the porch in 1960 to serve as a gallery for Edith's growing modern art collection. This new interest in art helped fill the void left by Edgar's death. Her collection concentrated on op, kinetic, and geometric pieces, with works by Victor Vasarely, Barbara Hepworth, Naum Gabo, Yaacov Agam, Jean Arp, and Alexander Liberman.

Edith and Edgar's corner bedroom upstairs combines comfort, luxury, and the latest innovations. Edith's dressing room contains a circular closet with a clothes rack that turns easily, whereas Edgar's bathroom, like the other family bathrooms, has an innovative built-in scale. And who could resist a night in the upstairs sleeping porch, with its charming hand-painted floral designs on the walls. Sleeping porches were common before air conditioning and were often used year-round for health reasons.

Longue Vue reflects Edith and Edgar's down-to-earth personalities; the formal and the casual blend nicely. And with all its elegance, the house does not have a distinctly "decorated look." No room is predictable, with each containing an assortment of casual furniture, Woolworth's knickknacks, and expensive antiques. Every object was selected for personal reasons, never because current fashion dictated it. For example, Edith defied convention in the elegant formal dining room, where she would often use her best tablecloth with its delicately appliqued birds. As part of the centerpiece, she would include an assortment of little ceramic birds bought at Woolworth's, a rare touch of humor in an otherwise formal room. Inevitably, guests would ask about the birds, assuming they were treasured antiques.

The library is lined with Norwegian spruce paneling bought at auction and originally from a house in England. The study has a collection of rare books, as well as a charming collection of cream ware and Staffordshire china. And as if to follow Ellen Shipman's advice that the house must never look too new or too formal, the study contains well-worn seating from Edgar's Harvard days.

The ceilings of the rooms are of different heights, set according to the proportion of the rooms: they are lower for small rooms and higher for large ones. The state-of-the-art air-conditioning system throughout the house made possible the flexibility in ceiling heights. To accommodate the AC equipment, the house has a basement, which is unusual for a New Orleans home because of the high water table. A photography darkroom and wine-tasting room are also in the basement, which flooded in 2005 during Hurricane Katrina.

In the upstairs drawing room is a historic mantle that Shipman bought serendipitously at a side-of-the-road South Carolina barn of a car mechanic. Nine coats of paint needed to be removed to discover it was made of carved wood and composite and signed by a famous Philadelphia cabinetmaker, Robert Wellford, in 1800. But what made the mantle very special to the Sterns is that it is a memorial mantelpiece to George Washington, with his initials and date of death inscribed. The Metropolitan Museum of Art has one like it in its American Wing. Above the mantlepiece is a portrait of Edith's paternal grandmother, Augusta Hammerslough Rosenwald, mother of Julius, painted by August Franzen in 1911.

In the later 1970s, when Edith vacated Longue Vue and moved to the Pontchartrain Hotel to allow the house to be converted into a museum, the only piece she took with her was her music box. It was a turn-of-the-century Swiss music box, cabinet intact, its repertory of brass cylinders in all the drawers. After her death, it was returned to its original place.

Both comfortably livable and elegant at the same time, Longue Vue was the perfect setting for a series of social events in which Edith, Edgar, and the house were at the center. A long, varied list of famous dinner and house guests visited over the years, such as Adlai Stevenson, Paul Newman (his assistant called ahead to tell the staff what kind of beer he liked), Pearl Buck, Pablo Casals, Ginger Rogers, Jack Benny, Moshe Dayan, and Eleanor Roosevelt. To make this lavish lifestyle work with grace and style, a full staff of thirty-five employees—Black, white, and Hispanic—were at hand, including two live-in housekeepers.

A Larger Purpose

Great care was given to the craftsmanship of the house itself and its furnishings. Unusual materials came from near and far. Brazilian rosewood is used for some floors, but the floors of the Blue Room are made of white oak. Friezes and plasterwork details in the ceiling were brought from New York, as was the millwork throughout the house. This was done for a larger purpose beyond the aesthetic. In their book about Longue Vue, Charles Davey and Carol McMichael Reese stated, "The Sterns also realized that the house could make a tremendous contribution to the preservation of traditional skills at a time when the Depression and lack of jobs were whittling away at the numbers of skilled craftsman."[10] William Platt, quoted in that book, said, "They thought if people were given a job, it would help train others, and it would help preserve the kind of building skills that were evaporating. And so, they believed in details of plaster, wood, hardware, doors, and floors, and all kinds of things that made an interior special."[11]

And it shows. Longue Vue is a marvel of artful details. As Edith wrote in "Autobiography of a House," "I have been told more than once [that Longue Vue] will, in time, be of historic value. It is said that it is the last big house in America planned and built prior to the end of [World War II]. . . . No more detailed craftsmanship done with artisan hands. Gone is the pride in workmanship. . . . Attention to details has been priced out of existence. In no house built after 1945 can one find the careful detailed planning or the execution by trained craftsmen."[12]

Edith's observation still has the ring of truth today, especially in New Orleans. Many Black skilled craftsmen brought their trades from Santo Domingo, Haiti, at the end of the eighteenth and early nineteenth centuries. They helped create the celebrated architectural landscape of this unique city and trained the next generations of craftsmen who undoubtedly built Longue Vue. Yet, their skills and knowledge are not being passed on as robustly as they could be, and the small apprentice training programs that exist today receive little, if any, public support.[13] In recognition of their contributions to the city's charm and beauty, in 2002, the New Orleans Museum of Art presented an exhibition titled "Raised to the Trade: Creole Building Arts of New Orleans." It celebrated the "rich legacies of artistry and craftsmanship of many generations of master builders."

Edith and Edgar were not just building a house or a showplace for its own sake. It was an expression of their own interests and tastes. They combined the kitsch with the priceless to demonstrate that the artful does not always come with a high price tag. They knew, as well, this was a house that would have a larger purpose, as a showpiece for the city; they established as early as the 1930s that they did not intend to leave the estate to family. They used it well and entertained both for their own sake and for fundraising for the causes they cared about.

And they surely knew how to entertain in a big way, especially for a meaningful celebration. Edith wrote:

> Longue Vue should be accordian pleated. It was either a feast or a famine; two living in solitary splendor or every bed taken. Children were adults by then but could get back now and then for the oyster bar—red beans and rice—fresh oysters, River Shrimp, Crawfish in season, and most often for New Years. But Longue Vue was also the center for serious, fruitful gatherings. Many times, it turned into the political, smoke-filled room on a state level; beautiful recitals and chamber music for the Symphony's small series; often fund-raising sales of garden clubs and Country Day boutiques.[14]

Edith did not leave a record of the many times she entertained but occasionally mentioned something about those occasions in her letters. Years later, on April 27, 1947, for example, Edith wrote to Philip, who was then serving in the US Navy, that daughter Audrey and son-in-law Tom were coming to New Orleans to celebrate Edith and Edgar's twenty-fifth anniversary: "Tom Hess and I decided suddenly to have a free-for-all in celebration. About 125 young folk in the Playroom, orchestra and all, and a huge reception in the main house for our friends." She added, as if in explanation, that they had just attended a wedding with more than eight hundred guests: "I assure you it was more painful than enjoyable. . . . Well, ours is pretty big but nothing like that."[15]

The Gardens

As interesting as the house is in both its design and its personalized décor, the gardens were really Edith's pride and joy from the beginning. After all, they were her major focus when she hired landscape designer Ellen Shipman in 1935. In addition, as mentioned, Edith hired Caroline Dormon, the wildflower specialist, in 1947 to supply native plants for the Wild Garden and consult elsewhere in the gardens.

Edith met both Shipman and Dormon through the local garden community. The Garden Study Club of New Orleans, which Edith founded, was at first denied affiliation with the Garden Club of America because the national organization did not welcome Jews. Edith's good friend Margery Stich recalled, "Since the latter did not accept Jews, Edith called a meeting of the group, and offered to resign, since she was the only Jewish member. The group caucused and decided that they would accept membership precisely as they were constituted, or not at all. The Garden Club of America accepted the group including Edith."[16]

One might be correct in thinking that the gardens meant more to Edith than the house. She cared about other people's gardens too, and generously so. For instance, she sent her gardener to her good friend Phyllis Dennery to replant her front-yard garden after sidewalk work had destroyed it.

To walk through the gardens around the house is to understand clearly what Shipman meant as the marriage of the interior and exterior. The gardens are largely the same today as they were in 1942 when designed and require a staff of sixteen to maintain. Each of the four sides of the house has separate entrances to distinctive gardens. The Pan Garden is easily accessed from the dining room through an opening created by a window that is lowered into the floor—resulting in the feeling that the dining room and garden are one room. The garden is modest in scale and does not overshadow the elegance of the dining room. Similar to a typical French Quarter garden room, the al fresco dining space is intimate and private. A sculpture of Pan, the Greek god of nature, by Gertrude Knoblock is surrounded by a profusion of pink azaleas. This was a favorite spot for dinner when it was just Edith and Edgar.

Just outside the modern art gallery and facing the golf course is a small terrace planted in 2009 to fit in with the sustainable pollinating goals of Longue Vue garden management; it is one of the landscape features that draw a host of butterfly species. Although small in scale, it is along the larger East Lawn abutting the adjacent gold course.

The formal Portico Garden opens from the library and extends onto the expansive Spanish Court. The doors of the second-floor drawing room, above the library, were always open when parties were held there. Spanish Court features thirteen fountains, manicured hedges, and brick and pebble walkways inspired by Granada, Spain. Each pebble was placed by hand.

Nearby but separate from it is the Yellow Garden that Edith designed in 1967 outside the glass door of the Whim House, the guest house. A bronze sculpture designed by Robert Engman is placed in a circular water feature designed to be silent so as not to disturb guests. Every detail reflected Edith's taste and concern for the experience of her house guests.

Various additional "garden rooms" are placed in the grounds, including the Canal Garden with a long water feature added in 1967; it was inspired by a Lisbon garden that Edith visited with William Platt. The Wild Garden features species indigenous to Louisiana. As a pièce de résistance, tucked away in the far corner, is a brick pigeonnier. Edgar used this as a quiet place to read the books found on the structure's interior shelves. The Iris Walk with its 3,500 Louisiana irises is a popular attraction every spring. The seasonal counterpart is the Camellia Walk, with its 120 winter-blooming camellia shrubs. The Walled Garden was once a kitchen garden and was transformed into a Victory Garden during World War II. Today the Walled Garden is filled with fruits and vegetables and is a source for ingredients served in the museum's garden café.

One sizable greenhouse remains where there were once three in what is now called the Discovery Garden. Created in 1998, the Discovery Garden was inspired by the Sterns' commitment to education and the natural environment and was designed for children of all ages. Pollinator plants, seasonal edible flowers, and insects are key areas of focus.

Altogether, Longue Vue is the height of elegance and style. In a significant way, it was Edith's substitute for the New Orleans lineage she did not have but that was so important to possess in this city. As she wrote in a foreword to "Autobiography of a House," the house "can boast of no historic past nor famous ancestors as can many in New Orleans, but a sincere attempt was made to capture the beauty, dignity and serenity of these noble homes which is our birthright. Opened Christmas 1942."[17]

Educational Breakthroughs

In matters of civic life, Edith participated where she felt she was needed and could do the most good. In many of her efforts, she followed her father's pattern of giving challenge grants—generous ones at that—that resulted in many New Orleanians giving more money to things than they intended. First, she recognized a need and learned more about it and then used her money and organizing skills to address it. When Edith had a new idea to address a pressing need, action followed. This seems to be a hallmark of her busy life.

When she decided that the available educational options were not suitable for her children, she founded two schools. As granddaughter Anne said, "She needed a place to send her children to school; it's as simple as that." Edgar Jr. had been born in 1922, Audrey would follow in 1924, and Philip in 1926. So yes, schools were high on her agenda.

First, she started the Newcomb Nursery School in 1926 in a small Uptown building near the Newcomb College campus. In an undated account, Irma Barnett recalls that Edith—a good friend—brought together "10 or 12 of her friends' children with graduate students [with] Newcomb's School of Sociology supervising."[18] There had never been an organized nursery school in New Orleans. Reportedly, it was the first one in the South.

THE IMPACT OF THE JOHN DEWEY MOVEMENT

In fact, the nursery school movement itself was brand-new. The John Dewey Laboratory School in Chicago, which Edith had attended, started what it called a preschool program for the youngest children in 1916. Rosenwald was an important funder of both this school and the University of Chicago. The Chicago Lab School was home base for the breakthrough progressive teaching philosophy of John Dewey that effectively changed American education. Hands-on attention to the individual child and learning as the byproduct of social activity were at the heart of the Chicago experiment, breaking with the regimented approach of the past. Students would learn as much outside the classroom as in. There was no preset curriculum; education was directed to the needs of each individual child. Edith would bring this philosophy to the two schools she founded in New Orleans.

Clearly, Edith's attendance at and familiarity with the Dewey school in Chicago had a major impact on her. After Dewey moved to New York to serve on the faculty of Columbia University, she visited the university's Institute for Child Welfare. There, Edith became acquainted with and then influenced by Patty Smith Hill, a leader of the progressive kindergarten and nursery school movement. The movement emphasized that preschool education should encourage development of the child's creative instincts. Edith took what she learned at this institute to New Orleans.

One can only understand how radical Dewey's approach to education was early in the twentieth century when one considers how schools were then run. Education was still primarily the "three Rs": basic reading, writing, and arithmetic. It was heavily structured, formal, and rigid. Each cohort moved forward together, whether individual students were ready or not.

Dewey's groundbreaking book *School and Society* offered a new vision focused on the individual child and his or her connection to real life. "Learning by doing" was the new catchword and was implemented in a variety of ways, such as skill development in cooking, art, or making furniture, along with the three Rs. Such a broad development of skills, including but not limited to basic book learning, would, Dewey believed, enable students to become active members of society. Education, beginning at the nursery school level, was meant to introduce a young child to the world of exploration and to guide each student's development.

A GRADE SCHOOL FOUNDED

The establishment of Metairie Park Country Day School in 1929 was of such note that two local newspapers gave its opening extensive coverage, spotlighting that students there were treated as individuals and were learning by doing.[19] One paper reported, "The children have engaged in practical illustrations of their subjects. The Second Grade pupils coagulated latex for an actual illustration of how rubber was made. The Third Grade pupils raised and sold canary birds in connection with their nature study. The first graders drew large pictures to illustrate the lessons they read."[20]

The school was located on fourteen acres in what were then beautiful woodlands that would evolve into the neighborhood of Old Metairie. The first building to be constructed looks like Edith and Edgar's first house but in brick. Eight white columns grace the front, and black shutters frame the windows, not unlike many historic southern dwellings. Edith would recall in her remarks at the Founders' reunion twenty-seven years after its opening, "This piece of land was truly in the wilderness—we were pioneers not only in the field of education, but geographically as well."[21]

In New Orleans, there were and continue to be a large number of Catholic and private schools that are popular alternatives to the public schools. The

Country Day Founders group was clearly a prominent crowd socially and financially; only one couple besides the Sterns was apparently Jewish. It is likely that if the group Edith gathered had included more Jews, some prominent families might not have been interested. But the members of this group could all write appropriately large checks, and of course, they believed in the school's educational philosophy.[22] These criteria were quite important, especially because the stock market crashed just two months after its first school year began.

Metairie Park Country Day School was not necessarily an alternative to either religiously oriented or public schools. Instead, it was an alternative to everything that education was about at that time. It embraced progressive ideas that had just recently taken hold in large US cities, rejecting the traditional practice of rote learning through memorization. As such, it was not just a new school; it was a mission, and Edith was its leader. As Edith reminded the gathering at the Founders' reunion, "Remember that methods of education were being strongly challenged around the area. The Country Day type of school was springing up all over the country; coeducation was considered a must; the approaches to reading and writing were radically changed. It was much the same atmosphere that one finds now—two generations later."[23] Bringing transformative ideas about education to New Orleans made sense to Edith.

"You have to remember that the whole country was in the throes of change," shared Howard Hunter, a history teacher for forty years at Metairie Country Day. Hunter and his father both graduated from Country Day. "You had progressive governors—Robert La Follette of Wisconsin, Charles Evans Hughes Sr. of New York, Hiram Johnson of California. The milieu was one of dramatic change. There was an optimism in America about new things. Oliver Wendell Holmes Jr. was espousing a new way to look at the law. And Dewey was at his height at Columbia offering a broader societal world view than was then the norm. The Progressive Education movement actually started among the elite and was considered modern."

The first head of the school was Ralph E. Boothby, who had graduated from Harvard in 1912. He had been involved ever since in education, promoting the progressive agenda. The search for a headmaster was national in scope. Although this was primarily Edith's effort, Edgar was very much involved, as letters in the archives indicate. So, it helped Boothby that he had gone to Edgar's beloved alma mater.

Boothby made Country Day a laboratory, with educators coming from around the South to visit and learn about it. He traveled extensively as well, giving lectures about progressive education. In 1938, he was chair of the Education Committee of the Conference on Human Welfare, which Eleanor Roosevelt attended. "It was probably the first bi-racial conference of any kind," Hunter explained. "It was looking at living conditions, economic and social conditions."

Boothby was celebrated nationally, and his progressive ideas influenced schools in Louisiana, both public and private. As Edith boastfully noted at the Founders' reunion, "Only the challenge of Country Day inspired the renaissance of our local private schools."[24] The original constituency of parents, noted Hunter, included liberal intellectuals, conservative professionals, and Uptown reactionaries. It was a school of Protestants, Catholics, and Jews at a time when institutional divisions between faiths were more defined.

Country Day had a slow start. The first year there were eight students (four boys and four girls), nine in the second year, then ten the next year, and gradually up to the full measure of several hundred that attend now. The first graduation was so unusual that it made local news. Noting the "distinct departure from the usual commencement" and that it lasted only seventeen minutes, a newspaper (unidentified) article reported, "In line with the educational philosophy of the school, there were no honor graduates, no awards, no long orations. The diplomas consisted of small pieces of parchment . . . tied with red, white and blue ribbon. Instead of carrying bouquets, the girls wore coronets of pale pink carnations."[25]

Edgar worked vigorously to recruit students by spreading the word about Country Day. He wrote long, detailed letters about how unusual and special it was. He then wrote to Boothby, specifying those whom he had contacted who had no interest, some possible interest, and occasionally those who planned to send their child to Country Day. Edgar, keeping an eye on the school's finances, periodically sent checks for funds that Edith had already committed from one set of Stern funds or another.

Edith donated many items to the school for educational purposes, including magazine subscriptions like *The Reporter* and books for the library. In one batch sent in June 1934, the fifteen books included what are now considered classics, although they were perhaps not then: Edna Ferber's *So Big;* DuBose Heyward's *Porgy and Bess;* Ivan Turgenev's *Fathers and Sons;* Jane Austen's *Pride and Prejudice;* Honoré de Balzac's *Père Goriot;* George Eliot's *Adam Bede;* and Theodore Dreiser's *American Tragedy.*

INTEGRATION

As "progressive" as Country Day was, it would be decades before the school integrated racially—eighteen years after the 1954 Supreme Court decision and only when pushed by its students.

In February 1970, the chair of Country Day's board (and Edgar's best friend), Monte Lemann, proposed a committee to study the "racial restriction clause of the charter." A week later, the school newspaper ran an unsigned column, "CD at the Crossroads," stating, "At a time when integration is the law of the land, Country Day remains lily white. At a time when even Gov. McKeithen says segregation is dead, Country Day's charter reads that the aim of the school shall be 'to promote the education of white persons.' Now that no laws remain to obstruct integration, Eh-la-bas! . . . [We] can only wonder at the failure of the board to strike this 40-year-old clause from its charter."[26]

Six months later, the board voted to admit Black students. The board minutes state matter-of-factly, "Racial segregation restrictions will no longer be a factor in admission of students to the school." The vote was fifteen in favor, with none opposed and one abstention. Edith must have been very pleased. The first Black student(s) entered in 1972.

Over time, both the nursery school and Country Day have become integral parts of New Orleans's educational landscape. Edith could not boast of having the right ancestors for the city's class-conscious society, but she could take credit for changing educational opportunities at the preschool, elementary, and secondary education levels. Edgar could boast of doing the same on the college level.

The Stern family in 1896.
Left to right: Solomon (known as S. Walter), Sara May,
Maurice, Hannah, and Edgar.

The Rosenwald family in Chicago, 1910.
Left to right: Lessing, William, Marion, Julius, Adele, Augusta, Edith.

Edith and Edgar on their wedding day, June 6, 1921.

Edith and Edgar with Audrey, Philip, and Edgar Jr.
on the lawn at Longue Vue, 1926.

Portrait of Edith taken by Dorothy Wilding, 1936.

Edith and Edgar in the Longue Vue Playhouse before a party, 1940s.

Edith at home, 1960s.

NEW ORLEANS STATES

Friday, May 15, 1953

SEAT HEADS OF VOTERS GROUP

—New Orleans States Photo.

NEW OFFICERS of the Voters Registration League were installed at a meeting at league headquarters yesterday. Left to right, MRS. ISIDORE NEWMAN II, treasurer; MRS. EDGAR B. STERN SR., president; MRS. MAURICE BAYON, secretary; and MRS. GLADYS REILY, vice-president.

Reforms in Vote Laws Advocated by League

Solis

Mrs. Edgar B. Stern was installed as president of the Voters Registration League yesterday.

Other officers are:

Mrs. Gladys Reily, vice-president.

Mrs. Maurice Bayon, secretary.

Mrs. Isidore Newman II, treasurer.

The newly-elected officers were seated at a meeting yesterday in Soule building, St. Charles and Lafayette, at which the group called for an overhauling of the primary election laws.

Propose Study of Laws

A study of the laws by the Louisiana research legislative council with the aim of relaxing some of the requirements for vote eligibility was proposed by the league.

Emmett Asseff, director of the research council, discussed the proposed study with the group and assured it that he will recommend the survey.

Taking part in the discussions were John Minor Wisdom, Louisiana's Republican national committeeman, Mrs. Natlie Dreyfous, president of the League of Women Voters, and Mrs. Bland Cox Bruns, 10th ward representative in the Louisiana Legislature.

Reforms Advocated

The league advised the research director that it was advocating reforms in provisions of the election laws covering absentee voting, residence eligibility and a cross file system which would allow candidates to enter either Democratic or Republican primaries regardless of party affiliation.

Newsclip of Edith and her fellow voter registration workers, May 15, 1953.
Left to right: Mrs. Isidore Newman, Edith, Mrs. Maurice Bayon, Mrs. Gladys Reily.

Emma Brown (*seated*) and Natalie Forcia at the Portico entrance, Longue Vue. Brown was the Sterns' longtime cook, and Forcia was Edith's personal maid and companion. Both were treasured members of the staff.

In addition to her work for the Sterns, Forcia was sought after by caterers for her elegant spun-sugar cake decorations. This elaborate bell topping for a wedding cake is typical of the intricate decorations she made.

The living room at Longue Vue with an oil painting of Augusta Rosenwald, Edith's mother, over the mantel. The two Loving Cups the couple received in recognition of their civic engagement are in niches adjacent to the fireplace.

The Longue Vue dining room. The table is set with an appliquéd tablecloth and papier-mâché birds purchased at Woolworth's. The bay window in the breakfast nook opens all the way up to overlook Pan Garden.

The west façade (main entrance) of Longue Vue, with fountain at center and live oak allée planted in the 1940s.

The east façade of Longue Vue, facing the East Lawn.
A bed for wildflowers along the base attracts butterflies and birds.

The south façade of Longue Vue overlooking the formal gardens,
with double staircase leading down from living room.

6

A UNIVERSITY IS BORN

In April 1930, Edgar was in the midst of a challenging fundraising campaign for the Flint-Goodridge Hospital, the only hospital exclusively serving the Black population in the New Orleans area and the first Black hospital in the South. Word came that Dr. William J. Mayo of Rochester, Minnesota—one of the founders of the Mayo Clinic—was then visiting the city. Edgar wrote to Embree, head of the Rosenwald Fund, describing what happened next: "We had a very lucky break in the sudden arrival in the city yesterday morning of Dr. Mayo, who arrived informally, on a pleasure trip. Edith heard of it in the morning and, with characteristic energy, jumped into her car and rode way down to the Industrial Canal, below the city, where Dr. Mayo's yacht was anchored, and got him to say he would speak at the [fundraising] dance."[1]

Created in 1896, the outdated hospital had just been taken over by Dillard University. Edgar had spearheaded the creation of Dillard and, as chair of its board, envisioned the building of a new Black hospital as key to the university's development. He planned and led a $2 million capital campaign for the hospital. The whites-only banquet attracted two hundred Orleanians to show support for the hospital plan.

Dr. Mayo gave the Flint-Goodridge plan a resounding but awkward endorsement: "It is to the material interest of everybody that the negro be taken care of," he is quoted in the *Times-Picayune*. "If you would be well, you must see that they remain well, for if they are left ignorant they will bring disease into your home and family."[2] Racism, you see, was not limited to the South.

Edgar knew well the difficulty of raising funds for a Black institution during a time of troubled race relations. In a letter he wrote to Embree, in which he enclosed a newspaper clipping about the dinner, he mentioned "an unwise effort of the Paramount Theater people to turn a white theater into a Negro one, right near the Roosevelt Hotel, [which] will stir up animated discussion of race relations. So far there are no indications of it, but it adds to the importance of watching closely every bit of publicity that is let loose in the campaign."[3] There is no indication whether Edith agreed with Edgar's sentiments.

Raising funds for the hospital and helping establish a Black university proved to be Edgar's longest and most challenging philanthropic endeavor. For thirty years, he spearheaded the creation and development of Dillard. Yet, he remained firmly opposed to the social mixing of the races. In 1931, he heard that the white wife of the white president of Fisk University in Nashville was seen "dancing with Negro men." He then wrote in a letter, "I was amused . . . that even Dr. Du Bois had some time ago told one of his friends, 'For goodness sake, try to take off those dances at Fisk,' at which I understand Mrs. Jones has been dancing with Negro men. Of course, this is going to the last limit, but I can sure tell you straight from the shoulder that the day the wife of the white president of Dillard University does this, you will find me among the missing of the trustees of that institution."[4]

To Edith, integration seemed to come naturally, having grown up seeing her parents entertain Black guests. She was used to the "mixing" of the races on many occasions, including social ones. Edgar, a product of New Orleans, clearly had a longer road to travel. During the early years of the Stern Family Fund, Edith did not try to push Edgar to embrace her liberal instincts. As his best friend Monte Lemann said of Edgar, "He is definitely a segregationist."

JR's influence on both Edgar and Edith was evident, yet Edgar would probably have been horrified that Booker T. Washington was both a dinner and house guest at the Rosenwald Chicago home. Edgar's enormous accomplishments in founding Dillard University and funding Flint-Goodridge Hospital made JR proud. If not as progressive as his wife, by New Orleans's standards at the time, Edgar was ahead of his peers.

To many people, Edgar's leadership in founding Dillard seemed incongruous. He was rich. His standing in the city was high. He was deeply involved in many other pursuits that seemed more appropriate for a man of his wealth and social position. There was surely nothing he could benefit from personally in founding Dillard. What seemed more fitting was his later major involvement in improving the deteriorating French Quarter. Yet, Edgar realized that broadening educational opportunities for Black youth merited the investment of his time, energy, and money. The founding of Dillard immeasurably changed the educational dynamic for Black students in the city and the region, just as building the Royal Orleans Hotel, the first new hotel in the French Quarter in fifty years, would change the future of that unique area.

Dillard University is today a highly regarded, historically Black liberal arts college. Its fifty-five-acre campus sits in a residential neighborhood, Gentilly, at what was the edge of the city in the 1930s. The modest, well-spaced homes in Gentilly resemble those in suburbs all over the country. Dillard is filled with imposing neoclassical buildings, each named after the notable people who shaped its history: Stern, Rosenwald, Alexander, Dent, Straight, and some of its prominent faculty. A tree-lined Avenue of the Oaks forms the focal point, giving it an eye-catching landscape of distinct southern beauty. Its sprawling, leafy campus matches those of much more well endowed universities. Its distinctive programs include a prelaw program with an award-winning moot court team, the Dillard University Center for Justice, and the National Center for Black-Jewish Relations.

A Long and Complicated Beginning

The founding of Dillard University and its affiliated Flint-Goodridge Hospital, guided by a mixed-race leadership committee headed by Edgar, required a delicate balancing act to succeed in Jim Crow New Orleans. In the late 1920s and early 1930s, any interest by white citizens to help Black ones was suspect and exceedingly rare. The Urban League of New Orleans, with its mixed-race leadership and focus on Black advancement, was then a decade away from formation. Black-white cooperation was a seemingly new concept.

Lynchings still occurred at that time. In fact, they were a state-sanctioned form of control. The aftermath of the 1896 *Plessy v. Ferguson* Supreme Court decision establishing the separate but equal principle had all but eliminated voting rights for Black citizens; voter rolls were purged, the poll tax was imposed, and land ownership was required to vote. The number of Black voters statewide fell from 35,000 before 1896 to 1,000. School integration was a distant dream. The NAACP had been founded in 1909 in New York, primarily prompted by the bold writings and influence of W. E. B. Du Bois and the support of progressive whites. But the aggressive legal push against various New Orleans segregation policies affecting transportation, public facilities, parks, and schools would not begin for decades.

Most colleges for Black students were started after the Civil War, primarily to train clergy. During Reconstruction, Clark Atlanta University, Morehouse College, Howard University, Fisk University, and Hampton College were founded with the help of missionary organizations and white supporters advancing the cause of education for both whites and Blacks.

The importance and impact of historically Black colleges and universities (HBCUs) were "huge," said Andrew Young, former US ambassador to the United Nations, in a telephone interview in 2021. "They created the Black middle-class." In addition, students who attended felt more comfortable and received much more attention than at predominantly white institutions, as Young experienced. He first attended Dillard, which was across the street from his New Orleans home, and then transferred to Howard University, another HBCU ("I needed to be away from home"). He also spent summer semesters at UCLA and Boston College during his undergraduate years. There, he recalled, "No one spoke to me," students and professors alike. "My academics didn't suffer, but I had no social life. Some of it was my fault because I was too young, sixteen and eighteen." In contrast, at Dillard and Howard, "I knew everybody and had a comfortable social life. Dillard and Howard contributed to my growing up and helped develop my leadership abilities to a degree that wouldn't have happened at a white school."

Two Schools Become One

It is within this context that Edgar Stern led Dillard's establishment—created by the merger of two small, religious-based Black colleges in New Orleans—and provided a small Black hospital with seminal financial support and strategic assistance of the Julius Rosenwald Fund. Edgar was a trustee of the Fund. "The real difficulty," Edgar wrote to Rosenwald Fund director Embree on April 4, 1930, "is that the city is not prosperous, and there are not many people who have any surplus profits for some time past."[5] Embree was receptive to Edgar's appeal because he was looking to expand the Fund's southern school initiative.

Not long before Embree took his trip around the South to explore how to implement the new Rosenwald Fund strategy to support and strengthen four major centers of Black colleges, a representative of Straight College came to Edgar to request a $500 donation. Straight was then one of several small Black colleges in New Orleans. "That's a rather small amount," he replied. "Your Board of Directors should be able to come up with that. But if you are ever interested in doing something bigger, I'd be interested." Clearly, Edgar was already a go-to person for the Black community. He seemed to be applying the same standard he used for everyone asking for funds, ensuring that others were also contributing and not just him.

Alerted by Edgar, Embree visited Straight College (affiliated with the American Missionary Association of the Congregational Christian Church) and the College of New Orleans (affiliated with the Board of Education of the Methodist Episcopal Church), both struggling to stay alive.[6] Building on what Edgar had already observed, Embree wrote the leadership of both schools to suggest they merge and requested a meeting with their leadership. The process leading to the establishment of Dillard had begun.

Both these small colleges had been founded by abolitionists and shared the goal of providing an education for Black students. "The white business community looks favorably on this merger to provide better educational facilities for the colored citizens," A. D. Danziger, head of the New Orleans Association of Commerce, wrote to Edgar.[7] But Danziger pointed out another advantage of the merger: if a new campus was created, the colleges would give up the valuable real estate they owned. Each school was located Uptown, where property values were rising as larger numbers of higher-income residents were seeking to live there.

As mentioned, Flint-Goodridge Hospital was the city's only medical institution exclusively serving the Black population. Charity Hospital in the downtown area served both Black and white patients in separate wings but did not integrate until the 1960s. Flint-Goodridge was located on Canal Street, where real estate was also increasing in value. The increased healthcare capacity of a new facility and its move out of the neighborhood were added incentives for the white community to support the hospital.

But the merger and subsequent establishment of Dillard did not happen easily or quickly. Complications arose every step of the way. During the protracted process of establishing Dillard, Edgar had to negotiate many thorny and often contentious racially charged issues. Navigating the social mores of the time was tricky. Edgar was in the delicate middleman position between the city's white and Black communities and the Dillard founders. Disagreements proliferated, which, given the times, was understandable: new ground was being broken. Dillard was clearly to be a Black college, but white students were not officially excluded. Many difficult questions thus arose. Should the staff be all-Black? Should the first president of the college be Black or white? Could a Black president preside over white faculty members? Did that matter? Should the president live on campus? Would a white president be more successful at fundraising than a Black one but then not win the confidence of the Black community?

In addition, the relationship between the two religious organizations that had founded the two merged colleges seemed always to be fraught with tension. That tension dragged on for years, even after Dillard opened in 1935. In a 1937 letter to Embree updating developments, Edgar wrote, "The church boards have . . . not shown that Christian brotherly love in their relations with each other that one might have hoped of them."[8] They paid their financial commitments slowly. After a prolonged disagreement with one of the Black ministers in which Edgar prevailed, he wrote to Embree, "Armistice achieved."

Money was being raised from both the Black and white communities, but socializing between them was out of the question. When pondering how this integrated group came together to form a new college, the late Sybil Morial asked, "But where did they meet? It was against the law until the 1960s for Black and white people to meet or eat together." This is a good question that a review of archival collections did not answer. Perhaps they met in the Playhouse at Longue Vue (where Marian Anderson performed) or at Temple Sinai where the Sterns were members or even at Dooky Chase's restaurant. Morial added, "This is why Leah Chase and her Dooky Chase restaurant were so critical during the later civil rights years, because she gave the mixed-race group of strategists a private dining room upstairs where they could meet beyond the eyes of the police."

Edgar's interest in Black advancement stopped at social gatherings. This was corroborated by Albert Dent, the third and longest-serving president of Dillard. Dent could attend the cocktail hours of fundraising dinners at

Longue Vue but was not invited to stay for the meal. It is difficult to know whether that was simply Edgar's preference or was due to the necessary deference to the white guests he was raising money from in the 1930s, or both. Yet, "A Personal Tribute" to both Sterns by Dent's wife Ernestine provided another view: "Albert's relationship with Mr. Stern over 27 long years became a very special friendship. It brought him into contact with a large group of prominent men, and also involvement in a variety of civic organizations. His work with them over the years, on a volunteer basis, led to his [receiving] the prestigious *Times-Picayune* Loving Cup—the only black person who has received the Award since its inception in 1901."[9]

Edgar Stays in It for the Long Haul

It was not Edgar's original intention to lead this all-encompassing effort, but he carried out that responsibility and remained chairman of the board—made up of twelve white and five Black members—until his death in 1959. The challenges seemed never ending, but no one was more appropriate for the task: Edgar was a highly successful, well-regarded New Orleans businessman. He had served as president of the New Orleans Cotton Exchange just before he embarked on this project. His business success made avoiding him difficult.

Edgar first turned to the city for help in acquiring a site for the college: Rose Hill, which was vacant land, except for a small, little-used Black cemetery. Although far from the city center of that day, it was close to the emerging white neighborhood of Gentilly. Protests were vigorous, and white homeowners' threats to sell and move were widespread.

Probably the only noncontroversial move in what would sometimes be a rocky process was the naming of the new university. James Hardy Dillard (1856–1940), both a Latin professor at Tulane and dean of the academic college, was an obvious choice. Born into a slaveholding family in Virginia, Dillard graduated from Washington & Lee University and went straight into teaching. Eventually, he landed at Tulane. While there, Dillard served as president of the New Orleans Public Library and promoted the establishment of a Carnegie Library for Black citizens. Most importantly, he was a board member of both merging colleges. He left Tulane to be director of two foundations that promoted interracial goodwill and supported vocational training for Blacks and training institutes for Black teachers. The Dillard name for the new university was something all participants could agree on.

Early on, Edgar realized that the easier project to fundraise for would be building the Black hospital. It was also the most needed. So, Flint-Goodridge became the first component of Dillard to open in 1930, with the university itself opening five years later.[10] Both operating boards of the two merging institutions committed $500,000 toward the new hospital and university. So did the Rosenwald Fund and the General Education Board of the Rockefeller Foundation. The New Orleans Community Chest, of which Edgar was head, committed to raising $250,000 from New Orleans citizens, Black and white. This was a rare if not unprecedented initiative. It was "an unusual thing for the South," Edgar wrote to Embree. "As a matter of record, [this was] the only time that the South has done anything of such large significance toward Negro education."

The Black Community Gives Very Generously

Fundraising within the Black community exceeded expectations. George Arthur, the Black staff member of the Rosenwald Fund, was key to the campaign's success. When he came to New Orleans to engage the local African American population in fundraising, he "earned the total confidence" of that community, Edgar wrote to Embree. Edgar led fundraising efforts among the white population. To everyone's surprise, the goals for both communities were exceeded, with $212,000 instead of the goal of $200,000 coming from the white community and $117,000, more than twice the original goal of $50,000, donated by the Black community.

In 1930, during the Depression, a new art deco Flint-Goodridge hospital opened in the primarily Black neighborhood of Central City—at Louisiana and LaSalle Avenues (today it is elderly affordable housing)—with one hundred beds and a separate building for thirty to fifty Dillard School of Nursing students. The Canal Street site at the edge of the Central Business District was sold, with the proceeds going to building the university that was still being designed.

Edgar's Conflicted Views on Race

Leading the challenging effort to establish Dillard and Flint-Goodridge, spending so much of his time and prestige to fundraise on its behalf, giving so much of both his personal wealth and the Rosenwald and Stern Funds' money to make it happen—all seem curious given Edgar's complicated views on race.

For example, in a letter to Dean Thomas F. Holgate at Northwestern University, Edgar wrote of this project's "interracial complications" and noted that he is vacillating on whether the first president should be white or Black. At first, he was convinced the president should be white, but after hearing arguments otherwise from Rosenwald Fund staffer George Arthur, Edgar noted, "A white president will be compelled, to a certain extent at least, to recognize his social obligations to the Negro members of the faculty and to the Negro students of the University. New Orleans is, I think, a rather conservative city about this sort of thing. We are going to have to be very careful in our relations with the white community if we are to maintain the good will that up to this time, I believe, we have established with them."[11]

He understood the difficulties of raising money for Black institutions primarily from the conservative white community; he recognized that his pitch to potential wealthy donors needed to be crafted in accordance with "the demands of local traditions." In several letters, he stressed the need to avoid "giving offense to the Southern tradition." Yet, he would not have devoted decades of his life to establishing Dillard if he had not recognized its importance to regional race relations, writing, "I visualize Dillard University as having the opportunity to do more than educate a certain number of Negro youth. I feel that if rightly directed it can be a tremendous influence in improving interracial relations in the lower South in the next generation, and this is just as much an educational problem as formal instruction is in the classroom."[12]

In 1930, the year before he wrote to Embree of his "misgivings" about the white wife of the president of Fisk University dancing with Black men, Edgar received the *Times-Picayune* Loving Cup for his "outstanding service in the establishment of Dillard University and its teaching hospital, Flint-Goodridge." Established in 1901, the award recognizes "citizens who have worked unselfishly for the community without expectation of public acclaim or material reward." Edith would be awarded the Loving Cup years later; the Sterns were the first married couple to both receive it. Yet even the Loving Cup, which both Edgar and Edith were so proud to receive, has a complicated history. It is highly valued and respected within white elite society, but it should not be forgotten that the *Times-Picayune* was initially proslavery, anti-Reconstruction, and anti-integration.

Edgar clearly worked very hard to create a quality university for the Black community while trying to maintain the strict racial traditions of the Deep South. He recognized that without the significant support of the prominent white community of which he was a key member, little progress for the Black population would be achieved.

In a letter dated March 16, 1931, to Fred L. Brownlee of the Rockefeller Foundation, Edgar shared, "I was absent from the city, when messrs. Howard, Lemann and Kearney so very vigorously espoused the Dillard cause against the apparently hopeless opposition of the Commission Council and finally secured the legal sanction of the city for establishing the university at Rose Hill." He also noted this contrast: "Mr. A. L. Moss, one of our leading Negro merchants, recited to me last year with tears in his eyes and despair in his voice the crushing defeat of himself and an influential Negro committee in attempting to get permission from the Commission Council to build a church in a logical neighborhood for one of the best Negro congregations in this city."[13]

In this letter, Edgar framed the building of the Black hospital as a matter of life and death for the Black population. He pointed out that the number of Black deaths from tuberculosis in New Orleans was three times the number of white deaths and noted the high rate of syphilis in the Black community. He told Brownlee, "Those who choose to chart this course of Negro isolation and the repulse of friendly Southern white interest, it seems to me, are assuming a gigantic responsibility—a responsibility not merely for the speed with which the Negro group may develop, but a responsibility for the very survival of the race itself, physical and economic."[14]

In 2000, Dillard published a short history of the university and offered an accurate evaluation of Edgar's thirty-year role as president of its Board of Trustees:

> The generosity of Edgar B. Stern and the Julius Rosenwald Fund was key to the success of Dillard University's founding and ultimately ensured the future of the institution. However, a careful examination of the issues surrounding this philanthropic giving offers insight into the complexities of race relations in 1930s New Orleans, suggesting, as have many, that while Stern was remarkably ahead of his time, he nonetheless was forced to undertake the reform within [the] context of that time. . . . Stern, who was both committed to Dillard University and keenly aware of the rigid social code of the South, was forced to be resourceful in his promotion of the institution.[15]

The Early Years of Dillard and Flint-Goodridge Hospital

An inspired compromise was made regarding who would serve as president of Dillard. The first president was white, but he only served for a year in an acting capacity. Dr. Will W. Alexander was a Southern Methodist minister, graduate of Vanderbilt University, and a member of the Rosenwald Fund board. He also was a leader in the formation of the Commission on Interracial Cooperation, which actively campaigned against lynching and had received $73,000 in grants from the Rosenwald Fund over the years. Alexander seemed to have been acceptable to all and was willing to serve in an interim role.[16] William Stuart Nelson, a prominent Black educator and administrator in higher education, took over after a year.

At the same time, Dr. Albert Dent was put in charge of the reorganized Flint-Goodridge Hospital, where, as mentioned, he impressed enough people to be chosen as the third and longest-serving Dillard president.[17] A native of Atlanta and graduate of Morehouse College, Dent gained national attention with the success of the hospital. As Charles Davey and Carol McMichael Reese noted of both Dillard and the hospital, "These institutions have long been acclaimed as critical milestones in the struggle for equality of opportunity, not only in New Orleans but in the region."[18]

Yet, building a new facility for the Flint-Goodridge hospital was only one of its many challenges. Yes, its 100-bed facility was modern, and it had up-to-date medical equipment. However, its dual mission of providing healthcare and training to Black doctors was difficult to fulfill simply because few Blacks had yet had the opportunity to attend medical school. And the few Black physicians in the city did not have access to medical libraries and current publications.

Rosa Freeman Keller, a member of the Uptown white elite, was outraged by this situation. At the request of Monte Lemann and Edgar, she agreed to serve on the board of Flint-Goodridge, determined to gain the access that Black doctors needed. She and a small group of Black doctors (Edgar was supposed to be among them but was ill) went to see Dr. Alton Ochsner, then one of the city's preeminent surgeons and head of the local medical society; Ochsner Hospital is named after him. She made the case for needed access, but Ochsner was "nearly apoplectic," Keller noted, and adamantly said no.[19]

A unique arrangement was developed in response to this rejection that did as much for race relations as it did for medical care. Experienced white doctors from Tulane and LSU hospitals were brought in as consultants to work side by side with the Black doctors to provide mentoring, skill training, and education. Essentially, an integrated staff was working together with mutual respect but without official acknowledgment of the arrangement. Over time, as the Black doctors gained the necessary experience, they were promoted to department heads, and the white doctors withdrew.

This remarkable collaboration, decades before the integration of New Orleans, had an almost immediate impact. Not long afterward and before Dillard opened, the local Boy Scouts emulated the arrangement: white Boy Scout leaders offered to train Black Scout leaders, despite "the threats by some of the white Scout Masters that they would quit the movement if Negro Troops were organized." Edgar ends his letter to Embree written on November 13, 1931, with this sentence: "THE WORLD DO MOVE."[20]

A Slow Beginning

The Black population did not embrace the hospital quickly, both because they could not afford its services and because they were accustomed to receiving medical care at home. Black women, for example, depended on poorly regulated and poorly trained midwives to deliver their children: "89.9 percent of the deliveries among colored women in Louisiana and 21.7 percent of those in New Orleans were being performed by midwives."[21] The typical cost of a midwife was $10, and most women could not afford to pay more. So, Dent hired a social worker to go out and form a Mothers Club and publicize that the hospital would handle all maternity cases at a flat rate of $10. In response, hospital births at Flint Goodridge rose 400 percent from 1932 to 1938.

In addition, Dent appealed to his hospital governing board for permission to sell hospitalization insurance to any group of Black workers. He wanted to charge one penny per day. The board balked and insisted that possible losses be underwritten. Dent then calculated that the most the hospital would lose was $45,000. He went straight to the Rosenwald Fund, secured a check for that amount, and instituted the program. Because it was so popular—by December 1, 1938, 3,231 people were enrolled—he never needed to dip into that Rosenwald contribution. Flint-Goodridge soon earned praise from the NAACP magazine, which described it as "a notable example of interracial cooperation."[22] The fact that both the board and the staff were racially mixed was cited as among its achievements.

Interestingly, Edgar had forged a strong bond—one might call it a friendship at a social distance—with two Black men who were pivotal in this long process: George Arthur and Alfred Dent. Arthur had been a highly respected director of Chicago's nationally acclaimed Wabash YMCA when Embree hired him for the Rosenwald staff in 1928. As far as we know, he was the first Black person with whom Edgar had a meaningful relationship. Edgar valued Arthur's knowledge of the Black community, listened carefully to him, and often followed his advice. Arthur gave him critical help in fundraising for Flint-Goodridge and Dillard from the Black community. At the same time, Arthur admired Edgar's role in this complicated process, writing this to him on October 19, 1931: "Each time I go to New Orleans I realize more and more . . . the tremendously difficult position you occupy; namely, that of an interpreter between two groups who are widely apart from almost every standpoint. . . . I am very much afraid that you will have to be for some time the 'hub' around which the wheel of progress, with its many colored spokes, revolves."[23]

Edgar's relationship with Alfred Dent was also close but in a different way. Edgar was somewhat in awe of Dent's management of Flint-Goodridge and was much relieved when Dent took the reins of Dillard in 1941, which he held until 1968. He was particularly proud of Dent's innovations, such as bringing in white doctors to mentor the Black ones. And, as noted earlier, he celebrated when white Boy Scout leaders embraced the model.

Dillard's Broad Impact

Dillard opened in 1935 and within a few years became much more than a university. "That's where we went to socialize," Andrew Young told me. His mother was a good friend of Albert Dent's wife, Ernestine Jesse Covington Dent. The Dents' son, poet and writer Tom Dent, was born the same year as Young and became his best friend.

Ernestine Dent was a concert pianist.[24] A graduate of both the Oberlin Conservatory of Music and the Juilliard Graduate School of Music, Ernestine organized all manner of cultural events for the Dillard campus and for the larger Black community. For young Black people growing up in the Jim Crow city where access to culture was essentially denied to them, these activities at Dillard were vital. "There was always great music there," Young recalled. In addition to enjoying the B Sharp Music Club (whose performances "my mother made me go to"), Young heard "Paul Robeson, Dorothy Maynard, Marian Anderson, everybody and anybody before they were ranked in New York or LA. But that was true of all the Black colleges where these entertainers performed."

Dillard hosted picnics and socials and a major lecture series. Eleanor Roosevelt, Thurgood Marshall, Haile Selassie, Mary McLeod Bethune, Paul Robeson, Martin Luther King Jr., Henry Wallace, Jackie Robinson, and Roy Wilkins all spoke there. At the time, Young did not realize how significant that cast of speakers was. There was an art collection that was more accessible to Black viewers than traditional museums. Initiated and led by *Art News* editor Thomas B. Hess, husband of Audrey Stern, the collection at Dillard focused on recognized artists still struggling to support themselves with their art.

Young's first job was mopping floors at Flint-Goodridge. "It was where I had my appendix taken out and my broken leg fixed," he noted with a laugh during our phone interview. He attended Dillard for a year before going first to Howard University and then to Hartford Theological Seminary.

For most of his youth, the Young family lived on Cleveland Street in Mid-City. His father's dental practice was in their home. "I would hang out in the waiting room of the dental office and get into a lot of conversations with the dental supplier salesmen who were mostly Jewish," he said. This was somewhat awkward because "the Nazis were just down the street at Deutsche House. I could hear them through the open window with their Seig Heils," the Nazi salute. But the experience served him in good stead years later. "I was with Martin [Luther King] and we were at a strategy meeting in Birmingham. King looked around the group and said, 'I need someone to talk to the businessmen in Birmingham. Can anyone speak to businessmen?' I was the only one who said 'yes,' so I was sent to talk to them and we got along fine."

Young, whose parents went to Straight College, was not surprised to hear about the complex questions with which the Dillard founders wrestled, but he pointed out, "All the early Black colleges had white presidents—Howard, Morehouse, Atlanta." The Rockefellers with their strong Baptist commitment were early supporters of Spelman and Atlanta, "probably under a certain guilt for slavery," he said, but also because "they saw these students as a connection to people of the world."

Young remembered hearing as a child about Edgar Stern, but he was too young to have any real idea who he was and did not remember ever meeting him. But when posed the same question as the late Sybil Morial, "But where did they meet?" he replied, "Good question." He repeated exactly what Sybil Morial had said but added, "The very wealthy . . . they do what they want to do."

A New Investment Beckons

Dillard was well on its way, still under Edgar's leadership. But the entrepreneurial side of Edgar beckoned. He took an enormous leap of faith to invest in the French Quarter. This investment would have as large an impact on the Quarter and the city's economy as Dillard has had on Black higher education.

7

RENEWING THE FRENCH QUARTER

In the early 1960s, New Orleans was still not complying with Supreme Court–ordered integration. It took until 1966 or so for integration to have an impact on the city. Black residents were having a difficult time finding formerly whites-only establishments that would accept their patronage. So it was for Walter Etienne Morial, a cigarmaker, and Leonie (Moore) Morial, a seamstress, who wanted to celebrate their fiftieth anniversary. Their son, Ernest Nathan "Dutch" Morial, and grandson, Marc Haydel Morial, would become the first and second Black mayors of the city decades hence, but in 1966, it was still mostly things as usual—except at the Sterns' Royal Orleans Hotel, a prominent hotel in the French Quarter.

"My grandparents celebrated their fiftieth anniversary at the Royal Orleans Hotel," Jacques Morial told me. "It was the only hotel at which they felt welcomed. The other hotels integrated eventually because the law made them."

The storied French Quarter was undervalued and neglected when Edgar began to build his new hotel here in the late 1940s and early 1950s. In yet one more arena, the Sterns were ahead of their time.

Forlorn and Almost Forgotten

The French Quarter (Vieux Carré) is a fragile remnant of a bygone culture. It is unique in America—one hundred square blocks of a mélange of French and Spanish influences. Settled in the eighteenth century by the French, this assemblage of mostly two- and three-story houses was built and rebuilt with a multiplicity of styles after a takeover by the Spanish and two fires.

After the Louisiana Purchase in 1803, Americans started to move from the North to New Orleans. Relations between the new arrivals and the locals were not friendly. And so, newcomers did not move into the well-established French Quarter but settled Uptown, on the other side of Canal Street.

Canal is an extra-wide boulevard that was once a drainage ditch between the Mississippi River and Lake Pontchartrain. Over time, it evolved into the city's central artery lined with grand department stores, magnificent movie palaces, and small shops and, at one time, served as a racial dividing line. With the streetcar line on it, Canal became the major spine of the downtown area that bordered the French Quarter. It became the dividing line between the French and American quarters and was called the "neutral ground." Ever since, medians on the major streets throughout the city have all been called the neutral ground. The division between the districts—one meant for the French, the other for the Americans—was so thorough that even the street names change as you cross Canal from one quarter to the other.

The city was transformed by the Civil War, but not so the Quarter. Many consider it the most authentic historic district in the country with its elaborate ironwork balconies, shuttered windows, lush courtyards, and carriageways. But its distinctiveness lies in more than its architecture:

> The genius of the Vieux Carré, architectural historians contend, is not the architectural worth of any one building or any group or cluster of buildings. It is the *tout ensemble,* the integration of buildings and environment, the total atmosphere of the whole district. This *tout ensemble* includes not only the height of the buildings, their color, texture, materials, and details, but also the environmental influences—the width of streets, the size of the blocks, the vistas, open spaces, the patios, and the harmony and symmetry of the building facades and clusterings.[1]

An unconventional group of mostly writers and artists, revolving around William Faulkner, Elizabeth and Sherwood Anderson, and Lyle Saxon, brought a bohemian character to the district. It became known as the Greenwich Village of the South.

Within the historically significant French Quarter, Edgar chose to redevelop the formerly lavish and prominent St. Louis Hotel, which was located only a few blocks from Canal Street. It was built in 1838 and described as "one long block of elegance." The hotel was designed to be as French as the year-old St. Charles Hotel on the other side of Canal Street was built to be American. Both had rotundas, but the one in the St. Charles—46 feet in diameter and 85 feet high—had the extra elegance of tall Corinthian columns and assorted shops on the ground floor.[2] The two hotels symbolized the hostility and competitiveness between the two neighborhoods.

At its heyday, the St. Louis was the center of haute-monde society with its lavish balls. It hosted the first Mardi Gras ball. But there was a dark side to its history as well. Before the Civil War slave auctions were held under its great rotunda.

Yet by the Civil War, the St. Louis was already failing. During the war, it was converted to a medical facility for the northern occupiers, and from 1874 to 1882, it was used by the Louisiana legislature. After standing empty for years, it was mostly demolished, except for one exterior wall that was left partially standing. This was the condition the site was in when Edgar bought the property in 1947, with no idea of how it could be used.

The French Quarter Changes

As the St. Louis decayed, so did the French Quarter. After World War I, most people embraced the motto, "Out with the old and in with the new." French Creoles of means were moving up and out to the newly built elegant and spacious mansions along Esplanade Avenue, parallel to Canal Boulevard but sixteen blocks away on the opposite side of the Quarter. Sicilian immigrants filled the French Quarter vacancies. Vestiges of their occupancy—restaurants, small groceries, and other stores—remain today. As population density increased, buildings became more crowded and rundown. Upkeep lagged. The Quarter's status as the most-desired residential district declined.

The Quarter enjoyed a renaissance of sorts in the 1920s and 1930s, however, when it became a popular café society locale where Edith and Edgar would go for a night on the town with friends to eat and listen to music. Its small cadre of artists and writers were joined by a group of die-hard New

Orleanian women. The earliest known organized historic preservationists, these women forsook their elite Uptown status and moved into the Quarter, championing its future. They were determined to preserve the architecture, artistry, and atmosphere of this unique neighborhood.

Interestingly, women had been in the forefront of the earliest development of the Quarter. New Orleans women had a unique economic advantage, as pointed out by Mary Gehlman in her book, *The Free People of Color:* "Because under French law a woman was sole owner of property which she inherited or brought with her from a former marriage, New Orleans women were free to sell, lease or rent their own property and to contract large building projects in their own names."[3]

The first big female-led development in the Quarter was the work of Baroness Micaela Pontalba, who built luxurious apartment buildings, one in 1849 and the second in 1851, paralleling the sides of Jackson Square, the central square of the original settlement. These buildings framed St. Louis Cathedral, establishing the cachet of the Quarter. Other financially independent women invested in the Quarter as well, yielding small but significant improvements over the years.

Women to the Rescue

In the 1930s, Uptown women initiated the effort that would save the Quarter's unique architecture and atmosphere. The first historic preservation efforts in the country started in the Quarter and in Charleston, South Carolina, with both initiatives led by women.[4] Their success inspired women in other cities, and the historic preservation movement was born and spread around the country.

In the French Quarter, women brought attention to and championed the historical significance and irreplaceable crafted details of each building's façade. "It took local women to see it as savable and restorable," noted author Frederick Starr. "This was a cornerstone moment in the history of the city."[5] Edgar clearly embraced the women's effort, respected their activism, and recognized the positive economic impact of historic preservation on his hotel development project.

In 1936, the state legislature had passed a constitutional amendment authorizing the New Orleans City Council to create the Vieux Carré Commission (VCC) and to give it control over building changes in the Quarter—an unheard-of concept at the time. The VCC's purpose was both to preserve the historic buildings and to ensure that any new buildings or renovations were architecturally in keeping with the old. It was the first landmark preservation commission in the country. In the 1950s, the VCC's strict regulations would prove to be a thorn in the side of Edgar and his architects when they were designing the Royal Orleans.

A slow but gradual renewal of the famous neighborhood took hold in the late 1950s and into the 1960s. Far-sighted residents—mostly women—bought and restored buildings, bringing national attention to the Quarter. Edgar's plans for the new hotel, the first one in decades, were seen as a vote of confidence in the Quarter's future and gave the nascent preservation movement a boost. "I always thought of Edgar Sr. as a preservationist," Nicholas Lemann told me.

Moon Landrieu, mayor of the city from 1970 to 1978, later hailed the building of the Hotel Royal Orleans as a game changer for the city. Its impact "cannot be exaggerated. . . . That was the first real commercial development in the French Quarter and it was done with such quality and style that it set a pattern," he told developer Pres Kabacoff, who interviewed him for a biography of his father Lester. The city's financial problems then were not much different from what they would be over the decades to come. As the senior Kabacoff recalled, "New Orleans was a relic from another age. Much of the wealth of the business establishment was inherited capital bequeathed from earlier generations that prospered from the city's port, from early oil discoveries, and from supplying the financing and factoring for the South's cotton and sugar cane growers. It was 'old' money held by families that already had it made and were disinclined to gamble on new developments." These families made up the "complacent economic elite."[6]

Out of the Ashes

Lester Kabacoff, hired as Edgar's executive assistant in the late 1940s, played an instrumental role in the new hotel endeavor. Kabby, as he became known, was a young prelaw student visiting New Orleans; he was introduced to the Sterns because he was a master tennis player. Both Edith and Edgar were avid and skilled players and had a tennis court. It was considered an honor to be invited to play on it. The three played frequently during the years that Kabacoff attended Loyola Law School. After spending some time as a Wall Street lawyer, he returned to New Orleans.

Kabby continued to be the Sterns' favorite tennis partner, playing with them both. Edgar was "probably the most charming man I ever met," he told his son Pres in his unpublished autobiography. Edith was "fine and generous" but "tough, made of tougher fiber than Edgar and she ran the household. She was a great lady, too. She wore the pants; I remember one of two occasions when he rebelled, but not often. Friends called her RAU—'right as usual.'"

Building the Royal Orleans was his first big challenge. Though he was a Jewish outsider, Kabacoff's eventual success made him a business star in this very closed city. When the Royal Orleans Hotel (now the Omni Royal Orleans) finally opened in October 1960, with an integrated staff, the city was still staunchly segregated. Edgar Jr., after serving in the Pentagon during the Korean War, became an integral partner in the project and took the lead after his father's death in 1959. Through it all, Kabby kept pushing the project forward at a time when investing in the French Quarter was considered a losing proposition. The city in the postwar years was at one of its lowest ebbs.

The Hotel Was a Hard Sell

The Port of New Orleans, the major source of jobs and businesses, was the heart of the city's economy. Commercial enterprises lined nearly the full length of the port, the most significant border of the city. By the 1950s, however, the port was declining as shipping by railways and trucks gained dominance. Synthetics were replacing cotton. Trade with New Orleans's major trading parters—newly communist Cuba and other Central American countries—was floundering. As a result, New Orleans's economy, which had never diversified, was also floundering.

Thus, building the Royal Orleans Hotel required a big leap of faith. Economic development across Canal Street was much more robust than in the Quarter. Edgar bought the site in 1947 without being sure of what to build in its place. At times discouraged and on the verge of losing interest, he remained committed primarily due to the determination and steadfastness of Kabacoff.

When he decided to build a hotel, Edgar told Kabby to make it happen:

"Get it done." Even though Kabby ran into one roadblock after another during his ten-year search for investors, he and Edgar remained true to their vision. Kabby showed the site to a long parade of out-of-town and local potential investors. Finally, Equitable Life Insurance in New York agreed to take on a mortgage, and investor interest emerged. Two socially and financially significant locals also signed on: Darwin Fenner of Merrill Lynch came up with $50,000; and A. B. Freeman, who owned the Coca-Cola franchise in New Orleans, put in $100,000. Two of the richest men of New Orleans—Greek oilman William G. Helis, after whom the Helis Foundation is named, and Gen. Kemper Williams, who eventually created the revered Historic New Orleans Collection—then joined as investors. It is no doubt a reflection of the high regard for Edgar that four of the richest men in New Orleans would take a risk and invest in his project. Likely, all four of these men were members of the Boston Club or another prestigious club to which Jews were not welcome. They could not invite Edgar for lunch, but they knew to follow his lead.

The same year that Edgar bought the hotel site, 1947, he purchased a radio station, which he intended that Edgar Jr. would run. The station would evolve into the first television station in the state of Louisiana, the first on the Gulf Coast, the first in the Deep South, and the forty-ninth in the nation. Edgar Sr. moved the WDSU offices into an elegant historic residence on Royal Street next door to the hotel. A new addition was built to house the studio.

That move into the Quarter of a prestigious business must have raised eyebrows; it was a major vote of confidence in its future that came to fruition more than a decade before the hotel was built. It was a very public sign of Edgar Sr.'s astuteness as a businessman. Clearly, his vision and money put New Orleans on the air before it would have otherwise been.

Once the financing was obtained, it was difficult to find a hotel chain to run the hotel. Kabby was ultimately successful in persuading Roger Sonnabend, head of Hotel Corporation of America (later the Sonesta), to sign on the dotted line, despite this prevailing wisdom: "None of the big companies wanted to touch the French Quarter at all. It was not a place for a hotel, nor did the French Quarter have much of a future."[7]

The ongoing challenges to building the hotel were complicated by a citywide debate that would continue for decades and, in this instance, would put father, son, and Kabby right in the middle. The debate centered on the preservation of what made New Orleans special: How closely did the design of new construction have to hew to the original? "In the loudest of public hearings over this style of roof or that precise measurement of height, the lines were indeed being drawn between those who saw the Quarter as a slum with a heritage too glorious to change and those who recognized a dazzling touristic enterprise whose wealth had scarcely been tapped."[8] What complicated the debate was that the people seeing a tourist opportunity in the development of the Quarter did not fully appreciate that its historic fabric would be its critical draw.

During the process of designing the new hotel, questions were raised about whether the Royal Orleans had to replicate the architecture and design of the historic St. Louis. In other words, how modern should the new hotel be? In the 1950s, midcentury modern was the hot design style.

In a shrewd strategy, the Sterns hired the city's two top architects, one in the field of historic preservation and the other in contemporary design. Arthur Q. Davis, a midcentury modernist, was a personal friend and frequent guest of Edith and Edgar, his next-door neighbors. He had also designed an unconventionally shaped swimming pool for Edgar Jr., but the hotel was one of his first commissions. He and his partner Nathaniel Curtis went on to design the city's iconic Superdome, the New Orleans Rivergate Exhibition Center, the Hyatt Regency and Marriott Hotels, and the Main Library, all modernist structures.

The second architect selected was Samuel Wilson Jr., with his partner Richard Koch. Wilson was often referred to as New Orleans's dean of historic preservation. He was a professor at Tulane's School of Architecture, an historian, and a dedicated preservation activist. He was best known for restoring the Pontalba Apartments and the Cabildo adjacent to St. Louis Cathedral, as well as the Pitot House, built in 1799. The Pitot House, now the home of the Louisiana Landmarks Society, is a West Indies–style plantation home and one of the state's oldest houses.

The goal, Davis noted aptly, was to design "a hotel that would have all the charm of the Vieux Carré, be reminiscent of the Quarter's historical background, and still be modern and efficient . . . one that retained the character and intimacy of scale typical of the Quarter."[9] In the end, it seems to have been achieved. The hotel's most notable feature was a partial row of granite arches taken from the old St. Louis façade that was still standing. The old arches became the template for the hotel's new arches along St. Louis Street. Wilson was mostly responsible for the exterior and Davis for the very modern and welcoming interior.

The hotel was an immediate hit when it opened in 1960. The staff was integrated, which must have caused a stir. Edgar Sr. had died the year before, and it is difficult to project how, by that time, he would have felt about having Black and white employees working together. But it was still illegal to accept Black guests. In fact, in 1963, the American Legion canceled its September convention planned for New Orleans because of "the Louisiana Legionnaires' inability to guarantee unsegregated facilities for delegates," the *Louisiana Weekly* reported on May 25, 1963. Three federal judges had just ruled the segregation law illegal, but it took some time for all hotels to comply. Yet, as soon as the public accommodations law passed in 1964, the Royal Orleans welcomed both Black and white guests.

Edgar Jr. was now in charge. Bill Borah and Richard Baumbach, then working for him to fight the expressway project planned for the Quarter waterfront, were in full agreement with his progressive racial attitudes. As they entered the ballroom for the first Christmas staff party, they stopped dead in their tracks. "Whoa, I said, as I surveyed the Black and white crowd," Borah told me a few years ago. "They are serious about this. It was revolutionary. It didn't happen anywhere else in this town. To say it was controversial was an understatement. And it was so honest and so straightforward. It's a symbol of what the Sterns did here and did nationally." In the 1960s, the civil rights movement had not yet made a significant dent in the city's entrenched segregation. It can be assumed that this rule-breaking antiracist policy made some New Orleanians unhappy.

With both the founding of Dillard and the building of the Royal Orleans, the Sterns were sticking to their path, blazed by Edith, of breaking rules, ignoring prevailing conventions, and taking a leap of faith where others did not dare to go. They took the city in a direction no one else thought of. This was the Stern family pattern. As Edith had told Kabby, "Money is wasted on many people. Our families always regarded wealth as a trust to be invested judiciously in humanity. We were reared in the tradition of good works, culture and public service."[10]

8

LEGAL PATHBREAKERS

In the 1960s, Judge J. Skelly Wright of the District Court for the Eastern Division of Louisiana blocked one attempt after another by the state legislature not to comply with the Supreme Court's 1954 ruling that segregation in schools was no longer legal. He effectively defied Louisiana's government on all levels—and certainly the state legislature, whose elected representatives hailed mostly from rural Louisiana.

For his efforts, he paid a high price: he was the target of a long siege of hate. A wooden cross was burned on the Wrights' lawn; this incident, however, was never investigated by police, according to Wright's nephew James E. Wright III, who later became a partner in a prominent New Orleans law firm. Federal marshals drove Wright to work, while local police guarded the family home and, at times, lived in it alongside the Wrights. The Wrights' twelve-year-son was attacked at a dance, but fortunately his Country Day School classmates immediately surrounded and shielded him.

The judge and his wife Helen, who once had social standing, became social pariahs because of his rulings. As Rosa Freeman Keller observed sympathetically, "She walked into church, and nobody would sit next to her."[1] Friends told Helen they were embarrassed to be seen with her in public.

Meanwhile Wright's son James, despite being attacked at a school dance, thought all this was "neat" and "great fun" and told all his friends, "We got a burned cross." When James was home alone one night, he happened to answer the phone. "Is that n——r loving communist there?" the caller asked. Without missing a beat, young James replied, "No, would you like to leave a message?"

James's response circulated in Washington, DC, spread by Wright's sister-in-law, who lived there. It was a source of great amusement. *Washington Post* columnist Drew Pearson gleefully included it in his column. The *New Orleans Times-Picayune* regularly carried the Pearson column but did not print that one.

No local sympathy was directed at this courageous and controversial judge. "He was the most hated man in the city," his nephew James told me. "He was considered a traitor to his people." Yet, his vilification was balanced by praise for his courage from those outside New Orleans. For example, the wife of Supreme Court Justice Hugo Black wrote Helen Wright how much she and her husband appreciated Skelly's "courageous fight to uphold the same constitution that Hugo is fighting for."

Unlikely Fellow Activists for Justice

Edith Stern had watched Judge J. Skelly Wright with great admiration as he challenged every attempt by the state not to integrate the schools, despite the *Brown v. Board of Education* 1954 ruling. "Wright was known as a low-key judge who wielded his authority quietly but nonetheless firmly."[2] He effectively defied the entire state's power structure.

Edith also knew what it was to be an outsider in a hostile society. She saw how Wright and his wife Helen were being vilified by the city's social elites. And when the Wrights were at their most besieged, when even their good friends were shunning them in private and public, when Helen's many volunteer efforts were no longer welcome, Edith called the judge in his chambers and invited Helen and him to dinner. In the elegant Longue Vue dining room, the Sterns and Wrights shared their personal stories, discussed the challenges following the *Brown* decision, and struggled to foresee a more equitable future.

An invitation to dinner at Longue Vue was considered a high honor. "Wright believed the Sterns supported him 'because they had felt discrimination over the years' and were still discriminated against in New Orleans in certain ways—socially and whatnot.'"[3] Yet the backgrounds of the Sterns and Wrights could not have been more different.

Born in 1911, Wright was one of seven children. He was fourth-generation Irish from County Cork—the "potato famine Irish," Wright used to say.[4] Like many early Irish immigrants, his parents were heavily involved in politics; his father probably got his position as an inspector for the Sewage and Water Board through political connections, and his mother was a ward leader. Nothing in his early history suggested Skelly would challenge the status quo.

The Irish Channel where the Wrights lived is a mile-long strip just downriver of the Garden District and close to the Mississippi. It was home primarily to Irish dockworkers who moved from the North before the Civil War to build the city's levees and canals. Generally looked down on, "the immigrant Irish, the reasoning went, came cheaper than native blacks for whom high prices had been paid at auction. The black workers were needed in the cotton and sugar fields, not to be wasted on such unskilled drudgery."[5] Most of the homes in the Irish Channel were modest but well-kept and came in assorted styles: Creole cottages, two-story balconied townhouses, and shotguns. There were also a few grander Greek Revival homes.

In the Irish Channel neighborhood, as in so many in New Orleans, white residential blocks were adjacent to or near blocks of Black homes. No one thought much about this or questioned it; it was just the way things were. Occasionally Black neighbors visited white ones, and vice versa, to pay respects when there was a death in the family.

A self-described "bad Catholic" in a dominantly Catholic city, Wright followed a traditional path to adulthood.[6] He attended Fortier High School, a public school. Then he went on to Jesuit-run Loyola University (the first in his family to go to college) on a scholarship and to Loyola Law School, graduating in 1934. After that, he taught history at both Fortier and Loyola University.

Wright and other less affluent classmates could not imagine that in this clannish city they would ever be asked to work at an upscale downtown law firm. Breaking into politics seemed a more promising path. Wright's uncle, a former state senator, was well connected in the Democratic organization and helped him land a job as Assistant US Attorney for the Eastern District in 1937. That conveniently separated him from the less savory world of Louisiana politics where "political corruption was a popular folk art."[7] Wright aggressively went after organized crime and Huey P. Long leaders. His nickname was the "Tom Dewey of New Orleans," after the three-term governor of New York who famously lost the 1948 presidential election to Harry Truman.[8] This era was the height of rampant voter fraud, with the rolls filled with dead people while being effectively closed to Black voters. Voter registration would become very important to Edith.

In contrast to her husband, Helen Patton was the daughter of an admiral and a product of upper-crust society in Washington, DC. She was working at the US Embassy in London when she met Skelly for the second time.[9] Her background helped the couple gain social acceptance in New Orleans's tightly closed society, which would never have been granted to the son of a plumber born on the wrong side of town.

A Transformative Moment

In his first job at the US Attorney's Office, Wright did nothing to change others' impression that he was "just another southern boy." He abided by the prevailing unwritten code of behavior. He followed the "rules"—separate water fountains, separate seating on buses, and separate schools—without questioning them. Growing up, he had witnessed but thought little about the assaults and abuse of all kinds that Black people suffered. As he later told Liva Baker, "Blacks were something apart. The injustice was lost on me basically. I took it like everybody else took it."[10]

That changed after Wright enlisted in the Coast Guard during World War II and served in New York and Europe. His conscience was awakened as he realized that the officers and soldiers were white, while Black servicemen were relegated to the kitchen and other menial jobs. He also witnessed how Black servicemen returning from overseas faced humiliation and violence in the unchanged Jim Crow South. Wright was slowly evolving a consciousness about race. His acceptance of the "southern way" began to falter soon after his return home and to his previous position at the US Attorney's Office.

Wright experienced a transformative moment while working at his office desk on Christmas Eve, 1945. The US Attorney's Office was having its annual Christmas party across the street, and the lights dancing in the windows distracted him from his work. He began to watch a disturbing little drama unfold at another Christmas party, also going on across the street. What he saw would stay with him for the rest of his life. This party was for the local branch of the Lighthouse for the Blind. He watched, fascinated as the sightless participants were segregated into white and Black groups. Even the blind, who were unable to see or be seen by other partygoers, were being segregated by race on this, of all nights, Christmas Eve.

In an interview with Baker, he recalled, "It didn't shock me. . . . It just began to eat at me. And it eats at me now [1979]. It began to make me think more of the injustice of it, of the whole system that I had taken for granted."[11] Soon after, in 1946, Wright left the New Orleans US Attorney's Office to go into private practice in Washington, DC. That was where Helen, his wife of one year, was from and where James would be born a year later.

During his time in the nation's capital, Wright was asked to help with a Louisiana lawsuit by a friend. The case was an appeal on behalf of a convicted Black man who was to be sent to the electric chair. Wright conceded that the man was guilty but believed he should have been given a sentence short of death. They lost the case. During that trial, he commuted back and forth, thereby maintaining ties to his native city.

Two years later, in 1948, Wright was offered the opportunity to fill a vacant US Attorney's Office slot in New Orleans, and the family moved back. A little more than a year later, a vacancy opened on the US Court of Appeals for the Fifth Circuit, located in New Orleans, and President Harry Truman appointed him to this position. So, it was in 1949 that Skelly Wright ascended to the Fifth Circuit Court just when challenges to how elections and public schools were being run in the South were increasingly coming to the fore.[12] Wright's tenure would elevate this court to national significance.

When Wright joined the Fifth Circuit Court, he was one of the youngest federal judges in the country. There he heard appeals from the lower courts of Florida, Alabama, Mississippi, Georgia, Texas, and Louisiana. He was also the only judge deciding school segregation cases after the *Brown* decision to live in the southern community for which he was ruling. In 1957, for example, District Court Judge Richard Davies of North Dakota had ordered the schools desegregated in Little Rock, Arkansas. This overrode Governor Orval Faubus's attempts to avoid integration. Unlike Wright, Davies faced no known social consequences in North Dakota for his desegregation order.

Sweeping Away Corruption

Edith's out-of-the-blue phone call to the judge initiated their transformative alliance. Yet, Wright was already aware of and impressed by Edith's involvement in advancing integration and Black voter registration.

Wright also knew about Edith's work to uncover and prevent voter fraud. Most likely, her activism in this area grew out of her involvement in Chep Morrison's 1945 mayoral election campaign; one of its key issues was cleaning up corruption in government, starting with the polling places. To make this issue visible Edith organized a "broom brigade," in which several hundred women marched down Canal Street with brooms (from Sears & Roebuck, of course) to the music of a jazz band, as they swept away corruption.[13] Clearly, this publicity stunt endeared her to Chep Morrison, and both she and Edgar became among his trusted advisers.

Several organizations—the League of Women's Voters, the Independent Women's Organization, and the New Orleans Civic Council—were working to eliminate voter fraud at the time, but Edith decided to form the Voters' Registration League in 1949. It would go on to address both corruption and voting rights for Black citizens. It is not clear why Edith felt the need to start an additional organization. Perhaps the existing groups were dominated by Uptown folks with social register status who did not make her feel welcome, or they likely did not have the mission of registering Black citizens.

At the time there was much anecdotal evidence for the local tradition of filling voter registration rolls with the names of dead, nonlocal, or fictitious people. So, Edith decided to undertake a thorough inspection of those rolls. She expected to find thousands of registration irregularities, but what she uncovered was even worse. For Edith, voting was a priority target for "cleaning up." As she told Elliott Hebert, "I had no idea we would hit the bull's-eye the first time."[14] They found nine thousand voters—"the famous 9,000"—who were classified as illiterate or disabled and therefore, by law, entitled to assistance in the voting booth, presumably by a poll worker. Yet, the requisite affidavits attesting to the disability were rarely, if ever, filed. The Voters' Registration League took the story to the press, which set off a sizable public outcry. Official state and city investigations followed, including court cases against a few deputies.

Edith and her friend Mrs. Isidore Newman took their case to the Governor's Mansion in Baton Rouge, where they met with then-Governor Earl Long, the brother of Huey Long. He challenged Edith, "How do you know all these people are not physically disabled or illiterate?" Her answer: "Mr. Governor, one deputy registered 32 voters in one day and 27 were listed as physically disabled. What would you think?" Probes revealed that some people did not even know they were registered as disabled, and the 9,000 shrank rapidly to 4,075, with more revealed as the investigation continued.[15]

Edith subsequently took the issue to the next governor, former judge Robert Kennon, in 1952. In an unsigned article in the Longue Vue files, "Cleaning Up the Voter Registration Rolls," the writer reports that Edith tried to be appointed as Orleans Parish Registrar of Voters.[16] Instead, someone with no record of any interest in political reform got the position. "So, with a chip on her shoulder, she called [the governor] . . . she came right to the point: 'This is what I want you to do,' and proceeded to outline some of the things needed to get the voter registration rolls in order. 'Okay,' he said, and to her astonishment, did exactly what she asked."[17] Edith could never be called shy, but on the strength of the public approval of the League's work, she, in effect, told the elected leaders what they needed to do and they did it.

The League that started as a small group of Edith and a few friends grew to include forty volunteer women who went on to create civics lessons and develop curricula about voting for schoolteachers. They brought model voting machines into schools for demonstrations, involved high school students in citizen surveys, and helped develop a nationwide campaign about modernized voter registration programs.

Obtaining Voting Rights for Black Citizens

Except for a few years during Reconstruction, most Black citizens in the South were disenfranchised. Southern states amended their constitutions to include new ways to stop Blacks from voting; there were poll taxes, property requirements, white-only primaries, and more. In the aftermath of the 1896 *Plessy v. Ferguson* decision, the effort to maintain segregation accelerated "more strongly than before." According to Judge Wright, "Blacks had just begun to get on the voting rolls in the latter half of the nineteenth century [but the

Plessy case] was used by the whites to get the voting rights of the Blacks who were registered taken away from them by having the laws repealed in various states. . . . In Louisiana alone there were 100,000 Black voters at the time of Plessy, and from 1900 on there were fewer than 5,000."[18] The judge applauded Edith's involvement in registering Black citizens. When interviewed by Gerda Weissmann Klein, he said that Edith "took particular interest in Voter Registration because she was smart enough to perceive that that is where the most important impact can be found."[19]

The Black community was also engaged in this issue. In the 1930s, African American residents of the Ninth Ward founded the Ninth Ward Civic League (NWCL), an early voter registration effort created with the sole intention of educating and registering Black voters. Throughout the 1940s and 1950s, "Black and white residents worked together to challenge the racial status quo . . . including National Urban League, Young Women's Christian Association, and the National Council of Jewish Women . . . by the time the Supreme Court handed down its *Brown* decision more than twenty-five thousand African American New Orleanians had successfully registered to vote."[20]

Voting rights took on new meaning during the postwar years. Louisiana was going through an economic transformation. As demand for cotton decreased and sugarcane harvesting became mechanized between 1940 and 1960, the "agricultural farm population diminished from about a third of the state's work force to 7.8 percent."[21] Black and white farm workers migrated either northward or to cities around the state and were competing for similar jobs. Racial divisions grew. As the demographics changed, the demand for voting rights grew louder.

Not surprisingly, voting rights were the subject of Wright's first case after his appointment to the Fifth Circuit Court in 1949, and not surprisingly, he ruled against the commonly implemented practice of denying voter registration to Black citizens. Wright reaffirmed a recent Supreme Court decision (*Smith v. Allwright*) outlawing the white-only primary. This may have been the law of the land, but it took a Wright ruling to guarantee it was applied to New Orleans. As mentioned, the white-only primary was just one of many maneuvers to prevent Black citizens from voting. This case did not make waves, nor did it bring Wright undue attention. That would come soon with his decisions regarding integration.

Wright Makes an Impact

With extraordinary courage, Wright struck down twenty-nine school segregation laws (the numbers vary according to how cases are counted) passed by the Louisiana state legislature. "Wright beat back each segregationist stratagem, even issuing a restraining order against the governor and every member of the legislature for good measure."[22] It was primarily Wright's decisions that finally led to a plan to integrate New Orleans's public schools by one grade each school year. Yet even this order would not be honored by the school board.

In October 1950, the three-judge Fifth Circuit Court ordered the LSU Law School to integrate. It was the first ruling expanding Black students' rights to an education since Reconstruction. The LSU Law School became the first law school to admit Black students in the Deep South. This decision applied to the professional and graduate schools of universities, such as the LSU nursing, journalism, and business schools.

This ruling was the opening wedge that would eventually widen to topple the separate-but-equal decision of *Plessy v. Ferguson*. It went further than the Supreme Court's earlier ruling that the University of Texas and the University of Oklahoma could not reject Black applicants. And Wright authored the opinion, writing in *Look* magazine, "Until that day I was just another Southern 'boy.' After that, there was no turning back."[23] This is when Wright began to make his mark on civil rights.

The LSU Law School suit was the beginning of a more-than-decade-long battle to integrate schools at every level. It also established the NAACP as the leading legal representative of the cause. "In courts throughout the country, the NAACP was the only national legal advocacy organization representing Negroes against the injustices of racial prejudice."[24] As mentioned earlier, Julius Rosenwald played a key role in the founding of the NAACP in Chicago, and Edith donated regularly to the organization.

On several fronts, Wright forced the South to loosen its fierce attachment to segregation. After World War II, whites in Louisiana were no more disposed to make concessions to Black demands than they had been before the war. They were not ready to equalize teachers' salaries. They were not prepared to let Black citizens vote. They were bent on using their political muscle in Congress to abolish the Fair Employment Practices Committee and defeat antilynching legislation.[25] These were all issues on which Edith stood on the opposite side, advocating for change.

Wright overturned the segregation of City Park and all public parks and swimming pools in 1957. His 1958 rulings put an end to forcing Black passengers to sit in the backs of buses and streetcars. Wright also ruled against the discriminatory purging of voter rolls, which facilitated Edith's voter registration efforts. He put an end to segregated sports games.

But it was his rulings to force compliance with the 1954 Supreme Court school integration decision that generated more than a decade of litigation and so many lawsuits. They stirred the most conflict, which convulsed the city.

Wright was appointed to the US Court of Appeals for the District of Columbia Circuit by President John F. Kennedy in 1962. By then, Wright was well known and much admired nationwide for his circuit court opinions. Most particularly, he is remembered for his eloquent "sad day for America" dissent in the 3–2 ruling that blocked the *New York Times* from publishing the Pentagon Papers.[26] His tenure was also notable for important decisions in environmental law, gender discrimination and human rights.

The NAACP national office identified lawyers in the southern states to be their local partners in suing the government for not enforcing the *Brown* decision. A. P. Tureaud became the NAACP representative in Louisiana shortly after being admitted to the bar in 1928. There were only three Black lawyers in New Orleans and one in Shreveport at the time; this number grew to six by 1951. Handling civil rights cases at this time required great courage, because violent reprisals were not uncommon. Yet progress had been made in integrating public transit, parks, and libraries, and there was hope that the public schools would be next. Tureaud fought, lawsuit after lawsuit, to desegregate the New Orleans school system. Edith followed his work with admiration.

A. P. Tureaud Front and Center

If Wright was the most important judge in the school integration fight in Louisiana from 1954 to 1960, then Tureaud was the most important lawyer—indefatigable, courageous, and brilliant. Like other Black lawyers of the time,

Alexander Pierre Tureaud went by his initials to avoid the humiliation of judges and white lawyers using his first name in the courtroom to imply his lesser status. The insults were endless. "'N——' was a common term used by whites on the street and in the courtroom. One judge even commented in open court, 'I didn't know they let you coons practice law.'"[27]

A. P. was born in 1899, just three years after the *Plessy* decision that guaranteed that his generation and those after him would grow up in the oppressive Jim Crow environment. He lived in an integrated neighborhood on Kerlerec Street near the French Quarter. His white friends went off to their white-only school, while he attended an all-Black private school that met in an old house on Bayou Road. Tureaud was one of twelve children of Louis, a local building contractor, and Eugenie (DeJean) Tureaud, daughter of the owners of a string of local pharmacies. She went to boarding school and Howard University and enjoyed other privileges of well-established Black Creole society. A. P. himself was so light skinned that he was often mistaken for white. As a youngster, he had a job delivering bread at a local store from which he was fired when the owner realized he was Black. Decades later, he was approached by a white lawyer in a courtroom and asked, "Where is that n—— lawyer I heard about?"

The Black Creoles formed a unique segment of New Orleans society, yet another dynamic layer in this multiracial, multicultural city. Black Creoles had European roots and light skin color and were different from American Blacks in many ways. Black Creoles "mostly traced their origins to 18th century unions of French and Spanish settlers with indigenous Indian women, African slaves, and Black refugees from political upheavals in the Caribbean. They were also called *gens de couleur*, people of color, and many carried French and Spanish names."[28]

Creoles were largely Catholic, often spoke French as much as English, and lived in separate neighborhoods—mostly downtown—from American Blacks. A. P.'s parents sent him to private school, thereby defying the prohibition against educating Black children. The Bayou Road School had been organized by the neighborhood. Thus, A. P. experienced a distinctly different childhood than most American Blacks.

A substantial portion of the Creole population—especially those living in the Seventh Ward like the Tureauds—was involved in the building trades. In fact, many would say they built the city. They were the craftsmen who created the architectural flourishes (as noted at Longue Vue) so celebrated today. They also created the popular styles that dominated the cityscape: double shotguns, Creole cottages, and camelbacks.[29] Louis Tureaud was a craftsman, and it was expected that A. P. would follow in his footsteps. But A. P. knew early on that the building trades were not for him; instead, he pursued his goal of working for racial equality and justice. He had the right temperament for this fight. With a calm but determined demeanor, he "almost never lost his temper or shouted in anger at others, as a youth or as an adult."[30]

Although he was better off than his American Black neighbors, A. P.'s life was still difficult. With no opportunity to get a high school education in New Orleans, he headed to Chicago alone as part of the Great Migration of southern Blacks. Deeply upset about how Blacks were treated there, he moved to Harlem. There he learned that he had passed the civil service exam he had taken before leaving New Orleans, so he moved to Washington, DC. After finishing high school there, he found a job in the library of the Justice Department.

While working at the library, A. P. discovered the law, and his destiny was set. In 1922, he entered Howard Law School. By the 1920s, according to Liva Baker, Howard Law School had trained more than 75 percent of the Black lawyers in the United States.[31] Tureaud soon met the renowned Harvard-educated teacher Charles Hamilton Houston. He joined the local NAACP, graduated in 1926, and moved back to New Orleans, ready to take on the injustices of Black life.

In the New Orleans that A. P. came home to, legalized segregation predominated. He immediately got involved in equalizing education, petitioning for new schools to be built for Black students and for existing ones to be improved. Because of the very few Black lawyers in the city and the fact that many Blacks sought out white lawyers whom they thought had more clout, it was difficult to build his practice.[32] But A. P. persisted, gained respect in the courtroom, and joined the local NAACP in 1927, becoming its state representative the following year. The New Orleans NAACP chapter, established in 1915, was the first in the Deep South.[33]

The NAACP Takes the Lead

Tureaud's first assignment for the NAACP was to be the local counsel in a lawsuit to equalize the salaries of white and Black teachers. The case, *McKelpin v. Orleans Parish School Board,* took almost a decade to be decided in favor of the NAACP, but it set a pattern of lawsuits based on the Equal Protection Clause of the Fourteenth Amendment. The issue had to be fought within parishes statewide in twelve individual lawsuits. This success established Tureaud's credibility as a civil rights lawyer and increased the NAACP's prestige. "For Tureaud to become a lawyer was a major step. And to become a civil rights lawyer and identify with the NAACP and the NAACP Legal Defense and Educational Fund with Thurgood Marshall took a great deal of guts and a great deal of courage."[34]

At this time, the Black community was split over the issue of working with whites. Was it appropriate, or would it jeopardize their support by pushing the racial boundaries beyond where white sympathizers were willing to go? But as A. P.'s son Alexander, also known as A. P., told me in a 2019 telephone interview, "In a quiet and understated way, [A. P. Tureaud Sr.] was all for building interracial coalitions." He came into close contact with the Sterns, working with them to establish and build Dillard University. A. P.'s wife Lucille, a Howard graduate and pharmacy school grad, organized lunches with white and Black professional women, according to her son, and "often invited white friends on family picnics." She was a volunteer at Flint-Goodridge Hospital and a member of the racially integrated YWCA. It is likely she crossed paths with Helen Wright.

In 1950, under the leadership of Thurgood Marshall, the NAACP made a pivotal policy decision to pursue "integration" and not the "equalization" strategy that many in the Black community advocated.[35] This was a controversial move, because many Black people preferred having equal schools with their own equal building facilities and their own teachers, rather than fighting for integration. Some thought that achieving integration would prove devastating for the Black students who currently attended white schools. Not so A. P.: he and the NAACP were solidly for integration. This was probably why Edgar Stern did not donate to the NAACP but instead provided sizable financial support for the Urban League, which focused more on job opportunities.

A Legal Giant Emerges

Thurgood Marshall seemed destined to lead this effort to secure school integration. Born in Baltimore in 1908, the grandson of a slave, Marshall had a brilliant legal career that led to his historic appointment by President Lyndon B. Johnson as the first Black Supreme Court justice. Yet in high school, perhaps because he was bored, Marshall was often banished to the basement for "time out" for misbehavior. The only reading material there was a copy of the US Constitution, which he read and memorized over time.[36] From then on, Marshall began to apply himself, graduating with honors first from Lincoln University in Chester, Pennsylvania, in 1930 and then from Howard University Law School in 1933.

Straight from law school, Marshall went to work for the NAACP, first in Baltimore but moving soon to the national office in New York. Within a year, he won his first major case against the University of Maryland, which had earlier rejected him because of his race. His suit led to the entry of the university's first Black student. In 1940, Marshall was appointed the first director counsel for the NAACP national office; in that position, he would become a critical partner for Tureaud in the spate of Louisiana cases that Tureaud brought to the courts.

In that same year, Marshall, with NAACP lead counsel Charles Hamilton Houston, won the first of twenty-nine Supreme Court cases. Together, they won cases ending the white-only primaries, disallowing racially restrictive covenants, and achieving graduate school integration. Then, of course, in 1954 came the *Brown* case. In *Brown,* Chief Justice Earl Warren famously wrote, "Segregation of white and colored children in public schools has a detrimental effect upon the colored children," and declared once and for all that the doctrine of separate but equal has no place, thus demolishing the *Plessy* doctrine of 1896.

The Louisiana Fight Begins in Earnest

Groundbreaking as the *Brown* decision was, it did not provide strong guidance on its implementation. President Dwight D. Eisenhower, a segregationist who was privately critical of and publicly unenthusiastic about the *Brown* decision, declined to endorse it. Chief Justice Warren, who needed every bit of support he could salvage for his Court, went to his grave still believing that "if Eisenhower, one of the most popular presidents in living memory, had spoken out in favor of the Supreme Court's ruling in *Brown*, and had urged 'every good citizen to help rectify more than eighty years of wrongdoing by honoring that decision,' resistance to it would have been substantially less, and 'we would have been relieved.'"[37]

Eisenhower made no effort to enforce the Supreme Court decision until southern defiance forced his hand in the 1957 Little Rock crisis. New Orleans native Louis Armstrong played a role in precipitating Eisenhower's involvement in Little Rock. The legendary performer was in Grand Forks, North Dakota, to give a concert and became the first Black man to stay at the finest hotel in town. A young newspaper reporter managed to get an interview with Armstrong and asked him to comment on the situation in Little Rock. It was national news that nine Black students there had been barred from the high school, despite the court order of a local judge. Arkansas National Guardsmen, ordered by Governor Orval Faubus, then surrounded the school to block the students' entry. Armstrong's reaction stunned the young reporter: "It's getting so bad a colored man hasn't got any country." He called President Eisenhower "two faced" and said he had "no guts." Then he said that he had been asked by the State Department to give a tour in the Soviet Union, but he had his doubts, adding, "The way they're treating my people in the South, the government can go to hell." That explosive remark hit newspapers and TV stations across the country. A week later, President Eisenhower ordered twelve hundred paratroopers from the 101st Airborne to surround the school and to escort the nine students into Little Rock High School. In response, Armstrong sent a message to the president: "God Bless You."[38]

In Louisiana, educational and political leaders of New Orleans and the state had no intention of letting the Supreme Court's decision change their segregation policies. The state legislature repeatedly found new ways to try to prevent integration. One after another, it passed new bills to delay or prevent enforcement of desegregation. No sooner did the bills become law, however, than Judge Wright annulled them. This was the kind of judicial action that Edith celebrated. It was also the kind of action that brought national attention.

By May 1960, six years after *Brown*, only "749 of the 7,016 school districts in the 17 southern and border states had desegregated," and none in Louisiana.[39] When Wright accepted the 1962 appointment by President John F. Kennedy to the US Court of Appeals for the District of Columbia Circuit, many people thought he did so to get away from all the desegregation cases. But this was not true, his son James told me: "He agonized about leaving New Orleans, but this was a very prestigious appointment, not one easily turned down." Actually, Kennedy wanted to appoint Wright to the Fifth Circuit Court, and Wright preferred that as well, but that appointment needed to be approved by Louisiana's two senators. No way would either Russell Long or Allen J. Ellender do that. Although the judicial spotlight moved away from Wright, he had left his mark, pushing back against every state legislative move and facing down the vicious racism that marked Louisiana's government. He played a key role in enforcing the *Brown* decision, "emerging to the national audience that saw him on the nightly newscasts as a man of mettle, one of the most courageous federal district judges in the South."[40]

Judge John Minor Wisdom Takes Center Stage

Soon after Wright left New Orleans, the judicial forum for the desegregation of educational facilities shifted to the US Court of Appeals for the Fifth Circuit, where Judge John Minor Wisdom played a leading role similar to Wright's.[41] Wisdom struck down numerous attempts to appeal lower courts' decisions, primarily those made by Wright. Frank B. Ellis, Wright's replacement on the court who was also the Democratic Party state chairman in Louisiana, turned out to be a big disappointment to the Kennedy administration that appointed him; he became known for falling asleep while on the bench and for his less-than-stellar judicial mind. Ellis reversed several Wright decisions only to be overturned by Wisdom, one after the other.

The state legislature and the federal government were at an impasse.

Wright had ordered the New Orleans school board to integrate grades one through six of all public schools by September 1962. One week after Wright left for the DC bench, the school board requested reconsideration of his last decree. Ellis not only delayed implementation of the order for two years but also ruled that only one grade be integrated at a time. It was then up to the Fifth Circuit Court under Wisdom to respond to an appeal of Ellis's decision modifying Wright's calendar by ordering a "staged" integration plan.

It is at this point that Wisdom replaced Wright on the front lines of court-ordered integration. For the next decade, he would lead the fight. Today, when people speak of the judicial history of integrating New Orleans's public schools, they often cite Wright and Wisdom together as the courageous and determined duo who fought the good fight: two judges with dramatically different backgrounds who led two different courts but with the same goal. Noted Fairclough, "Skelly Wright and John Minor Wisdom developed a deep sense of the historic injustices inflicted upon blacks, and their legal thinking reflected a determination to right past wrongs."[42]

Politically and socially, Wisdom and Wright were complete opposites. As described, Wright grew up in the working-class Irish Channel of shotguns and camelback homes on the river side of Magazine Street; Wisdom spent his childhood on the other side of Magazine in the Garden District, where the city's social elite lived in an elegant neighborhood graced by Greek Revival architecture.

Wisdom was born in 1905 into the privileged class. The family wealth derived from Virginia plantations and also from the cotton trade. Two centuries of financial prosperity and social position gave Wisdom an impeccable pedigree and all the right credentials. Ironically, even though the family would never socialize with Jews, Wisdom's maternal grandfather, David Cohen Labatt, was Jewish. In fact, Tulane Law School's first law degree was awarded to Labatt.[43] In 1929 Wisdom graduated first in his class from Tulane Law School and became a registered Republican. He then accepted membership in the Mardi Gras krewes of Momus, Comus, Rex, and Proteus—the most exclusive in the city—as well as the Boston and Louisiana Clubs. His serving on the board of the racially mixed Urban League local branch was apparently not held against him, even though the Urban League was evicted from the Community Chest after being part of it for twenty-five years.[44]

Nor did Wisdom's law partnership with Saul Sokolsky, his best friend from law school, seem to damage his social standing. Sokolsky was the son of Jewish immigrants who fled Poland and lived in a working-class neighborhood in the city. He later changed his name to Stone, and he and Wisdom remained law partners for twenty-eight years. Stone's son Harvey told me in a phone conversation, "When Wisdom saw Stone get the highest score in the first set of exams he said to him, 'Let's study together.' They became best friends."

Wisdom's choice of law partner was one indication of his independent thinking; another was his strong belief that segregation was wrong. "Wisdom was part political functionary, part social and political historian particularly conversant with the southern experience, part constitutional scholar, and part avid student of Shakespeare and Marlowe, and he knew how to employ all the parts as superstructure for his judicial opinions. Scholarship and civil rights soon became his specialty."[45] Yet, after being appointed to the Circuit Court, Wisdom retained his exclusive memberships; his only concession was to cease riding in all the Mardi Gras parades.

In contrast to Wright, Wisdom did not seem to suffer socially from judicial rulings in favor of integration. Reportedly they never cost him a friend. According to Baker:

> Establishment New Orleanians were much more accepting of their fellow elite. John Minor Wisdom, who, though somewhat insulated on the appellate court and safely removed from the front lines at the district court, was fully as adamant as Skelly Wright in upholding the civil rights he also believed were mandated by law and the Constitution—approving Wright's rulings in the school desegregation case whenever they were assigned to him, voting rights and trial procedures at other times. Wisdom got a good deal of mileage out of the membership in an old New Orleans family, the right carnival Krewes, the right clubs, and the right social circles.[46]

The story goes that one friend greeted Wisdom at the Boston Club, smiling and asking, "Well, John, what have you done to us white folks today?" According to Baker, "Wisdom extended his blueblood hand in friendship to

Skelly Wright during this troubled time, and they became friends as well as colleagues. Wright was appreciative, even encouraged, but their association could not shore up his position among white New Orleanians. It was too late for that."[47]

Interestingly, some New Orleanians attribute Wisdom's liberal thinking to his Jewish relatives. Wisdom did not agree, but he was aware that whatever support he had for his positions on local school desegregation came primarily from members of the New Orleans Jewish community. The Save our Schools organization (described in detail in the next chapter) was his most vocal backer, and it had many Jewish members. They included Rabbi Feibelman at Temple Sinai; Sam Rosenberg, who was on the school board; and Edgar and Edith Stern.[48]

Wisdom, for years, devoted considerable time and effort to strengthening the Republican Party in Louisiana. He believed strongly in the need for a two-party system. As President Eisenhower's Louisiana campaign manager, he was credited with helping win Louisiana's support for Eisenhower at the 1956 Republican convention. Eisenhower then won Louisiana by 40,000 votes. That earned Wisdom the tag "Ike's best friend in Louisiana" and a plum judicial appointment, placing him front and center in the snail's pace implementation of racial integration.

Over the course of the next several decades, the Fifth Circuit assumed the preeminent role in the decades-long struggle to desegregate public schools and other segments of American society. It issued more opinions in civil rights cases than any other federal circuit court. Most of those cases had first been decided by Wright. Wisdom, by upholding those decisions, brought the battle over the finish line.

9

AN UPFRONT ACTIVIST

"You fought your war and I supported you. This is my war, and someone has got to do it. I've gone too far to stop," Rosa Freeman Keller told her husband, Charles Keller, referring to his military service in World War II.[1] At that time, Rosa was experiencing hateful incidents similar to those directed at Edith. Her husband, who feared for her safety, wanted her to discontinue her activism.

Edith had met her match—an aggressive changemaker of another sort whose impact on the city was as visible, if not more so, than hers. Sixteen years her junior, Rosa Freeman Keller was out front and open as a fighter for social justice, while Edith acted mostly quietly and behind the scenes. Rosa was the ultimate insider, Edith the ultimate outsider. One was Presbyterian with the best social credentials money cannot buy, and the other was Jewish with an estimable pedigree. They were like opposite sides of the same coin, but they became friends. And their husbands partnered to build one of the most significant Black residential developments in the country, Pontchartrain Park.

Rosa was not the only southern white woman to courageously stand up and fight against racism in the 1930s, '40s, and '50s. For example, Virginia Foster Durr from Montgomery, Alabama, had all the social trappings of a southern belle but chose to join several progressive organizations over the years—fighting the poll tax, promoting antilynching legislation, working for trade union rights, opposing segregated bus transportation, and helping reduce the mistreatment of Black people. The sister-in-law of Supreme Court Justice Hugo Black, Durr was vilified at a US Senate hearing by Senator James Eastland of Mississippi. He accused her of being a Communist sympathizer. She worked with the early Black civil rights leader and educator Mary McLeod Bethune, Eleanor Roosevelt, the Southern Conference for Human Welfare, and the Southern Regional Council, whose work was supported by the Stern Fund. She was an inspiration for many others. As Fairclough notes, "The Association of Southern Women for the Prevention of Lynching had slowly but inexorably changed white attitudes. The ASWPL repeatedly refuted the traditional justifications for lynching: that lynching 'protected' southern white womanhood; that southern courts could not adequately punish Negro criminals; and that southern sheriffs were powerless to stop lynch mobs."[2]

A New Orleans Socialite

Rosa Freeman Keller was to the manor born in 1911 but rejected it all when she took up the cause of racial integration on several fronts in her native city of New Orleans. In turn, the society she was born into rejected her. Rosa's father, A. B. Freeman, had moved with his wife Ella from Georgia early in the nineteenth century, bringing with him the Coca-Cola Company bottling franchise for Louisiana. He subsequently built it into one of the largest bottling companies in the world. This conferred on him and his family the ultimate social status—so much for bloodlines being more important than money in New Orleans. Despite their relatively recent arrival to the city, the various Freemans in New Orleans were at the top rung of the social ladder.

Rosa's background could not have been more different from Edith's. She had the requisite coming-out party as a debutante the same year—1932—that her father was King of Rex, the elite Mardi Gras krewe. These were twin achievements in a city where these status markers were the coins of the realm. Her gold-star status was secure, but then she married a Jewish engineer, Chuck Keller, a graduate of West Point (where few Jews were admitted) from the Midwest. Both her parents fully approved of the marriage, but her father worried what kind of backlash it would bring.

Chuck Keller unwittingly provided the catalyst for his wife's metamorphosis into a civil rights liberal, both through his cultural-religious background and his choice of profession. As the Protestant wife of a Jewish husband, Rosa learned about antisemitism from him and his family. She listened attentively to the ugly thoughtlessness of casual antisemitic remarks that were commonly uttered in the 1930s. And she heard about what was happening to the Jews in Europe. Rosa thus developed a heightened sensitivity to prejudice in all forms. As an army officer's wife, she also experienced life outside the South. In the decade that Chuck spent in the US Army, the couple lived in Massachusetts, Panama, Michigan, and Colorado, experiencing life free of de jure segregation.[3] During these years, Rosa Freeman Keller liberated herself from the conventional life that New Orleans had intended for her.

When she returned to live in New Orleans in 1941, Rosa's activism emerged slowly as she grew aware of the racism all around her. She first joined the League of Women Voters, the Independent Women's Organization, the PTA, and the Girl Scouts. She was also a poll watcher and civil defense volunteer. But then she followed in the tradition of her mother. In her mother's memory, Rosa joined the biracial board of directors of the local YWCA, a rare integrated board on which her mother had served. That service, embarked on out of filial duty, changed her life. There, Rosa met and mingled comfortably with "very attractive [Black] women with educational backgrounds equal or better than [her] own."[4] Delighted to make new friends, Rosa became quite upset when she realized she could not have lunch or socialize in any way with them. It also sensitized her to the limited world to which white and Black people in the South were restricted. "My outrage was enormous. The more I learned about what a small world [they had,] I wondered how they could tolerate this and keep the genial attitude."[5]

Rosa was beginning to see parallels between Black experiences in the South and the social, political, and economic barriers faced by Jews. This was the 1940s when the horrors of genocide in Europe were exposed, as were the injustices faced by Black servicemen after they returned home. And like Edith, Rosa befriended the Wrights, clearly putting her out of step with her social crowd.

J. Skelly Wright had already endured more than five years of being reviled, cursed, and isolated. Keller agonized over the family's ostracism, which weighed particularly heavily on Wright's wife, Helen; Keller saw that it was nearly crushing her. At one point, Rosa and her husband spirited the Wrights away for a weekend in New England. There, the hotel staff, without prompting, brought out a bottle of champagne on a silver tray for the judge and his family. This was immensely satisfying to Keller, demonstrating that Wright was honored elsewhere for actions that had earned him infamy at home.[6]

At the invitation and encouragement of her friend Edgar Stern, Rosa joined the board of Dillard University and then became managing chair of Flint-Goodridge Hospital. The board had both Black and white members. In her leadership capacity, she was incensed to discover that Black doctors were denied membership in the Orleans Parish Medical Society. That meant they had no access to medical libraries or informative lectures. She led a group that included Black doctors to visit and appeal to the head of the society, Dr. Alton Ochsner, "one of the elitist of the city's social elite" and a leading surgeon for whom a hospital system was later named.[7] The appeal was for membership for Black doctors in the medical society. "He sputtered with rage and just about threw [us] out of his office," she reported in an interview.[8] But she was persistent on several fronts, often taking Black friends and colleagues to visit bankers and civic leaders to plead their cause. Like Edgar, she served as a liaison between the white establishment and the Black community.

Rosa Targets the Libraries

Rosa was active, along with Edgar and Edith, in the 1945 anticorruption campaign to elect Chep Morrison as mayor. In gratitude, Morrison appointed her to the city's library board. Initially, she served quietly among her segregationist colleagues, "trying to look nice and doing my homework." But she eventually started lobbying the board members to integrate the libraries. The League of Classroom Teachers and an ecumenical delegation headed by Monsignor Henry C. Bezou were also pushing for integration. And since the *Brown* decision, Black leaders had been pressuring the mayor on the library issue. Yet, the board was strongly opposed to integration. She went to the mayor, telling him of the board's opposition and that she would have to resign. To her astonishment, Morrison agreed to end segregation in the libraries, making it city policy that they would be open to all. He was able to withstand the expected outrage of most of the white voters. "It was the only public facility in New Orleans that desegregated without a court suit or a threat of one," noted Liva Baker.[9]

Efforts to advance integration seemed to consume Rosa's life. She served as the only woman on the board of the Urban League, assuming its presidency in 1953. She was used to being shunned by the white aristocracy who had celebrated with her at her debutante ball and dined with her at white-glove affairs. She watched people whisper behind her back on many social occasions. Not even Chuck's urging that she step back could stop her. Nor did appeals made by friends of her father have any effect. Even when her children were the targets of hatred, she continued her activism.

But the scariest incident occurred after a meeting of the Orleans Parish School Board in 1955, when a board member showed up at her front door, threatening her with a gun. She kept that incident a secret from her family for years.

A New Orleans Case Becomes Part of the *Brown* Decision

The school integration fight in New Orleans began before the 1954 *Brown* decision. In 1952 A. P. Tureaud filed the lawsuit *Bush v. Orleans Parish School Board* on behalf of sixteen-year-old Earl Benjamin Bush, who had been denied entry into an all-white high school. The *Bush* case, along with integration lawsuits from around the country, were folded into *Brown v. Board of Education of Topeka*. In fact, there had been many lawsuits around the country, all filed on behalf of female students:

> That almost all of the early cases—the radical first attempts that earned both the biggest headlines and the most backlash—were filed on behalf of girls went unremarked upon in the officials' records of the NAACP. . . . By approaching white universities, speaking with white officials, and engaging with white students on campuses in the 1940s; by testifying in court and responding to inquiring white reporters in the 1950s; and by choosing to enroll in previously all-white schools in the 1960s, girls and young women initiated and enacted school desegregation so that others might be able to envision themselves doing the same.[10]

The 1954 Supreme Court decision covered them all.

By 1960, the state had tried every possible tactic to prevent integration in both Wright's and Wisdom's courts; no options remained. The segregationist strategy then became to close all the public schools, rather than allow four young Black girls to integrate two white schools in a low-income neighborhood. A way would then be found to fund the reconstituted "private" schools, the segregationists believed. The school board also refused the appeal of several Uptown women to send some Black students to schools Uptown.

New Orleans no longer had any choice but to implement integration. The eyes of the nation were on the city, waiting to see whether peaceful integration would be possible there. Little Rock, after a violent televised confrontation in 1957, had complied under duress, and Baltimore did so voluntarily.[11] But responding peacefully was unthinkable for Louisiana. It had a rabidly racist governor, Jimmie ("You Are My Sunshine") Davis, who had invited Black citizens not to vote for him. There was Leander H. Perez, legendary political boss of Plaquemines Parish, the local pitbull of segregation and the segregationist czar of the South. Perez was supported by the White Citizens' Council. Together he and the governor led the state's "red hot defiance," as Baker called it.

Pushing to keep the schools open was the equivalent of advocating integration at a time when both notions were anathema to the school board and its followers. WDSU radio and TV, owned by Edgar Stern Jr., had already run more than fifty editorials in support of keeping the schools open. Noted Baker, "WDSU was taking its first tentative steps toward what was to become over the next year one of the few voices for law and order in New Orleans." WDSU's persistent advocacy of integration amplified the voice of Edith Stern. In one editorial, WDSU lamented, "Most community leaders are trying to look the other way. Few people want to talk about it. The newspapers play it down. . . . It seems to us that New Orleans is drifting in an atmosphere of unreality toward a catastrophe which, if it occurs, could seriously hurt this city."[12]

Again, the Women Take Charge

Up stepped many brave white women of New Orleans.

The Orleans Parish School Board, political leaders, and most of the city's population were acting as if school integration would be the end of the world and, certainly, of their world as they knew it. In response, an elite group of white Uptown women formed Save Our Schools (SOS) in 1960. Its mission was to ensure that all children, Black and white, would receive a public school education during the integration process. At its peak, it had a membership of about 800, mostly women. Its leaders, aided by the Southern Regional Council, which had played a similar role in the integration of Atlanta's schools, strategized about how to ensure that integration would proceed in New Orleans.[13]

One of SOS's key strategies was never to use the word "integration" in its brochures and posters. "SOS members took pains to avoid saying anything that could characterize them as 'integrationist,' fearing that such a label would discredit them with the whites they hoped to sway. Thus, SOS deliberately refused to offer an opinion on the merits of the *Brown* decision."[14] The leaders of SOS also decided that Black women's involvement should be welcomed, but never publicly. Indeed, the Black community contributed $1,000 to the effort.[15] Albert Dent, president of Dillard, led the fundraising effort.

SOS's first action was to mount a massive public relations campaign to convince white parents not to withdraw their children from the public schools that were expected to be integrated. This PR campaign was funded by the Stern Family Fund and designed by an advertising agency. "In all its propaganda, SOS hammered away at one basic theme: school closing would inflict catastrophic damage on the economy and social fabric of New Orleans."[16] Pamphlets were distributed throughout the city, their message supported by a major telephone campaign encouraging parents to support keeping the schools open.

The SOS women attended legislative sessions in the state capitol building in Baton Rouge, demanding that the public schools remain open. This notable group of women included Betty Wisdom, niece of the judge, and Katherine Wright. Forty SOS women traveled with them in support. But, of course, they were "only women."[17]

SOS also deployed creative tactics such as organizing carpools to take students to school. The name-calling mobs of white parents were so hateful that it was difficult to get past them and into the school buildings. When four Black girls were assigned to two schools in New Orleans's Ninth Ward, the SOS women initially escorted them into school. But the women were besieged with telephoned threats, and their harassment was so egregious that

US marshals took over that responsibility. This was the time that a cross was burned on Judge Wright's lawn.

The SOS's efforts failed to change public opinion. Most of its members were already identified as liberal integrationists, and some—like Rosa Freeman Keller, Peggy Murvison, and Gladys Cahn—were also active in the Urban League. Still others were well-known Catholic integrationists, such as Father Joseph Fichter and lawyer John P. Nelson. "SOS also evoked anti-Semitism: it had too many Jews and liberals to be of any help, explained one school board member."[18] Perhaps this is why Edith stayed out of view and even left town for a while.

Yet, behind the scenes, the Sterns provided funds to support a second, purportedly more neutral, citizens' group: the Committee for Public Education (COPE). No known integrationists were involved in it, and it distanced itself from SOS but effectively lobbied for the same goal. However, integration seemed designed to fail. As a "highly placed official in the Kennedy Administration" told a *Wall Street Journal* reporter, "The worst possible schools were selected to start desegregation. They were in the poorest neighborhoods where bad race relations resulted partly from Negroes displacing white workers by working at lower pay. By having only two desegregated schools, extreme elements could easily focus their hate and pressure tactics; if desegregation had been ordered throughout the school system such tactics would have been much more difficult and much less effective."[19]

Mayor Chep Morrison: A Steadfast Segregationist

Throughout these turbulent months, Mayor Chep Morrison laid low. He maintained that integration was a school board issue, leaving Rosa Freeman Keller, SOS, and others on their own. Morrison was a segregationist, but he seemed to be open to advancing improvements for the Black population, as long as they had nothing to do with the schools. In fact, what projects he did support reinforced the separation of the races, as in the case of Pontchartrain Park.

In the 1950s and early 1960s, Morrison focused public attention on physically reshaping the city—and away from public education. New Orleans was caught up in the urban renewal movement sweeping the country. As in other cities, highways bulldozed their way through Black neighborhoods. Claiborne Avenue, lined with large, majestic live oak trees and thriving Black businesses, was the heart of the Black community. Interstate 10 ripped through Tremé, the oldest African American neighborhood in the country, and destabilized for decades the communities whose roots there ran so deep. The suburb of Metairie grew, undermining New Orleans's downtown. Its schools drew middle-class taxpayers out of the city, particularly after integration occurred. Yet, urban renewal was considered a progressive program and the key to the national economic recovery so needed after World War II. Morrison took every opportunity to boast about these projects and deflect attention from his lack of involvement in the school issue.

School integration ever so gradually became a reality. New Orleans was no longer a poster child of die-hard racism. Fairclough describes the "grudging acceptance of inevitable change" by the city's business elite as a means of overcoming the "ugliness" of the school crisis:

> These were men, however, of small compromises rather than strategic vision. Collectively, they wielded great power. Judge John Minor Wisdom, who knew them intimately, described them as a kind of "interlocking directorate" or "closed corporation," for the same people could be found on the governing bodies of the Hibernia and Whitney banks, Tulane University, the Orleans Parish Levee Board, and the Board of Liquidation of the City Debt. Many belonged to the same social clubs (Boston and Pelican), sent their children to the same private schools (Newman and Country Day), and masked in the same Mardi Gras krewes (Rex, Comus, Momus, and Proteus). This concentration of old wealth made New Orleans one of the most conservative cities in the South. More exclusive and tradition-bound than wealthy whites in other southern cities, such people were slow to embrace change and, in Wisdom's view, "never really assert themselves in favor of desegregation."[20]

These were the men of Rosa's world, most of whom were appalled by her progressive ideology and commitments. But Rosa was indefatigable. She kept working hard to achieve integration at the high school level. With the support of civil rights activist John Nelson, Rosa funded a successful lawsuit to force the integration of Tulane University (both her brother Richard Freeman and Edgar were on its board) in 1963. In fact, Tulane voluntarily integrated its student body before the decision was handed down, motivated apparently by a potential Ford Foundation grant available only to integrated universities.

The Tulane lawsuit seemed like the end of the school integration conflicts. Edith was out of town but heard about it. She wrote on a postcard to Rosa: "I feel so guilty basking in this relaxation while you faced the firing squad. . . . You never cease to amaze me, my love. My congratulations—you have made history. We are all grateful."[21]

10

EDITH AND THE ARTS

Dawn DeDeaux is among the most important and successful artists in New Orleans; her solo and group exhibitions both in the city and across the country span fifty years. She is a self-identified "eccentric"; the media in which she works are decidedly conceptual, avant-garde, and out of the box. Her artwork reflects her environmental and social justice values.

DeDeaux burst on the art scene in the 1970s with her *CB Radio Booths* series, which brought "art to the people" through the mass communication means of telephone booths. "We had people talking to each other in different neighborhoods from outdoor booths," she explained. Then there was her *MotherShip* series, installations containing all sorts of mixed-media mechanisms, especially ladders, to escape the "ruined planet." *Free Fall: Prophecy and Free Will in Milton's Paradise Lost* was an outdoor collection of sixty-four tilting concrete columns, with verses from the blind poet's famous "Darkness Visible" poem in reflective vinyl so that cars passing by at nighttime could read them. The columns were installed as a falling colonnade in front of the Superdome in the center of the city. And DeDeaux created an art program generating poems, photos, and drawings for prisoners at Angola, the Louisiana State Penitentiary, a maximum-security prison located about two hours from New Orleans. It is named "Angola" after the former slave plantation that occupied that land. After the importing of slaves became illegal, the enslaved were "raised" locally.

DeDeaux's work is daunting, somewhat mysterious, and filled with meaning. One might think that it would be too unconventional and challenging for potential donors. But she received generous support, primarily from the Jewish community, including Edith.

When I interviewed DeDeaux, a twinkle-eyed, white native New Orleanian with long hair pulled to one side and dressed all in black, she told me, "The Jewish community stood by me through all of my work," whether they understood its complexity or not. "They were role models for me," she added. "If not for the Jewish community and key Jewish patrons, I would never have made it in New Orleans. In fact, I don't think I would have stayed in New Orleans without the Jewish community. I was eccentric, a free agent. I hung out with the downtown bohemian crowd of artists and writers but went Uptown to school and parties. I was a crossover person."

"Without the Jews there would be little culture in New Orleans" was a comment made many times to me by non-Jews as I was researching this book. Of course, Mardi Gras is its own culture, and clearly Black culture, especially in music and food, is as rich as in any city in the country. In fact, the culture of New Orleans is Black culture. But the Jewish community played a major role in supporting the traditional arts—museums, theater, and the symphony.

The list of Jewish funders of the arts in New Orleans is long. Edith was a patron of DeDeaux and provided major support to the New Orleans Museum of Art (NOMA), as well as to the symphony, helping rescue it from bankruptcy. She had a major impact on the traditional arts in New Orleans.

Art: Edith's New Interest

Edith and Edgar lived a life very much intertwined from the day of their marriage forward. Even though they each had their own passions and causes, they supported and applauded each other in these efforts. When Edgar died in 1959, there was a void in Edith's life that she filled partly with art.

Edith showed no real interest in art or in art collecting before Edgar's death. Until she traveled to Europe to purchase art in 1963, only one picture hung in Longue Vue, her grandmother's portrait. Perhaps Edith developed a newfound interest in art merely to occupy her time. Or she might have started collecting art earlier if Edgar had also shown an interest in this pursuit. Or perhaps it was driven by her competitive spirit: her siblings were avid collectors and equally serious philanthropists.

Brother Lessing Rosenwald, the oldest, succeeded his father as chairman of Sears from 1932 to 1939. He retired to concentrate on collecting rare books and art but continued to head the Rosenwald Fund; this was during the period when it was making its innovative grants and fellowships to an array of artists.

Lessing later donated to the Library of Congress his collection of 2,600 rare books, which trace the history of the illustrated book through the last six centuries, as well as 5,000 reference books. This collection is housed in the Rare Books and Special Collections division in a room that replicates the one in Lessing's home that housed his rare book collection. Lessing also donated what is considered one of the finest print collections—27,000 prints and drawings—to the National Gallery of Art, for which he was one of the founding donors when it opened in 1941. That is a formidable legacy.

Sister Adele Levy amassed an extraordinary collection of French masters and served on the board of trustees of the Museum of Modern Art (MOMA) in New York City for twenty years, including as its first vice-president. She was instrumental in securing for MOMA half of the Jacob Lawrence collection. After her death, she donated her collections to museums around the country. In 1961, MOMA mounted a memorial exhibit, *From Degas to Picasso,* which included not only the five works she donated to it but also those given to other museums around the country.

Brother Philip and his sculptor wife Helen ("Leni") were serious collectors, amassing works by Josef Albers, Marsden Hartley, Morris Louis, and David Smith. Together they founded the Washington Gallery of Modern Art. Philip was a serious political activist and philanthropist as well; he and Helen produced a photographic book spotlighting the disparities between the slums in the nation's capital and those near the White House.

Edith's daughter Audrey was married to Thomas Hess, editor of *ART News* and later curator of contemporary art at the Metropolitan Museum of Art. Edith and Edgar occasionally called on him for guidance—Edgar to help create an art collection for Dillard and Edith when she launched her own collecting venture. As the late William Fagaly, a curator of African art at NOMA for more than fifty years, noted in his memoir, "Edith felt left out, and being

Edith, she didn't like being the black sheep of the family. So, she went about changing that deficiency."[1]

Edith was not only a prominent member of the NOMA board, beginning in 1962, but was part of the "recognized triumvirate of 'grand dames' of New Orleans of their day—Muriel Bultman Francis, Sunny Norman, and Edith Rosenwald Stern—who almost triple-handedly, so to speak, ran the New Orleans culture scene, including the art museum, symphony, opera, ballet, and theater, in the 1960s, 1970s, and 1980s."[2] Muriel Bultman Francis was both a philanthropist and public relations expert with a New York City agency representing primarily classical musicians, the New Orleans Symphony, and the New Orleans Museum of Art. Sunny Norman was a major art philanthropist and supporter of Loyola University.

Fagaly recalled, "I dare say a day never passed when these three women were not on the telephone talking to each other and any other parties involved in addressing the latest 'crisis' that one of these cultural institutions were faced with. They worked tirelessly 'behind the scenes' until the problem was alleviated. If they were on the problem, one could almost rest assured the problem would be worked out if at all possible. Many times, it was their checkbook that came to the rescue."[3]

When Fagaly arrived in August 1966 from Indiana to join NOMA's staff, the "triumvirate" was already at work. "Edith was their leader simply because, let's face it, she had the most money and consequently the most power as a result of her being the heiress to the Sears & Roebuck fortune. She 'ruled the roost' in New Orleans, not only with culture but with politics as well. She was the queen bee." And he noted, "It didn't take Edith long to become an expert" in art.[4]

John Bullard, NOMA director for thirty-seven years, added in a 2023 interview, "There was a coterie of young women—Margery Stich, Phyllis Dennery, Dorothy Shushan—all vying for Edith's attention. . . . [They were part of] a wonderful group of women who were serious collectors." However, Bullard did not consider Edith to be a serious collector. "It didn't fit with her décor," he said. "When she didn't want to see the art, she just closed the doors." The door, that is, to the special room she created to display her collection of paintings and sculpture.

Edith's First Art Venture

Interestingly, Edith's first venture into collecting was of an artist close to home. Tulane art professor William Woodward (1859–1939) was painting local scenes, especially of the French Quarter, with a modest Impressionistic touch. He was an early advocate for the preservation of the French Quarter. His romanticized views of the Quarter helped advance the preservation cause at a time when demolition was in high gear.

Edith was also an advocate for preservation, occasionally buying a building in the Quarter and having it restored. The Woodward paintings could easily have fortified Edith's interest in preserving the past. Through the Stern Family Fund, she purchased a collection of forty-four oil crayon paintings and more than one hundred drypoint etchings depicting historic New Orleans, particularly the French Quarter, and donated them to NOMA. She underwrote the publication of a pocket-size catalog of these works as a guidebook to the Quarter. It generated revenue for NOMA.

Edith's art-collecting appetite had been whetted, and although she could easily have embarked on collecting the "masters," she instead was inclined to artwork that was considered modern in the 1960s, especially op art. She turned to her son-in-law Tom Hess for guidance, almost in defiance of his earlier critique of her lack of interest in art. As she wrote in "Autobiography of a House," "My son-in-law . . . said to me one day, 'I've gone through this house, and you will go to any means to avoid putting up an oil painting. You have glass. You have wood. You have paper.' So, after Mr. Stern died, a few years after that, I thought that I really had to go and look at some art."[5]

She did, in fact, have artful wallcoverings at Longue Vue—the "paper" Hess was apparently referring to. She and designer Ellen Shipman had done an extraordinary thing: they had Chinese wallpaper, which depicted beautiful birds, painstakingly removed from the walls of Shipman's New York apartment and rehung in the Longue Vue dining room. Edith picked up the bird theme for her tablecloth appliques and the Woolworth centerpiece. And on three walls of the upstairs hallway is a detailed mural block-printed in 1823 by Felix Sauvinet conveying a full view of the city of Lyon, France. As magnificent as these two artful wall coverings are, they are not considered traditional art.

To Europe on a Mission

Edith enjoyed buying art for NOMA and had loved acquiring the Woodward collection. By 1963, she was ready to go on an international shopping spree for art in Europe, but she did not know where to start. She enlisted her New Orleans–born friend, artist, and shoe heiress Lillian Florsheim to go with her to Europe. She also consulted then-NOMA director James Byrnes, who gave her a list of galleries to visit in Paris; she was supposed to send him photos of available works for his approval, but she did not. Byrnes also suggested that she visit artists Joan Mitchell and Sam Francis, but that did not happen either. Edith, being Edith, only partly followed Byrnes's advice. But she did purchase for the museum and herself works by op artist Victor Vasarely and light sculptor Julio Le Parc. She also purchased for the museum a marble Jean Arp sculpture for $20,000, which she described as "the one real thrill I've had."

In addition, she bought an oil drawing, *Several Circles*, by Wassily Kandinsky. When the Russian-born artist living in Germany fled that country in 1933, this oil drawing was rolled up in his satchel. According to Fagaly, the circles "grew out of what he called his fascination with the circle's connection to the cosmos. Of the three primary forms, Kandinsky said, 'The circle points most clearly to the fourth dimension.'" Fagaly also noted the importance of the Kandinsky for Edith: "Edith had a special affection for the Kandinsky painting. . . . It was the first painting she claimed she ever bought for herself, and it remained her favorite. She always seemed surprised with herself for being attracted to this colorful abstraction, painted by an artist she admitted she had never heard of before its purchase."[6]

Degas Was Next

In 1964 Edith launched a citywide campaign to acquire *Portrait of Estelle Musson Degas*, by Edgar Degas; its significance stemmed from its being painted while the artist lived in New Orleans in the 1870s. Degas's mother was born in New Orleans, and the Estelle of the painting was Degas's cousin. The Freeman family had set up the Ella West Freeman Matching Fund, the first of its kind, for acquisitions like this and challenged the museum and the city to provide a match of $200,000. Edith stepped in to meet that challenge, invited the appropriate crowd to Longue Vue for a po-boy lunch, and told them to bring their checkbooks. That began the citywide "Bring Estelle Home" campaign. It even reached into the public schools, where children were asked to contribute their pennies. The campaign succeeded not only in raising the needed funds but also in spreading awareness of the importance of culture in the city.

When NOMA hosted a Jacob Lawrence exhibition in 1975 that had been organized by the Whitney Museum in New York, John Bullard hosted a dinner in honor of Lawrence at the Pontchartrain Hotel on St. Charles Avenue. Lawrence came with his wife, and the invited guests included a fair number from the Black community. Edith commented to Bullard as she looked over the integrated room, "I never thought I'd see this day."

Tom Hess Helps Shape Edith's Direction

Edith was always looking for new ways to strengthen the museum, and she turned to son-in-law Tom for advice. William Fagaly described him as "urbane, witty, erudite and, during the third quarter of this century, universally recognized as one of the leaders of the New York (and, consequently, international) art world." Given that New Orleans had proclaimed itself the "Gateway to the Americas," Hess suggested the museum look south of the border to establish a collection that no other American museum had.

A collection of Cuzcanian Spanish colonial paintings was then up for sale. Edith tried to persuade the museum board to acquire it, but it declined to do so. Not wanting to give up, Edith turned to friend and architect Arthur Q. Davis to partner with her on its acquisition. Interestingly, in 1945, Edgar had pulled some strings to enable Davis's acceptance by Harvard's School of Design, where he would study under the legendary architect Walter Gropius of Bauhaus fame. Gropius accepted only twelve students, and with Edgar's help, Davis was one of them.

The Cuzco collection is now considered quite significant. The Cuzco School was active from the sixteenth to the eighteenth centuries in the heart of the Inca Empire; the artworks fused Indigenous and European styles. After a formal appraisal was made of the collection's value, Edith and Davis provided half the funds to purchase it, with NOMA providing the other half.

This was classic Edith: not donating funds unless they were matched. As Davis told Gerda Weissmann Klein, "Since the people of the Delgado [the original name for NOMA] had a stake in the purchase they are much prouder of the acquisition than had it been an outright gift. . . . Through Edith's guidance and imaginative conceptualizing, the entire Cuzco experience was not only a pleasant and exciting one but also a great contribution to the Museum as well."[7]

But what Edith wanted did not always come to pass, and sometimes that was all to the good. Bullard noted, "Edith was privileged and arrogant and always got her way"—but not every time. In the early 1970s, she wanted the museum to drastically alter its interior by ripping out the grand central staircase in the Great Hall and tearing down some walls. This would make it possible for visitors to go directly to the new addition paid for by the city in 1970. Saner heads prevailed. As Fagaly noted, "Her ideas to commandeer the entire museum were rejected."[8] However, she did make a large contribution to build the Stern Auditorium and office wing that also opened in 1970.

"The Ultimate Hostess"

William Fagaly spent a lot of time with board members, especially Edith and the other two "grand dames." He often escorted them to the symphony, the theater, or other social events and, of course, attended many of their dinner parties. As friend Tommy Lemann told me, "Edith was the ultimate hostess. She made people feel important and special." In his memoir, Fagaly provided a very apt description of a classic Edith dinner party:

> Edith loved parties and entertained with frequent lovely dinners in her beautiful home, occasionally with celebrities in attendance. Being a single man, I was at times invited and have very fond memories of those glamorous evenings. While dinners took many forms from serving po-boys to Isaac Stern to an affair comparable to a "state dinner" for Adlai Stevenson, there was a predictable pattern. . . . Upon arriving at Longue Vue, one was ushered in for cocktails and hors d'oeuvres to the second floor drawing room with a large glass window overlooking the extensive garden, the Spanish Court, with its water fountain creating

> a double-arched allee of cascading water in the distance. When dinner was announced, guests descended the grand circular staircase to the dining room off the main corridor. After dinner on special occasions, Edith would offer to make cafe brulot [a flaming after-dinner drink] herself in front of the bay window looking out onto the Pan Garden. She made it with much flourish, adding the necessary spices and liquor to the large silver bowl and allowing the flaming brew to twist down the curly rind of an orange. Bravo! Later the guests were led into the blue sitting room with the Kandinsky over the mantelpiece for after-dinner conversation and digestifs.[9]

On less formal occasions, Edith loved to play Twenty Questions, charades, and other games. After Edgar died, she learned to play bridge.

The Symphony Gets Edith's Attention as Well

NOMA was indeed Edith's passion, but she had a family commitment to the symphony. Edgar's mother had been a charter member in 1935 when it became the New Orleans Philharmonic Symphony, the successor to several earlier orchestras. And so, Edith grew as dedicated to raising serious money for the symphony as for the museum. Her gifts enabled the symphony to hire top-rated performers, enhancing its national standing. In 1957, Edith and Edgar donated $300,000, the largest gift by far in the orchestra's history. That "put them on the map," one observer reported.

Edith was always finding novel ways to raise money for the symphony. On one occasion, she brought Raymond Oliver, owner of the prestigious Le Grand Véfour restaurant in Paris, to New Orleans for a week of demonstrations of French cuisine. Chefs from all over the country came to learn from him. The week's final event was a black-tie dinner limited to one hundred people who paid $100 each. Edith secured all the culinary equipment for the week of demonstrations from Sears & Roebuck and auctioned it after the event, raising another $20,000.

She held conventional fundraising dinners as well, but occasionally a gimmick was added. One dinner was organized around the raffle of a Rolls-Royce. Only two hundred tickets were sold at $200 each. A key was presented to each ticket holder, and at the end of the evening, the person who held the key that fit the car was the winner. And in honor of Edgar's seventieth birthday, the New Orleans Symphony, Harvard, and Tulane each received $70,000.

Longtime general manager of the New Orleans Symphony Thomas Greene recalled the generosity of the Sterns:

> In my twenty years as general manager of the orchestra I frequently made requests to individuals or heads of companies for favors of financial support, only to meet with the response, "We can't do that . . . if we did it for the Symphony, we'd have to do it for everybody." This would seem to say that the person making that reply was, in fact, helping nobody. The Sterns *could* turn down an appeal, if they were so inclined. That seldom happened. . . . They were more likely to make a value judgment and let the size of their gift reflect their opinion.[10]

Edith loved to entertain visiting artists both for a formal meal and sometimes after a performance. In "Autobiography of a House," she lamented having not created a guest book or diary and then quoted a note she found that she thought was written in 1963: "Am truly getting childish about my party giving, but the house is so beautiful and seems to spread a glow over those who come here. The Casals luncheon not only went well, but there never was anyone more appreciative. He noticed and enjoyed every detail, even the table décor—I used the little glass bowls what [*sic*] fit onto the candlesticks, with white mums, the daisy kind with pronounced yellow hearts—three on the big table and one on the small."[11]

And then there is a recollection of an after-performance meal: "All records for Po-Boys [go] to Isaac Stern at a post-Symphony supper—all artists are ravenous after a performance. It seems they cannot eat before (though not sure if this is true of 'Cousin Isaac'). That time we again gathered in the playroom and, after three plates of gumbo, and his Po-Boy record, individual pecan pies hit just the right spot."[12]

Edith not only loved entertaining visiting artists but was also determined to make sure their needs were met. When Werner Torkanowsky became the music director and chief conductor for the New Orleans Symphony, Edith held a welcome party. Their son David Torkanowsky told me in a 2019 interview that Edith asked his mother if they were settled in and all was well. All was well, came the reply, but unfortunately, they were unable to get David into Metairie Park Country Day School. The next day, that was accomplished, and David, now a celebrated New Orleans jazz pianist and composer, happily attended the school.

Broadening Citywide Support for the Arts

There is no doubt that Edith spread her support for the arts over many New Orleans institutions, but because she left no specific records of her donations, one finds the evidence only serendipitously. By structuring her gifts with a matching challenge, she used her philanthropy to encourage buy-in from other people. She was always looking for a way to get as many people involved as possible in her many interests, and they were broad; she also served on the boards of Dillard University, the city's Parks and Parkways Commission, and the New Orleans Housing Projects.

In the early 1960s, Edith turned to Margery Stich, whom she had not yet met but had heard about, when she needed help to manage a new cultural fundraising effort. She asked Margery, "I need someone to help me with a helluva job right at this moment, so can you have lunch with me tomorrow?" Margery was one of the group of women always vying for Edith's attention, so, of course, she said yes. Edith was then president of a new organization called the Cultural Attractions Fund that she helped found. As Stich explained in her memo to Gerda Klein, "It was a kind of miniature United Way dedicated to raising the funds ONCE ONLY for all of the cultural organizations in N.O. We had our symphony, Opera Association, libraries, public television station, etc. . . . And to date it had not packed the wallop it needed." Edith asked Stich to organize a publicity campaign for the organization, and together the two had some significant success. That first encounter apparently led to a long friendship. Stich recalled, "I believe that our personal friendship was firmly based, because I treated her like an equal rather than a queen. We were twenty years apart in age, and vastly separated in intellect, yet there seemed to develop a mutual respect, admiration and caring for each other."[13]

Establishing a genuine friendship was apparently not easy for Edith, who worried that she was sought after by many people because of her money, connections, and festive parties. Stich, who considered Edith the smarter of the two of them, continued:

> People tended to hover over Ede at social events, almost smothering her in their eagerness to sit beside her, or to get her ear. . . . I felt that she was lonely, and that she did not wish to be relegated to the older woman, widow variety of guest . . . nor to be fawned over. . . . She was good company, and a great raconteur. No one told a story better. Often, they were about members of her own family, and often jokes upon herself and/or Edgar.[14]

The National Spotlight

Edith's hostess credentials were known near and far, and in 1968, she scored a major coup. The January 26, 1968, issue of *Life* magazine featured Edith as one of "The 'Grandes Dames' Who Grace America." She was the only Jewish woman so honored. Her social standing was in no way a match for the other seven featured in the article, but surely she matched them in good works and philanthropy.

In the photograph accompanying the article, Edith is seated on her living room sofa, with her silver punch bowl on the coffee table as she is poised to make her famed café brulot. Noting that Edith is the daughter of Julius Rosenwald, the article states that Edith was "raised in the tradition of good work and public service" and then lists several of her favorite charities such as the New Orleans Opera.

Being presented as an equal among the rich and socially eminent women of America must have been a proud moment for Edith. The other seven women were as follows:

- Mrs. Christopher Temple Emmet, grandniece of Mrs. William B. Astor, who made her debut at her great-aunt's famous 1892 ball of the original Four Hundred. Presented to Queen Victoria at age twenty, she was also active in the women's suffrage movement.
- Mrs. Nicholas Longworth (known to the public as Alice), daughter of President Theodore Roosevelt. She made her debut at the White House

and was wed there. She was quite the individual, defiant of her father at times, politically active, and well known to the public.

- Mrs. Harper Sibley, president of the United Council of Church Women, a celebrated Rochester, New York, philanthropist and active in interfaith and civil rights causes.
- Mrs. Malcolm Peabody, mother of both Massachusetts governor Endicott Peabody and Marietta Tree, US representative to the UN Trusteeship Council and grandmother of Pulitzer Prize–winning author Frances FitzGerald. A spirited civil rights activist, Mrs. Peabody purposely got arrested sitting at a lunch counter in St. Augustine, Florida, in 1964.
- Mrs. August Belmont, an English actress who, as Mrs. Belmont, devoted her time to the Metropolitan Opera Guild and the American Red Cross.
- Mrs. Lytle Hull, a founder of the New York Opera Company and the New York City Center, a trustee of the Metropolitan Museum of Art, and similarly involved in a host of performing arts organizations.
- Mrs. Thomas Armstrong, granddaughter of Captain Richard King, who created the famous King Ranch in the 1860s in south Texas, the largest ranch in the country. As chair of the board, she presided over the enterprise, which covered more than one million acres of prairie and grassland and included much livestock.

All came from prominent families and were mostly known for the well-positioned men that they married or were the daughter of, and for the good works they performed and the grand soirees they held. Living in a city where the accepted social class turned up their nose at her, a Jewish upstart from Chicago, one can only imagine Edith's sense of satisfaction for being listed among these upper-crust women.

Annabelle Bernard

Edith was not one interested in supporting individual artists; she was oriented to funding communitywide projects or specific organizations. In fact, she vowed never to sponsor a single artist of any kind, and she abided by that until she encountered New Orleans–born Annabelle Bernard. In 1955, Annabelle sang the lead in the opera *Ouanga* at New Orleans's Xavier University, the only Catholic HBCU in the country. *Ouanga* was written by a distinguished Black composer, Dr. Clarence Cameron White. Trained at the Oberlin Conservatory of Music, White spent three years on a Rosenwald Fund fellowship in Paris as a student of the French opera composer Raoul Laparra. It is quite possible that Edgar and Edith knew about that fellowship and were thus motivated to attend the performance.

In the audience that night, Edith was smitten by Annabelle's voice. "There was this voice and this child," she told Margo Miller. "I couldn't resist."[15] A five-foot-two lyric soprano who liked to wear her hair in a chignon, Bernard was the oldest of four. Her parents were of modest means, but they worked hard to secure the best possible education for their children. After attending public elementary schools, in eighth grade Annabelle won a scholarship to Gilbert Academy, a private school for exceptional Black students in New Orleans. Among the top ten students in her class, Annabelle was offered scholarships to three colleges. She chose Xavier because of its music department led by the well-known Sister Mary Elisa. After the opera that night, Edith sought out Annabelle and told her she wanted to be involved in her career.

When Edith became involved with something, as we have seen, she got involved in a big way. She did not just become Annabelle's sponsor—she effectively adopted her. She introduced her to the right people. She guided her training, paid for her clothes, and covered her living expenses as Annabelle sang in operas all over the world. In many letters over the course of years, Edith gave her advice and often lectures, as if Annabelle were her own child.

After the Xavier performance, Edith went to work and secured Annabelle an audition with Boris Goldovsky, a producer and conductor well known in the opera community. He accepted her for the 1956 season at Tanglewood in the Berkshires and, in the fall, brought her to the New England Conservatory of Music. There, she received a master's degree in 1958 and the artist's diploma in 1959. Edith and Edgar had a summer home near Tanglewood, and during that first summer Annabelle was under Edith's watchful eye.

Before World War II, Edith and Edgar had a lavish, sprawling summer estate on a lake in upstate New York where they had guest cabins, staff quarters, and a boat. Edgar named the boat "RAU," as in "Right as Usual," which he always called Edith. But after the war, they settled for a more modest place near Lenox, Massachusetts: a clapboard cottage with views of the mountains and plenty of acres of rolling landscape. More casual than the earlier place, this one was called "Austerity Castle," which Edith expanded, of course, and furnished totally with Sears & Roebuck's best. Here, they also had guest quarters and an additional house just for the five live-in summer help. Best of all, for Edith, was the proximity to Tanglewood, the legendary summer music venue with both inside and lawn seating. Edith reserved two boxes every season.

So, it was only natural that she would ensure that Annabelle performed at Tanglewood. Edith was enmeshed in the summer music world and often entertained musicians visiting from France and Germany. She could converse a bit with them, although not fluently. She put all her strong ties to work for Annabelle, and her efforts succeeded. The United States was not yet welcoming to Black opera singers, although a few notable singers had overcome racial barriers. But Annabelle was clearly on the right trajectory, winning awards and scholarships to study at noteworthy places in this country and abroad.

Before she moved to Europe, Annabelle performed at Longue Vue, accompanied on the piano by Robert Evans in May 1959. This performance of Schubert, Strauss, Charpentier, Chopin, and others, along with spirituals, was still illegal in New Orleans, as the Marian Anderson performance had been years before. But it did not turn heads as strongly and was well attended and appreciated.

Occasionally, Annabelle would visit Longue Vue and have tea with Edgar and Edith. Edgar was interested in opera and closely followed her career. In an oral history in the Longue Vue files, Annabelle said it was clear that Edgar loved Edith very much: "He loved America and his favorite song, when I came out to have tea with them, he would say 'Annabelle, sing for me "God Bless America"'; that was his theme song and he would stand and sing it with me with watery eyes, just lovely."[16]

On May 13, 1962, Annabelle wrote to Edith (her salutation being "Dear Mrs. Stern") to let her know that she had "finally made a few difficult decisions for the betterment of my health and career." She had decided to stay in

Berlin where she then had a contract with the West Berlin Opera "because these Germans I find nice and easier on the heart and mind." She pointed out as well that the "music world is at its height here and I've had such a marvelous success for a beginning." She also told Edith of her forthcoming performance in *Aida* and expressed hope that she would come to Berlin to attend it.

Annabelle's performance in *Aida* in 1962 was resoundingly successful. Both Edith and Annabelle's mother flew over for it. Edith told Margo Miller, "She came from so little, a very modest home, and she hasn't let herself become spoiled. During 'Aida' I cried the way I did at my daughter's wedding. That little figure on the stage! It was an experience."[17] Annabelle remained with the German opera company until her retirement in 1968.

Several letters in the Longue Vue Archives reveal that Edith felt no less possessive of Annabelle after she moved to Europe. In March 1963, Edith wrote in a long letter that "for the first time I have to give you a lecture." The lecture was all about not spending money quickly and foolishly, just because Annabelle was having some success and earning a nice income. Edith wanted her to make sure she put money away for the future when she would no longer be performing. Edith wrote that she was "shocked" that Annabelle had used up the 1961 letter of credit for $2,500 from Edith in a year and a half. The money was supposed to be untouched unless an emergency arose. "You did the same thing," Edith wrote, "the minute I gave you your Sears stock—you wanted right away to sell it to help your sister." After going on about why Annabelle must "protect" herself, Edith added, "It is for your sake that I am herewith telling you that I will not come to your rescue in the future and, during my lifetime, you cannot sell your Sears stock without my permission."[18] And then she affirmed her warm feelings for Annabelle.

Annabelle responded with a detailed explanation of her expenses in 1961, which seemed to equal her income, given the travel and accommodation costs for various performances around Europe. She was able to save some money in 1962, even with the expenses of travel and coaching. She even itemized her health insurance, gas/electric, and agent costs. There were no further letters, at least in the archives, about Annabelle's spending, and their relationship remained as close as ever.

Annabelle Bernard became something of a local heroine—local Black girl makes it big on the world's opera stage. She was a standout among Xavier's graduates and, after her retirement from singing, returned to teach in the department that nurtured her. A performance series and awards are now presented in her name.

When she felt comfortable doing so, Edith went public with her pet projects. She could be open about her relationship to Annabelle because white New Orleans did not pay much attention to graduates of the Black universities, even those who were making it big in the world of art and music. She was open, as well, with her service and generosity to NOMA. After all, the museum did not alienate its white patrons by putting on Black art exhibitions. In fact, NOMA did not have an integrated staff or board until the late 1960s. Before then, Dillard University had to make special arrangements for sculptor Elizabeth Catlett to bring her students to the museum on Mondays when it was closed. Perhaps Edith helped make that arrangement happen.

Edith was happy for the world to know about her work founding progressive nursery and elementary schools, on voter registration, and, of course, on Longue Vue and the Garden Club. For those efforts she left an extensive archive. However, her efforts and personal philanthropy on behalf of Black advancement, integration, and the arts are known only through the records and stories of others. She left no official record, no archive; she must have wanted it that way.

Edgar's efforts are better known because they were so public. His roles in the founding of Dillard and the development of Pontchartrain Park and Homes are highly celebrated. Edgar did not seek the spotlight, but what he did on behalf of New Orleans thrust him into it.

Together and separately, their mark on the city runs deep.

11

OVERCOMING THE MASQUE

Bill Borah was a tall, handsome man with blue eyes, thick white hair, a puckish sense of humor, and courage and integrity to spare. He was also a member of the New Orleans elite. Son of Fifth US Circuit Court of Appeals Judge Wayne G. Borah, he was also the great-nephew of Senator William Borah from Idaho, who famously opposed President Woodrow Wilson's proposal to create a League of Nations.

But Bill stepped out of line to help lead the fight against the Robert Moses–designed highway that would have decimated the French Quarter. It was not the first or last issue on which he deviated from the straight and narrow. He fought for good city planning and for the city to have an official master plan that officials then ignored. He fought against building a Walmart in the 2000s near the Mississippi River and the historic Garden District. After Hurricane Katrina, he fought to save Charity Hospital and its surrounding residential neighborhood, a monumental loss from which the city has still not recovered.[1] He was indeed a fighter who always gave credit to the many others who fought alongside him. But he also had a contagious zest for life and good food.

For his activism, Bill experienced the fate of anyone in this class-conscious city who stepped out of line, did not play by the "good old boy" rules, and followed his or her own path. Yet Bill never expected to experience the level of ostracism he did. "Many of my parents' generation just stopped talking to me," he told me in conversation in 2014.[2] His fledgling law practice suffered. The message was clear: "If you straighten up, we'll love you again." Yet, once he got involved in the highway fight and recognized the validity of its cause, he was not going to be deterred. He had never had an interest in playing by the rules of what he called the "Velvet Rut." This made him the perfect collaborator with the Sterns, particularly Edgar Jr. Defying convention, Edgar Jr. worked arm in arm with Bill, his friend Richard Baumbach, and a whole host of New Orleanians who were either not of the elite or not afraid to defy it. Edgar Jr. financed the fight against the highway and pushed it to a successful conclusion. A fight to the finish, it was a battle like no other and is often referred to as the "Second Battle of New Orleans."

Robert Moses was in the vanguard of the national push to build interstate highways across the country and tear up streetcar lines to be replaced by rubber-tire buses. However, Moses opposed the removal of New Orleans streetcars; because they rode on the neutral grounds, they did not take space away from cars. When hired by the Louisiana Department of Transportation as an engineering consultant to "devise an arterial plan for the city," Moses decried the removal of New Orleans's streetcars in his report, filed June 24, 1946:

> We see no advantage in this scheme. In fact, those who have wrestled with the free, mobile franchise bus on city streets envy New Orleans a separate right-of-way which completely segregates streetcars and at the same time serves as a safety zone. Franchise buses where no separate lanes are provided for them have a tendency to confuse traffic by weaving, stopping and doubling, and to preempt the curbs of ordinary streets. It is the vogue, no doubt stimulated by shrewd advertising and lobbying, to scrap all trolleys in favor of buses. New Orleans with its separate neutral ground right-of-way would gain nothing by shifting from streetcars to buses and giving up a unique and on the whole very successful local rapid trolley system.[3]

The Biggest Break with the Establishment

Edith and Edgar changed the educational landscape in the South from nursery school through college. Edgar Sr.'s pathbreaking development of Pontchartrain Park reverberated around the country. Edgar Jr.'s progressive editorials on WDSU were heard throughout the South. His helping his father build the Royal Orleans Hotel in the French Quarter challenged the negative assessment of that iconic neighborhood's future. But perhaps nothing was as significant or controversial as Edgar Jr.'s opposition to the proposed expressway through the French Quarter that was part of the federal government's campaign to drive highways through the heart of American cities—through downtowns, low-income minority neighborhoods, waterfronts, and parks. Nothing Edgar Jr. did was as bold and such a direct slap in the face of the power elite of New Orleans. Bill Borah and Richard Baumbach were his perfect partners.

The Claiborne Expressway

It is important to point out that the conventional wisdom today in New Orleans—that white preservationists saved the French Quarter at the expense of Tremé, which came to be bisected by the Claiborne Expressway—is false. Yes, the Claiborne rammed through that thriving Black neighborhood, once considered the "Black French Quarter." And yes, Claiborne Avenue in the Tremé was "one of the most beautiful and culturally significant boulevards in New Orleans."[4] Two hundred majestic live oak trees were lost and 155 properties seized to build the highway. Of the 143 places of business lining the avenue, only 44 remained after it was built. This tragedy was repeated in thriving Black neighborhoods across the country as highways were rammed through anything that stood in their way.

Yet, Claiborne Avenue was an expressway target long before the French Quarter was, and the Claiborne Expressway was more than halfway completed by the time the riverfront fight began. Richard Campanella, a widely respected Tulane geographer and historian of New Orleans, calls this conventional wisdom "the entrenched myth." In a 2025 phone interview, he pointed out that a highway through Tremé was first proposed in 1957 in the "Prospectus" prepared for the New Orleans Chamber of Commerce. Because the earlier proposed Riverfront Expressway would likely overwhelm the Quarter with traffic, a third leg, Claiborne, was added to the planned system. At that time, the Riverfront link was stalled because of opposition to it. In the meantime, it was full speed ahead on Claiborne, and the live oaks were removed in 1966. In 1968 the Claiborne pilings were pounded in, and by 1969 the expressway was more than 50 percent complete, when Borah and Baumbach were just beginning the fight against the French Quarter roadway. By the time President Richard Nixon's new transportation secretary, John Volpe, canceled the Riverfront Expressway, the I-10 through Tremé was complete.

Recognizing the Wrongheadedness of the Country's Highway Plans

Unlike most members of New Orleans's ruling class, the Sterns were not seduced by the false promises of a downtown revival that these expressways would bring and the offer of 90 percent funding from the federal government for their construction. Just as they had done before in redeveloping the French Quarter, advancing integration, and building a middle-class neighborhood for Black homeowners, they followed their own path.

The 1950s and 1960s were times of change for urban and rural landscapes across the country. After World War II, the country had to retool from a wartime to a peacetime economy. America had won the war by thinking big and growing from the top down. Why should that strategy not work domestically? What better domestic alternative than to redirect the economy from tanks to cars? The expected job gains and auto industry profits help explain the popularity of this vision of the future promoted by Madison Avenue, by automobile manufacturers, and by government leaders. Most leaders of downtowns across the country believed that tearing up their city to provide a roadway to the suburbs would save their businesses. Those that followed that course are the very ones today trying to revive the downtowns they turned over to cars and parking lots. They are building back housing, cultural venues, and street-level shopping that they once demolished. Urban neighborhoods have reclaimed their voice.

The Ultimate Sabotage

As part of this vision, the country's extensive network of trolley systems, once one of the world's finest, was purposely destroyed to give automobiles more road room. Stephen B. Goddard, in his revealing and extraordinarily detailed book *Getting There*, put it bluntly: "In the 1920s, General Motors, under the leadership of Alfred P. Sloan and his fellow automakers, decided to do nothing less than reorder society to alter the environment in which automobiles are sold by replacing light rail systems with cars and buses. So, in the early 1930s, GM approached railroads and electric utility companies, which owned most urban trolleys, and offered to buy their electric streetcar lines, which GM would then replace with buses."[5]

Initially, resistance to doing away with trolleys was strong. Buses were a hard sell: they jolted, smelled of gas, and were not nearly as comfortable as trolleys. But Sloan would not be daunted. If the streetcar systems would not willingly sell their lines, they would be taken over from within and dismantled. With Greyhound and Yellow Coach bus companies, Standard Oil, Phillips Petroleum, Mack Truck, and Firestone Company as partners, General Motors secretly formed the National City Lines (NCL), which bought up streetcar lines in eighty-three cities. NCL cut services, left repairs undone, raised fares, and took money out of each system.

A 1947 court case later confirmed that this secret partnership had "schemed to create a motor monopoly in nearly four dozen cities . . . taking over more than 100 electric transit systems in the process."[6] The pattern was set, the direction unstoppable. In a stark case of twentieth-century waste, light-rail systems being built today are recreating only a fragment of what was destroyed unnecessarily. New Orleans's St. Charles and Canal Street streetcar lines are rare survivors but still only a remnant of what was a robust New Orleans transit infrastructure.

Detroit, once a vibrant industrial center producing a variety of goods, was transformed into the car manufacturing center of the world. Car ownership mushroomed, and with it came the need for roads and highways. A 1956 congressional act under President Eisenhower established the interstate highway system. An admirer of the German Autobahn during the war, the president saw the need for fast-moving connections *between* cities as a national security issue. The big-city power brokers in New York, Detroit, Philadelphia, and other cities saw the highways as a cash cow—but they could only share in the federal bounty if the highways went *through* the cities.[7] Politically, the easiest places to situate those highways was through low-income neighborhoods, parks, or waterfronts. Black neighborhoods were frequent targets. Their housing stock was declared to be "slums" to comply with the law; even strong communities with bedrock institutions and solid but landlord-neglected housing met this fate. Thousands of highway miles tore through these neighborhoods, crippling them in ways that initiated or accelerated deterioration.

Not every place fell under the highway spell, and some downtowns famously succeeded in fending off the destructive dividers. In Savannah, for example, the late preservation activist Lee Adler told me years ago, "We fought urban renewal highways like a Communist plot." Today, many of those cities thrive with a diversified downtown attractive both to residents and tourists.

New Orleans Under the Spell of Robert Moses

But the modern allure of these highways was too seductive for many New Orleanians. Of course, they did have some benefits. Thousands would be employed demolishing mixed-use urban neighborhoods and building the highways. Big money was to be made by contractors. Handling the bonds, insurance, legal documents, and administrative costs of the highway would necessitate the creation of white-collar jobs.

For local officials and businessmen, there was money to be had when the federal government was paying 90 percent of the cost of building the highways. Who could resist that deal? No such comparable offer was forthcoming for increasing and improving mass transit, upgrading or refinancing inner-city housing, or making infrastructure repairs. Just the opposite. Every federal and state agency seemed to be blackballing the urban core by building into their provisions the denial of Black ownership or residency. The difficulties in developing Pontchartrain Park illustrated this, providing enormous stumbling blocks that Edgar Sr. so deftly overcame. Demolition and rebuilding were the name of the game.

Robert Moses, the planning czar of New York State and New York City, was the overarching figure during this postwar reshaping of American cities. He had so much power that he headed twelve New York city and state agencies at the same time. Just as significantly, he was an adviser to federal officials developing urban renewal and highway building programs. First there was Title I of the 1949 Housing Act, the primary vehicle for turning over neighborhoods to developers to demolish and build anew. Intentionally, the new high-rise housing was always less dense than what was torn down; the goal was to thin out minority and poor neighborhoods on the erroneous assumption that less density and fewer people would mean less crime. Even today, deteriorated public housing projects are being rebuilt as less dense communities, even while more density is advocated for higher-end neighborhoods.

Then the 1956 Interstate Highway Act unleashed more funds to demolish great swaths of urban America to make way for highways. Moses was not only an adviser to those who wrote the federal legislation but was also the first in line to get financing, receiving a lion's share. New York was transformed, and the appeal of this change reached cities across the country, including New Orleans. Thus, it was considered very progressive to invite Moses to bring his ideas southward. And so was born, in 1947 under Mayor Chep Morrison, a proposal for three highways through the city—the Pontchartrain most inland, the 610 through Tremé, and then the six-lane elevated highway along the waterfront of the French Quarter, all based on a Moses-led study of New Orleans. That was Moses's stock solution everywhere, but no other city had the unique French Quarter as its signature downtown district.

The voices counteracting the vision were drowned out and ignored by the press, which favored the new vision. After all, mainstream newspapers stood to reap a great deal of automobile advertising revenue. Think of all those ads showing attractive women next to shiny new vehicles.

The forces aligned in favor of this highway included the entire power structure of the city, in addition to the leading daily newspapers: the Chamber of Commerce, regional planners, labor unions, transportation bureaucrats from every level of government, and past, present, and future mayors. That was a formidable force. The plan to build a highway was clearly going full speed ahead when Bill Borah and Richard O. Baumbach Jr. got involved. It is not surprising that initially they could gain no traction.

Seeing Through the Promises

Yet, the Sterns saw beyond the seductive rhetoric and generous federal funding. They understood that the French Quarter would be key to reviving the city's economy, if it was left intact. That is why they were investing in that neighborhood. The Sterns also understood that this one proposed highway would become a national issue.

If the Riverfront Expressway were to be built, the French Quarter would lose nine of its eighteen square blocks, nearly 3,000 residents, and 1,100 businesses. The sweeping vista that connects St. Louis Cathedral and Jackson Square to the river would have been cut short by a roaring beltway, six lanes wide and forty feet high. Even the modified versions that tried to pacify the opposition would have blocked pedestrian access to the riverfront. A permanent, oversized impediment would divide the heart of the original city.

In addition to the blow that it would have dealt to New Orleans's still evolving tourism, convention, and entertainment industries, the expressway would have done almost nothing to revive the downtown department stores—Maison Blanche, D. H. Holmes, and Krauss's. Expressways did not bring people downtown but had the opposite effect; they accelerated the migration of retail to suburban strip malls and made white flight easier. Diehard preservationists—the Louisiana Landmarks Society, VCPORA, and others—vigorously opposed the highway in the 1950s when highways first became feasible. Yet, in downtowns across America where highway opponents organized, including New Orleans, preservationists were labeled obstructionists by the business community and social elite. And they were laughed at by government officials who insisted they did not understand what was best for the local community.

No one listened to Borah and Baumbach's arguments until Edgar Jr. got behind them, adding a game-changing dimension to the fight. He *was* part of the Establishment. He had clout. He was a highly respected businessman. He enjoyed membership in a host of prominent organizations, including Rex. He was a political animal, and he knew people in Washington, DC. Of course, he was still an outsider as a Jewish businessman, but his success and money could not be ignored.

After Edgar entered the fray, the anti-highway campaign gained national attention. *Washington Post* architecture critic Wolf Von Eckardt sounded the alarm about "the monstrous ribbon that is to recklessly slash through the city's picturesque Vieux Carré." This nationally syndicated columnist had some hope it could be stopped. In a column titled "Battle of New Orleans: Turning Point in the Freeway War," Von Eckardt wrote that the "revolt against freeways started in San Francisco and then spread to other cities—notably Washington, New Orleans, Philadelphia, Cleveland, Boston, Baltimore and New York." The New Orleans battle, he noted, "attracted national interest because of the Vieux Carré's significance as the last remaining legacy of historic French culture on American soil."[8]

Taking On the Establishment

Bill Borah understood how lucky New Orleans was to have escaped—so far—the worst ravages of the urban renewal era. It retained its extensive street grid, streetcar system (even if reduced), and incomparable architecture. And he understood how much the city had to lose if the highway were to be built. "New Orleans grew one neighborhood at a time along the oldest light rail system in America," he argued. "The neighborhoods were often mixed income and definitely mixed use. When planners come in to tell us about models for development, I say the best model for New Orleans is New Orleans itself. In fact, it is the best model for the nation, as well. It's just good urbanism."

In 1966, Borah and Baumbach, son of a well-established businessman, were home for Christmas vacation—Borah from the London School of Economics and Baumbach from Columbia University's MBA program. Both were Tulane Law School graduates, and Borah was a Marine veteran. When the two met for lunch at the famed Napoleon House in the Quarter, they learned of the highway plan from the restaurant owner. They immediately recognized its destructive impact; soon, they began to research alternative routes and to strategize how to expand the opposition beyond the small, hearty band of preservationists who were having little success. Journalist Jed Horne, in the foreword to the 2019 edition of *The Second Battle of New Orleans,* written by Borah and Baumbach, noted that, once engaged, they "pioneered new tactics and led a guerrilla resistance to the arrogance of the very elite into which they had been born."[9]

Borah then unexpectedly got a call from David Hunter, director of the Stern Family Fund since 1964. Hunter came to be considered the godfather of progressive philanthropy, taking early positions against nuclear energy, promoting socially responsible corporate practices, and devising programs to help poor neighborhoods. He went beyond the bounds of traditional philanthropy by identifying needs, the people who could satisfy them, and working with them to implement their ideas. The Fund even paid the salaries of those activists. "Hunter knew smart people everywhere," Borah told me. "He would seek out activists, like us." Borah later described the Stern Fund as "the shock troops of foundations. It would go where other foundations did not but they eventually followed. It was ahead of its time."

In that telephone call, Hunter informed Borah that Edgar Jr. was so impressed with their work that he wanted Borah and Baumbach to come work for the Stern Family Fund and carry on this fight. And so they were hired not only to oppose the New Orleans roadway but also to bring attention to the impact of highways on cities nationwide. "We at the Fund," Hunter told Bill and Richard, "are concerned about the impact of interstate highways on the urban areas in this country and we would like you to come work for our fund and specialize in areas of urban transportation policy to move this nation away from virtually almost unlimited financial support for the construction of highways and the support of the automobile." Edgar Jr. then met with Borah and Baumbach to convey his commitment to their work and asked them to join the Stern Fund board.

At those board meetings, Borah sat next to Edith. He told me, "She had great energy, was outspoken and well informed. She did her homework and was controversial," adding, "If you were promoting Black rights, you were thereby controversial in this city. The kids were as well. It was not Edgar Jr.'s style. He was overshadowed by her. Edgar Jr. was conservative, quiet and had a little grin." "Courage" is the word Borah used most often to describe the family. "If you supported integration at that time, you were taking a big stand. Edith was out in front on the issue, like her father."

One of the Biggest Battles in the City's History

With the financial support of the Stern Fund, Borah and Baumbach launched a broad and more comprehensive PR campaign and had the means to travel where necessary. Even more important were Edgar Jr.'s connections to the power centers in Washington, DC. His Washington lawyer, Louis F. Oberdorfer of the firm of Wilmer, Cutler and Pickering (the former assistant attorney general in the Kennedy administration), brought a lawsuit on behalf of Edgar Jr. and a citizen group to delay construction of the highway until it met all the necessary federal requirements.[10] Lawsuits like this were common in highway fights; their purpose was to put off construction while other opposition strategies were pursued.[11] Oberdorfer threw every possible wrench into the highway approval process, asserting that the Secretary of Transportation made no effort to study possible impacts on a national historic site or a mass transit alternative. Both actions were required by Section 106 of the National Historic Preservation Act, which created the National Trust for Historic Preservation, passed by Congress in 1966.[12] Meanwhile Borah, Baumbach, and others were calling on highway resisters in other cities to support their efforts.

The fight went on for several years, with Edgar Jr. monitoring closely the work of Borah and Baumbach. There were some small victories and big defeats until July 1, 1969, in the first year of President Nixon's first term, when Secretary of Transportation John Volpe canceled the Riverfront Highway plan. It was a momentous announcement provided with little explanation. Attempts to revive it under different programs failed. One such effort was led by Rep. Hale Boggs (D-La).

Business Week reported on the significance of Volpe's decision: "DOT officials said the cancellation of the French Quarter expressway was the first time any segment of the 42,500 mile Interstate System had been rejected for purely 'environmental' reasons."[13] Indeed, it had a national impact; after this, many expressways were canceled or stopped before they had begun or were completed.[14]

Making Television History

As if working to stop the highway did not ruffle enough feathers, Edgar Jr. stirred up perhaps even more controversy by using WDSU, purchased by his parents, as his personal mouthpiece in favor of integration in the early days of television. People today still remember how the stream of on-air WDSU editorials urging compliance with the *Brown* decision resounded throughout the city. "Keep the schools open" was the message, because doing so meant that integration would follow, as ordered by the courts. "In the news media, only WDSU radio and television campaigned vigorously against school closing, endorsing SOS and carrying more than fifty editorials on the subject of desegregation."[15]

Edith and her son may have disagreed on electoral politics, but she must have been thrilled with how he used television as a medium to broadcast his views on integration. There was no elaborate Stern family plan to acquire a radio and then a TV station. The Sterns bought the WDSU radio station first and then founded WDSU-TV simply to give Edgar Jr. the opportunity to run a business on his own. He was twenty-five when he returned to New Orleans after graduating from Harvard and serving as a Signal Corps officer in the Pacific during World War II and at the Pentagon during the Korean War. He was interested in technology and science and went to work as an electronics engineer for an offshore oil company.

Edgar Sr. asked his chief assistant Kabby to explore business opportunities for Edgar Jr. Kabby identified the emerging opportunity of television, even though most homes did not yet have a TV set. And so, Edgar Sr. founded the WDSU television station, which began broadcasting in December 1948. It was the first TV station in the Deep South, in New Orleans, and on the Gulf Coast, and was the forty-ninth station in the country.[16] Until Edgar Jr. sold it in 1972, the station was, on many fronts, one of the most innovative in the country. Surely, it had displayed formidable courage during the most divisive issue in the city's history.

Edgar Jr. had a vision of journalistic excellence that is rarely seen today. Three news directors—Bill Monroe, John Corporon, and Ed Planer—broke new ground in many directions. "He just said, 'This is my prize pony, and I want to win all the blue ribbons," Corporon told Mark Lorando of *Electronic Media*. "In its heyday, it was widely recognized as one of the finest local TV operations in the country. Making a difference wasn't a marketing slogan, but a business philosophy."[17]

Edgar Jr. provided the funds to make such excellence and innovation possible. Weekly children's shows, daily talk shows, and continuous news initiatives were just some of its ground-breaking initiatives. WDSU-TV broadcast the first live congressional hearing (Senator Estes Kefauver's hearings on organized crime) in 1951. The station introduced TV cameras on the floor of the state legislature in 1956, after Governor Earl Long's reelection. And it opened a full-time Washington, DC, bureau in 1958 to cover the activities of the Louisiana congressional delegation.

Its news team also created special reports that ran for several days. The Ku Klux Klan special report exposed its political infiltration strategy, revealing that there were KKK members in the state legislature, the state police, and local governing bodies. A thirteen-part series focused on loan sharking in New Orleans. A documentary revealed shocking conditions in the parish prison. WDSU, according to *Newsweek*, "had taken on the governor, the state attorney general, the district attorney and assorted judges, police officials and city councilmen. One state official was indicted on seven counts of malfeasance and extortion as a direct result of a WDSU exposé."[18] The blue ribbons that Edgar coveted came steadily. In the 1960s, the station won two Emmy Awards and a Peabody, journalism's equivalent of the Pulitzer Prize.

What is most remembered today and is often cited for its impact was the stream of on-air editorials that themselves were an innovation. They were the brainchild of the station's first news director, Bill Monroe. Not only did Monroe lead WDSU into uncharted on-air territory, but he was also outspokenly critical of the two daily newspapers. "What kind of newspaper is it that will send its man to the Kentucky Derby but won't send anyone to Little Rock?" Monroe asked publicly during the integration crisis precipitated by then-governor of Arkansas Orval Faubus. When the crisis began, WDSU newsmen were the only ones on the scene from New Orleans. In his editorials, Monroe "called for calm during the early days of civil rights conflict, 'generating a bit of hatred toward the station,'" as *Electronic Media* reported.[19] The Peabody Award soon followed.

Unfortunately, Monroe's pathbreaking editorials are not included in any official archive—only the news film footage is. Nor could I find editorials written by John Corporon during the school crisis.[20] Those written by Ed Planer, starting in 1967, were fortunately kept in a scrapbook by his daughter Marcy Planer, a former WDSU reporter.

The significance of those early editorials and the station's news coverage of the school controversy cannot be overestimated. At the time, the two major newspapers were advocating closure of the schools to avoid integration and called for state funding of private schools. Some claim that WDSU was the first station to have on-air editorials. In addition, the station crafted its news coverage to avoid giving the anti-integration protestors much exposure.

The editorials of the late 1960s had an impact in other areas of governance, as they questioned the expenditures of the New Orleans Tourist Commission, the levee board, and sources of financial support for judges. Editorials also focused on the need for a state board of censors; posed ethical questions to the state attorney general; shone the spotlight on local organized crime and on sordid conditions in public housing; and endorsed an antidiscrimination public accommodations law. Highlighting these issues inspired public debate.

A Chip Off the Old Blocks

As the only one of the Sterns' three children who stayed in New Orleans, Edgar Jr. was a close partner to both his parents. After his father's death in 1959, he became deeply involved in helping Edith manage family affairs. He also remained on the board of Sears & Roebuck.

Father and son worked together for years, so when Edgar Sr. died, Edgar Jr., a tall, often-smiling man with dark hair and penetrating eyes, was able to step in and fill his place. Building on both parents' commitment to improving the lives of Black citizens, he took a more activist position in the 1960s as a new phase of the civil rights era was beginning. Some people set things in motion and then step back. This was Edgar Jr.'s style, but he still had a great impact. Edith had a different personality and style. She stayed connected.

The two men had been very close, and not just as business partners. Letters in the archives demonstrate Edgar Jr.'s eagerness not only to please his father while he was away at school but also to argue with him politically. In an undated letter he sent from his boarding school Hotchkiss to "Dear Pop," Edgar Jr. reported, almost gleefully, "Guess what? The first quarter marks came out today, and I yanked down a 75 average. I even passed English with a 60. It is sneaking by, but it is there." This chatty letter continued: "The work is pretty hard, but I got on to it pretty quickly. . . . [the] English master is a marvelous fellow . . . funny as the devil sometimes." Edgar Jr. wrote equally enthusiastically about football: he was playing "first string," and the team was scoring victories. "Well, Pop, to sum it all up, I am having a swell time."[21]

Years later, Jr. wrote to Sr. a much more serious, two-and-a-half single-spaced letter from Harvard that began "Dear Sir." Edgar Jr. explained in detail why Roosevelt was the better choice over Dewey in 1944, even though he would have preferred to vote for a Republican. He wrote, "I am much more afraid of Mr. Dewey than I am of Mr. Roosevelt." He noted that "Dewey would not pin himself down on anything," presenting himself as an "isolationist" in the Midwest but an "interventionist" on the East Coast. He was "too much of a compromiser." Edgar Jr. concluded, "Republicans are very much dissatisfied with Dewey."[22] Without question, father and son were both Republicans and remained so. Edith, in contrast, was clearly liberal; after all, she gave the equivalent of a state dinner for Adlai Stevenson.

Jewish Observance Was an Alien Concept

Just about every member of the Stern family was Jewish in name only. As Sandra remembers: "The funny thing about our family. We didn't talk about who we were. You got hints about our Jewish heritage, but it was really just that, hints. I once overheard people who had just been talking to my father. One asked, 'Who was that?' The reply was, 'Oh that's old Edgar Stern, the Jew who married a Gentile.' That was the total summation of who my father was. Whoa. They didn't know who we were." Nor, evidently, that Edith was also Jewish.

Her Jewish identity was important to Edith in various ways; for example, she insisted that a rabbi officiate at grandson Bill Hess's wedding and that granddaughter Sandra get married under a modest chuppah, even though her partner was not Jewish. When Edgar Jr. wanted to marry Pauline (Polly) Stewart, her being Presbyterian became a real problem.

Born March 1, 1925, in Mapleton, New Jersey, Polly was a "tomboy who loved to climb trees." One sibling said she was a "playful sister, a lot of fun but somewhat reserved. It was the Scottish in her."[23] Edgar Jr. and Polly met at a dance and immediately fell in love. They were married in May 1947, but, as Sandra reported, "Things did not go well. My grandmother's sun rose and set on her sons. I found letters from her about Polly, and they were not kind. She was not welcomed." There is no indication how Edgar Jr. reacted to his mother's actions, but Polly took matters into her own hands.

Sandra explained, "The big thing in New Orleans was the society page picture in the newspaper, the engagement photo, and details. Edith never sent one in about Polly. [My] Mother [Polly], bless her tough soul, sent it in herself. She wrote it up as if it came from grandma and mailed it in. So that must have been a rough beginning." Yet, Sandra added, "While Edith was a dominating mother, Edgar Jr. admired her greatly. He ran her business and her household. They were business partners after Edgar Sr. died."

The Hate Was Real

Edgar Jr. was part of the social elite not only as a member of the Mardi Gras krewe of Rex but also as the "captain of the little float of Rex, a prestigious position," his brother Lessing remembered. "And I never heard negative conversations about Mardi Gras. He was very involved."

Yet Edgar Jr. had already irritated the Establishment by funding the opposition campaign to the Riverfront Expressway, building the Royal Orleans Hotel, and locating WDSU in the French Quarter. His WDSU's on-air editorials ratcheted up his social ostracism. But there was no turning back, nor any inclination to do so: Edgar Jr. faced the disfavor of the elite, something Edith was used to doing.

Bill Borah, who did an oral history interview at Longue Vue in 1987, described Edgar Jr.'s difficult situation:

> Edgar Stern was on the board of directors of Tulane University. But he ate and drank with the leading proponents of the Riverfront Expressway. To oppose that highway when virtually every major civic leader and politician supported it and then have to eat with those people too and sit on the Board of Tulane meeting after meeting and to take a position that they opposed and to do it virtually alone was an amazing act of courage. He did it time and time again. . . . You have to have incredible respect for that kind of guy. He didn't have to do that.[24]

Noted Lessing, "The culture was incredibly embracing when you did the things the culture liked but if you stepped outside it, as my folks did, you were shut out."

Edgar Jr. and Polly, like other members of the family, were victims of hateful graffiti and death threats. At least twice, their home on Garden Lane, only steps away from Longue Vue, was burglarized. Their home was one of the first ones in New Orleans to have a built-in burglar alarm system. It seems that someone from the alarm company staff stole the codes and broke in. Lessing said he was not sure whether the KKK instigated the death threats or if they were issued by "another hate group, but my parents were fearing for their lives."

Sandra, seven years older than Lessing, reported a frightening incident: "My grandparents one Christmas gave the three kids a phone to share. We started getting these vicious, hair-curling phone calls. 'We're going to kill you and your grandparents, you n—— lover.' You just froze, you didn't know what to say to that." Whether the hatred was motivated by antisemitism is not clear. Yet, antisemitism exists in different ways even today. As Bill Hess says emphatically: "If you were to say it didn't exist, that would be a lie. . . . Even today it still does exist. It's just more subtle."

Edgar Jr. and wife Polly began spending more time in Aspen, perhaps because of the tense atmosphere in New Orleans and his feeling some burnout. He told Mark Orlando of *Electronic Media,* "Television just devours ideas. It got so just about anything you could think of had already been done. The creative fun had gone out of it."[25] He ended up selling the station in 1972.

Aspen then became the couple's favorite place to vacation. They loved hiking and other outdoor adventures. Edgar Jr. got involved in the music society there and supported the hospital financially. There was much in Aspen to encourage both Edgar Jr. and Polly to move there.

Edgar Jr. was a developer at heart, and he pursued his passions out west. He developed the Starwood residential subdivision, the Park City ski resort, and his and Polly's sprawling Red Mountain Ranch. He became active culturally and philanthropically, particularly as chairman of the Music Association of Aspen. In the 1970s, he developed both the high-end Stanford Court Hotel in San Francisco and the Deer Valley Ski Resort outside Salt Lake City. Deer Valley was a new concept in ski resorts, in which haute cuisine and hospitality were as important as the sport, and it was often rated as the number-one ski resort in the country.

That the Sterns left because it was just too politically and socially uncomfortable and that they really liked Aspen proved a bitter pill for New Orleanians to swallow. Many people of a certain age will recall their departure and attribute it to their being excluded socially because they were Jewish. Yet, even though antisemitism was a constant in New Orleans in both obvious and subtle ways, Edgar Jr. and his family did not experience the degree of ostracism that other Jews felt. As noted, Edgar Jr., before his strong opposition to the highway and his on-air editorials, was accepted in many ways, particularly in Rex.

About a decade ago, a Stern family member who had moved from New Orleans told me, with strong conviction, what he thought was the real reason that Edgar Jr. and Polly relocated: in 1966, the FBI had warned them to leave town for their own safety. I found this hard to believe, and so I made a freedom-of-information request and secured the FBI report.

This report indicates that no such warning was issued, but the file had some information that was never made public: in 1966, Edgar Jr. was being considered for a presidential appointment. Sandra did not recall knowing anything about this but said that it was not unusual "for the kids to be uninformed about such things." There is no indication that Edgar Jr. even knew about it. In its investigation of Edgar Jr.'s activities, the FBI seemed most concerned about the Stern Family Fund's donations to liberal groups, particularly the Students for a Democratic Society (SDS) and the League for Industrial Democracy; the latter contribution was for "a conference of local leaders engaged in community development programs in various northern cities and Appalachia." This accords with Sandra's impressions. "The Stern Fund was mentioned in Watergate Hearings along those lines," she recalled. "When I was on [the] Stern Fund Board we did get heavily redacted [a] Freedom of Information report on our FBI file," she adds. "The general drift was that our donations treaded close to the line of being more political than charitable and definitely left leaning." Ironically, the politics of the Stern Fund apparently did not jibe with the politics of Edgar Jr. Sandra noted, "My dad was totally unhappy with the radical approach the Stern Fund was taking [he was a conservative Republican, in the old sense of the term] and he resigned from the board [in 1969] as a result." By then he had moved to Aspen.

So, fear of retribution for the Sterns' progressive actions was a given. It had not alone driven away any of the family members, but Lessing said, "I thought our exit from New Orleans was more consensus that it was not the safest place to be for us." Both Lessing and Sandra believe that offending the Establishment, taking stands that the city elite opposed, being unwilling to go along to get along precipitated the family's departure—certainly more so than antisemitism. Not following the social rules of the elite was a Stern family tradition begun by Edith when she first landed in New Orleans in 1921.

CONCLUSION

Three devastating historical events had the greatest impact on the mindset of southern Jews, regardless of where they emigrated from or how they began new lives in this country: the lynching of Leo Frank in Atlanta in 1913, the case of the Scottsboro Boys—nine Black teenagers falsely arrested for raping two white women—in Alabama in 1931, and the Temple bombing in Atlanta in 1958. In response, wariness was a constant element in their lives—sometimes consciously, other times not.

The Leo Frank case—for which Julius Rosenwald paid part of Frank's legal fees—was, as NYU professor Hasia Diner asserts, "the most traumatic event in American Jewish history."[1] Leo Frank, a native of Texas, was raised in New York in a traditional Jewish family. After earning a mechanical engineering degree at Cornell University in 1908, he moved to Atlanta. There he married Lucille Selig, also Jewish. He was very involved in the Atlanta Jewish community and was president of the Atlanta chapter of B'nai B'rith, a Jewish fraternal organization.

In 1913, Frank was falsely accused of the rape and murder of Mary Phagan, a thirteen-year-old worker at the Atlanta pencil factory he then managed. The case was front-page news across the nation. Antisemitism was not new, but this case fanned the flames. Jews everywhere were on edge.

The trial was purposely contrived to make Frank look guilty, and it succeeded. He stayed in jail for years, while his lawyers asserted his innocence and appealed his sentence. It was eventually commuted by the governor, but as he was being transported between detention sites, a lynch mob seized and hanged him. Edgar Sr. was then age twenty-seven, and Edith was twenty-one years old.

The case of Leo Frank—an innocent man wrongly convicted of murder—evoked the conditions from which Jews had escaped czarist Russia and their longstanding persecution in Western and Eastern Europe. This tragedy not only made American Jews feel more vulnerable but also as Diner pointed out, they

> became acutely conscious of the similarities and differences between themselves and blacks. While Jews had been involved in black affairs for years before the Frank murder, and since the beginning of the twentieth century had participated vigorously in efforts to change the racial status quo in America, that affair precipitated an upsurge in Jewish interest in blacks. They recognized that both identifiably separate groups were profoundly affected by their marginal status in society.[2]

The nation as a whole in the late 1920s was experiencing racial turmoil, characterized by lynchings and the growth of the Ku Klux Klan. Then in 1931, a very grave injustice occurred when nine Black teenagers from Scottsboro were arrested on a freight train from Memphis to Chattanooga. A racially charged fight had broken out in one of the cars, and the white youths were forced to exit the train. Enraged, they found two white girls, who were themselves facing arrest on various charges, and persuaded them to accuse the nine Black teenagers of rape. By the time the train arrived at a station in Alabama, it was met by an angry mob.

The boys were not all tried together, so various sham trials went on for years and were covered on the newspapers' front pages. Samuel Leibowitz, a nationally known New York defense attorney, was brought in to handle one of the appeals. The southern Jewish community perceived his involvement as a matter of pride, but of course, southern racists felt differently. Even Leibowitz's brilliant and eloquent courtroom performance could not change the verdict.[3]

Leibowitz then appealed all the way to the US Supreme Court, where he argued that justice could not be served by all-white juries. The Court agreed with his argument, ruling that all-white juries were illegal based on the Equal Protection Clause of the Fourteenth Amendment. All the cases were sent back to lower courts for retrial. Leibowitz also used his court appearances to show respect for his Black clients. He demanded that prosecutors address the Black defendants and witnesses by Mr. or Mrs. Soon the two women recanted the accusation of rape, and eventually all the Scottsboro cases were dropped.

Although the Jewish community applauded this outcome, Leibowitz's involvement made it a target as well. In the following decades, little attention was paid to the many cross burnings at Jewish sites and to the synagogues and temples throughout the South that were bombed. Then in 1958 a group of white supremacists, calling themselves the Confederate Underground, bombed the Temple, Atlanta's oldest and most prominent Jewish house of worship. It was also a hub of civil rights activism. Rabbi Jacob Rothschild was an outspoken advocate for the cause, and Martin Luther King Jr. had spoken there. Fortunately, the fifty sticks of dynamite exploded in the early morning hours when the Temple was empty.

For Atlanta's Jewish community and for Jews throughout the South, the event evoked memories of the lynching of Leo Frank a half-century earlier. Fortunately, public outrage at the bombing and support for the Temple were strong. The entire city of Atlanta came together to raise money to restore the building. Even President Eisenhower issued a strong condemnation. That communal support was impressive, a far cry from the response to the Leo Frank case. Nevertheless, the Temple bombing was another wake-up call for Jews across America. In the South, this history unavoidably hung heavily on Jews. It shaped the context in which the Sterns and all the Jews of New Orleans lived.

The Sterns' Impact on New Orleans

On the wall of my New Orleans apartment is a poster titled "Putting Philanthropy on the Map." It is a map of New Orleans showing the sites that Edith and Edgar built and "ventures they supported," thirty-five in all, ranging from Pontchartrain Park to WDSU and the Royal Orleans Hotel. Surrounding the map is a frame with thirty-five photos of people and places whose lives they touched, along with text descriptions of their impact, including Edith's "Broom Brigade," the New Orleans Philharmonic Symphony, Dillard University, and Annabelle Bernard. It is indeed a powerful visualization of the Sterns' continuing impact on this unique city and of their varied consequential projects, some they started and some they generously supported. It would be difficult to imagine the city without this rich assortment of places and institutions.

Yet, to accurately measure the Sterns' impact on the city, one needs to ask these questions: How different is New Orleans today than when Edith and Edgar were alive? Did they really change the city in ways they cared most about?

When I embarked on this inquiry, I knew through New Orleans friends that the Sterns were revered in the older Black community. In fact, in some ways they were better known and appreciated in that community than in the white one. That fascinated me.

But I never expected to find the depth of involvement of all three Sterns—Edith, Edgar Sr., and Edgar Jr.—in that Black community. Dillard, Flint-Goodridge Hospital, Pontchartrain Park, voter registration, funding for the school integration campaign, advocacy for Black access to public amenities, the early acknowledgment and celebration of Marian Anderson and the generous support of Annabelle Bernard—these were actions of significant import that made a real difference in the lives of Black citizens. They set an enviable example long before the civil rights era. Edgar Jr.'s early integration of the staff of the Royal Orleans Hotel and WDSU's standing up for school integration were huge game-changers. Surely, integration would have come eventually, at least with the passage of the 1964 Civil Rights Act. But leading by example was a Stern hallmark, a principle to be admired and one that accelerated change in New Orleans.

When I started my research, I assumed that the Sterns' involvements and philanthropy were responsible for major changes in New Orleans. Now I see the complexities of that assumption. Yet, the reality remains that Edith and Edgar, Edith's father before them, and their children after them comprise one of the most fascinating families to grace the American scene in the twentieth century and certainly one of the most impactful philanthropically.[4]

There are many generous Jewish philanthropists in New Orleans today. As mentioned earlier, socially well-placed friends told me at the start of my research journey, "Without the Jews there would be little culture in New Orleans." Yet some generous donors may say under their breath, "Enough with the Sterns." Resentment at being overshadowed may account for the almost complete absence of the Sterns from the story of southern Jews at the Museum of the Southern Jewish Experience. After my aggressive questioning of the museum staff, a photo of Edith and a small description appeared. Certainly, the Sterns' contributions merit more than a short paragraph about Edith alone.

Their philanthropy set a pattern in New Orleans by following Julius Rosenwald's matching-grant approach, which challenged others to give more generously than they might have on their own. The Sterns were the first couple to receive the Loving Cup given by the *Times-Picayune* newspaper. Edgar received his in 1930, primarily because of his efforts on behalf of the founding of Dillard University and the Flint-Goodridge Hospital. Edith received hers much later, in 1964, primarily for her philanthropic support of education. That the *Times-Picayune* had earlier been racist and segregationist did not seem to diminish the honor for the Sterns: two cement replicas of the cups grace their gravesites in Metairie Cemetery. Interestingly, there is nothing on their tombstones to indicate their Jewish identity; there is no Star of David or any Hebrew inscriptions. The tombstones of their daughter Audrey and son-in-law Thomas Hess are similar in that respect. This is true of all the German Jewish tombstones in that cemetery.

The Jewish Peddler Impact

In the twentieth century, New Orleans had its own brand of Reform Judaism, of which the Sterns are an example. In many ways, southern Jews and those in New Orleans, in particular, are different from northern Jews; one observer noted, "New Orleans Jews were probably the most assimilated of any city in America." As a Reform Jewish New Yorker, I was fascinated by this difference, which led me to read and learn more about southern Jewish history. The Stern family's relationship with the Black community, a bond beyond color, was also fascinating. It was a byproduct of a shared history in the South of being an outsider or worse. The historic roots of the Black-Jewish relationship go back to Jewish immigrant peddlers. This intrigued me as well.

When Jewish immigrants started arriving in the South early in the nineteenth century, there were few factories to provide opportunities for employment, in contrast to the North. Yet, in some ways, the South offered more opportunities for advancement: "Persistent agrarianism, its fairly small commercial class, and its lag in industrial and urban development as compared with other American regions made it a particularly attractive magnet for young Jews looking to gain a foothold in American commerce."[5]

And so, Jews turned to peddling. Picking up an "old style trade but in radically new settings," they would buy—mostly on credit—an assortment of goods from a local supplier to carry in a bag on their back. The goods would be anything from cooking utensils to fabric for making clothes. Because the South was not as densely populated as the North, the peddlers had to travel very wide circuits to sell their goods. If they made a little money, they would graduate to a pushcart and, later, to a horse and wagon.

At first the peddlers were viewed with suspicion by their customers, small farmers and emancipated slaves. But because they offered goods not found in the distant general stores, usually undersold those established stores, and, most importantly, sold on credit, they soon were welcomed by their customers. In the pre-newspaper days, they also brought news from the town they started out from—including gossip, jokes, and reporting on the status of runaway slaves. And as has been observed elsewhere, the peddlers were probably the first white people to treat Black people with respect. The peddlers ate meals with whomever invited them and slept in whatever accommodations they were offered.

In time, the immigrants' English improved. As they traveled, they absorbed the ways of their customers, learning to be Americans in the process. Really, they learned to be southerners, never stepping out of line with prevailing customs, even though selling to both Black and white customers was already breaking tradition:

> No one crossed the Southerner in his native land. The Jew was conditioned to fear authority from the boot of the tsar and the emperor; he knew his place, the perpetual visitor, tentative and unaccepted, his primary concern to remain and survive. Subconsciously, the region would stake a claim to a corner of his soul, too; for he was white and he would acquiesce and become like them in many ways. Yet he was conscious of the differences, of the permissible boundaries of attitude and act, of just

how far was too far, and protective enough of his own body and time to take on whatever colors were necessary to get through the day.[6]

When peddlers had amassed sufficient profit, they would open a general store—often called "the Jew store" by both Blacks and whites—in which they would follow some southern customs. That might mean designating certain days to sell to whites and others to Black customers. They would also violate such customs by allowing Black customers to try on clothes and sit at lunch counters. By the time of the Sterns' marriage, the descendants of Jewish peddlers had built most of the high-end department stores along Canal Street, which catered to the moneyed class and would not let Black customers try on clothes or ride the elevator lest it offend white shoppers.

Dryades Street, away from the city center, was filled with just the kind of small Jewish-owned stores where Blacks could shop with dignity. Ironically, it was the target of the first Black protests in the 1960s against the absence of Black employees. When I asked someone who was part of that movement, "Why did you target Jewish businesses when they were already treating you better than the others?" he replied, "Because we knew they'd be easy." He was correct: the store owners hired Black employees immediately.

Thus, the bond between the Black community and the Jews endured throughout the civil rights era. Yet not all sympathetic southern Jews advocated publicly for equality; some feared a loss of business or becoming targets of hostility.

The Rosenwalds and the Sterns did not share the peddler experience. Their forebears emigrated and went straight into business: Maurice Stern into cotton brokering and Samuel Rosenwald into the retail business. Yet both were seeking refuge from discrimination, which gave them a head start in empathy for the less fortunate. That empathy might have been heightened by the Sterns' feelings of being outsiders in a closed New Orleans society.

Perhaps, the most profound impact of the Sterns dates from "the most difficult years" of the 1950s and 1960s. "Conditions were volatile, and there was more opportunity for ugly things to happen. Things could have gone more sideways. The white elite would not have been able to muster the courage to lead," one New Orleanian observed in an interview with me. "The Sterns truly moved the needle in race relations. And it would have been much worse if we didn't have Dillard, the YWCA, Pontchartrain Park, WDSU and more."

The Sterns' greatest impact may lie in the educational arena. New Orleans is the only southern city outside Atlanta with two Black universities: Xavier and Dillard. Today, more than four thousand Black students graduate from them each year. Unfortunately, at least half depart the city to find professional opportunity elsewhere. Edith and both Edgars would certainly have done something to increase Black career opportunities in the city.

Failing the Black Community

As expected, a 2023 study released by the New Orleans Data Center showed that Black income in New Orleans is lower than white. However, it also showed that it is way lower than Black income in other southern cities, such as Houston, Charlotte, Nashville, and Atlanta:

> Black income in Metro New Orleans is not only well below White income locally, but it is well below incomes of Black peers in comparison metros. Notably, if Black per capita income locally equaled that of Metro Atlanta's Black population, Metro New Orleans' total Black income would be 22 percent higher than it is currently and the GDP of Metro New Orleans would increase by an estimated $5 billion. If Black per capita income locally equaled Metro Houston, New Orleans Black income would increase by 15.6 percent and local GDP would increase by $3.3 billion.[7]

Thus, the low economic standing of the Black population has the effect of lowering the economic performance of the entire city. This should be a cause not only for embarrassment but also of alarm among the civic elite.

By every important standard, New Orleans is failing its Black community. According to various measures—the ones that really count because they reflect living conditions, salaries, educational level, and employment opportunities—New Orleans ranks last or nearly last among American cities. The reality is never so glaring as when a national event takes place in New Orleans. Desperately needed infrastructure work around the city was put on hold for four months to prioritize the area surrounding the Superdome in which the 2025 Super Bowl was held—so tourists would not see a city in disarray. What was accomplished in those four months staggered locals, who are accustomed to repairs dragging on for months and even years. On the Crescent City Connection—the pair of bridges spanning the Mississippi River—new color lights were installed at a cost of $21 million, assuring that the bridges would shine in backdrop photographs during the Super Bowl. "Disneyland meets Vegas," one observer noted. Streets were paved and street signs hung in the French Quarter; crumbling pavements, water mains, and many potholes were fixed; flower and tree plantings appeared in the city center; and, of course, litter was picked up—all improving the city's appearance mightily. Some public murals in downtown were restored. The road to the 1930s lakefront airport, an Art Deco masterpiece, was repaved to improve the drive into the city for those arriving in private planes. All of this was great stuff, and all was targeted for the downtown tourist experience. What was done for the Super Bowl was another beautiful New Orleans masque. Was it merely lipstick on the pig?

For the Super Bowl, even the Lower Nine, across the Industrial Canal, one of the city's most fascinating mixed-income neighborhoods, got rare attention with a cleanup of some of its overgrown empty lots.[8] Before Katrina, the Ninth Ward had the highest rate of homeownership in New Orleans; after Katrina, it was the most devastated neighborhood in the city. Whatever recovery it has made has been because of the community's own efforts and its relentless pressuring of city hall. But all-Black neighborhoods in the city have been either ignored or only assisted nominally. The schools with the highest percentages of white students seem to get the lion's share of attention.[9]

In the historic Seventh Ward, for example, one outside investor bought up a whole block of homes to turn them into Airbnbs. Because Airbnb has forced up rental prices and limited the number of homes for sale, the city council has cracked down and restricted their numbers, particularly in tourist neighborhoods. Nor does the city receive revenues from the tax on Airbnb stays. Unfortunately, enforcement has to date been negligible, and rising home prices across the board are pushing more and more residents into neighboring parishes.

Great disparities between the white and Black communities, brought to national attention after Hurricane Katrina, remain. In August 2025, nearing the twentieth anniversary of the storm, one anonymous observer noted online:

> It is time to recover the loss of affordable housing, public services and population the official "Katrina Recovery" has inflicted on New Orleans. The University Medical Center's 450 hospital beds is nowhere near the 2,650 hospital beds Charity New Orleans' had as Hurricane Katrina approached the city. The 2,200 public housing units in New Orleans today is not a recovery of the 8,000 public housing units the city possessed on August 28, 2005. The 73 public schools in 2025 New Orleans is a far cry from the 124 schools the city had in 2005. The list goes on and on. All of this points to the need for the people of New Orleans to demand and receive nothing less than a full and real Katrina Recovery!

The New Orleans economy has become primarily a tourist economy, with out-of-town ownership of most of the hotels and bars. The musicians, who are a vital part of this industry, are significantly underpaid. As one musician said at a public forum, "New Orleans loves its music but not its musicians." A city so totally dependent on tourism and conventions is, indeed, as one New Orleanian noted earlier, a "failed city." The negative impact of these trends falls primarily on Black residents, who are mostly dependent on that low-wage visitor economy. Even though New Orleans is reportedly the most lucrative location for hotels in the country, minimum wage is still only $7.25/hour. The city's business class seems to want nothing more than for its all-charter public school system to produce hotel maids and bartenders. By every possible measure, the city is failing its Black population.

Today's New Orleans is counterproductive to the Black advancement that Edith and Edgar were working so hard to achieve. They strove to increase the number of Black homeowners, college graduates, and trained healthcare professionals. They wanted to make the accumulation of wealth possible for some Black families and to improve the health of the entire Black community. Either their impact was not lasting, or it dissipated once the Sterns were gone. Too many Black (and white) youth have had to leave town to find opportunity and a better life. The most celebrated New Orleanians today—Louis Armstrong, Michael Lewis, Trombone Shorty, Walter Isaacson, Wynton Marsalis, Mahalia Jackson, the late Cokie Roberts—all left the city to become a national success.

As Much as Things Change . . .

The social hierarchy of New Orleans persists. The same circles of power brokers rule. The dominance of the krewes has hardly changed. The luncheon clubs remain the mainstay of the power structure. A select group of quasi-governmental bodies still set the rules and divert too much of the city's taxes to their organizations or state authorities that legally cannot be touched. The Convention Center with a $200 million surplus since 2002, the tourism agencies, the stadium all overflow with cash.[10] These surpluses could be reinvested in meaningful ways to lift up the city's population in need or to make physical improvements to a deteriorating, flood-prone infrastructure. Instead, they are being used to create a new neighborhood next to the Convention Center that will only benefit the politically potent white upper class and outside investors.

"This city will break your heart," the former NPR correspondent and editor Gwen Thompkins told me. She continued:

> Outsiders come to New Orleans with a vision to make it better, but the city—for all of its dynamism in the streets—resists change. Sometimes local resistance is a good thing, like when Robert Moses tried to run a highway through the French Quarter. That was a terrible idea. But the resistance more often means that the same people end up on top and the same people end up on the bottom. Some of those outsiders get defeated and they'll stick around, regardless. Others leave. The Sterns knew New Orleans needed them more than they needed New Orleans. They knew when it was time to back away, as Edgar Jr. did.

The Stern Legacy

Maybe the question should not be about Edith, Edgar Sr., and Edgar Jr.'s impact but this one: What would New Orleans have become if the next generation after Edgar Jr. had stayed and followed the pattern set by Edith and

Edgar? Or, if another super-rich power couple of conscience had come forth to take up their mantle? Rosa Freeman Keller lived until 1998 and remained an iconoclast and effective rule breaker, and her descendants are generous philanthropists. New Orleans is graced with plenty of people who donate to good causes. But the unique flame of the Sterns died out after Edgar Jr. left. Perhaps their impact came not just from being wealthy and making big donations but also having the conscience to go along with their giving. Positive change does not happen unless someone pushes for it. No one among the current power brokers seems to do that in the same way.

In truth, the real meaningful change that happens in New Orleans comes from citizen action. The top echelons push for development that benefits their own kind, not the broad citizenry, hence, the new waterfront development by the Convention Center. Government operatives and the social elite care more about what the tourist sees than how the city functions for its residents.

Fortunately, the tradition of local activism is strong in New Orleans, particularly since Katrina. After the storm's destruction in 2005, thousands of energetic young people came to the city determined to rebuild; many of these changemakers remain.[11] Local groups fight for better storm drainage to prevent street flooding after heavy rainfalls. They fight for protection and expansion of the critical tree canopy citywide, so needed to maintain bearable temperatures. They fight for street signs to be replaced, something even tourists need. They fight new development that threatens the human scale of the historic neighborhoods. They fight for the preservation of the city's incomparable historic buildings and neighborhoods, all of which make the city so visually distinctive. They initiate sustainability efforts like recycling, cleaning up after Mardi Gras, and planting new trees. They fought for the reopening of Charity Hospital but lost, and healthcare services in the city have remained less extensive post-Katrina.

Edgar and Edith were not interested in curating their legacy. In fact, the archives at Longue Vue include papers and objects mostly recovered from waste baskets or unorganized desk drawers. They probably assumed their accomplishments would speak for themselves, which they indeed do. But their example is needed today more than ever. As one wealthy Uptown New Orleanian said after Katrina, "New Orleans will come back smaller, richer, and whiter." It has.

Notes

Introduction

1. Recollection of her friend Lucille Blum told to Gerda Weissmann Klein, *A Passion for Sharing*, 61.

2. Klein, *A Passion for Sharing*, 267.

1. Pontchartrain Park

1. Rosa Freeman Keller, taped autobiography, Amistad Research Center, Tulane University.

2. Stevenson, Lynching in America, 2.

3. Claire DeLucca, "Both Sides of the Barbed Wire: Lives of German Prisoners of War and African Americans in Camp Claiborne, La., 1944–46," 2018, University of New Orleans Theses and Dissertations 245 https//scholarworks.uno.edu/id/2454/.

4. Dozens of long-forgotten Black communities and towns are being rediscovered today, many of which were bulldozed to build everything from new highways to shopping centers.

5. Pierce, *The Wind in the Reeds*, 82.

6. Rothstein, *Color of Law*, 74–75.

7. Memo to deLesseps S. Morrison from W. Ray Scheuering, 3/23/49, Manuscripts Dept., Tulane University Libraries. A copy of this letter was made years ago by Jacques Morial but was apparently in the files lost or damaged by water during Katrina. They are off-limits to the public. Morial had found the memo in box 9, folder 1, Morrison Papers (LaRc) series 3: mayoralty 46–60, Afr-Am, 48–55.

8. Memo to deLesseps S. Morrison from W. Ray Scheuering, 3/23/49.

9. Haas, *DeLesseps S. Morrison and the Image of Reform*, 74.

10. Memo from W. Ray Scheuering to Mayor Morrison, 2/28/50, Manuscripts Dept., Tulane University Libraries, box 9, folder 1, Morrison Papers (LaRc) series 3: mayorality 46–60, Afr-Am, 48–55. (Lost since Hurricane Katrina.)

11. Davey and Reese, *Longue Vue House and Gardens*, 174.

12. Fairclough, *Race and Democracy*, 153.

13. Memo to Morrison from Stern in same folder as lost Morrison memo, read and copied by Jacques Morial.

14. Keller, taped autobiography, Amistad Research Center.

15. Fairclough, *Race and Democracy*, 152.

16. Davey and Reese, *Longue Vue House and Gardens*, 189.

17. Davey and Reese, *Longue Vue House and Gardens*, 188.

18. Khaton, "Wonder Years," 29.

19. Davey and Reese, *Longue Vue House and Gardens*, 189.

20. Pierce, *Wind in the Reeds*, 82.

2. Behind the Masque

1. Gwendolyn Thompkins, "Where Everyone Was Having Such a Good Time: De-Segregating the Dew Drop Inn," unpublished thesis, June 7, 2023.

2. Starr, *New Orleans Unmasqued*, 89.

3. Starr, *New Orleans Unmasqued*, 153.

4. Trillin, "U.S. Journal: New Orleans," *New Yorker*, March 9, 1968.

5. Eaves, *Singing Out Loud*, 56.

6. Barry, *Rising Tide*, 218.

7. Diner, *In the Almost Promised Land*, 26.

8. Some members of the Stern family did not emigrate to the United States but remained in England. The Longue Vue Archives indicate that Edith and Edgar stayed in touch with them and visited them when they went to Europe.

9. In the Longue Vue Archives, Collection 235, box 15, Maurice is said to have arrived in 1872 at age seventeen; he became a mailboy at Lehman, Newgas Co. and a firm member in 1880. I used the information provided by his grandson Walter C. Stern in his chapter, "The Worlds That Built Edith and Edgar," in *Longue Vue House and Gardens*, by Davey and Reese.

10. Stern, "The Worlds That Built Edith and Edgar," in Davey and Reese, *Longue Vue House and Gardens*, 167.

11. Richard Campanella, "A French Chateau Style of Architecture: Thomas Sully's Long-Forgotten Liverpool & London & Globe Insurance Building," *Preservation in Print*, October 2017, https://richcampanella.com/wp-content/uploads/2020/02/article_Campanella_Preservation-in-Print_2017_Oct_LLG-Insurance-Building.pdf.

12. Sylvania Williams was a Black educator and women's rights advocate.

13. Klein, *Passion for Sharing*, 50.

14. Stern, "The Worlds That Built Edith and Edgar," in Davey and Reese, *Longue Vue House and Gardens*, 170.

15. Stern, "The Worlds That Built Edith and Edgar," in Davey and Reese, *Longue Vue House and Gardens*, 171.

16. Williams, *Huey Long*, 21.

17. Williams, *Huey Long*, 4.

18. Baker, *Second Battle of New Orleans*, 320.

19. Powell, *Troubled Memory*, 369.

20. Bauman, *Quiet Voices*, 25.

21. Powell, *Troubled Memory*, 367.

22. Cohen, *The Fish That Ate the Whale*, 100.

23. Chapman, *Bananas*, 166.

24. Chapman, *Bananas*, 119.

25. Luxenberg, *The Story of Plessy v. Ferguson*, xvii.

26. Fairclough, *Race and Democracy*, preface.

27. Fairclough, *Race and Democracy*, 9.

28. Fairclough, *Race and Democracy*, 110.

29. Fairclough, *Race and Democracy*, 9.

30. The streetcar line was added to the National Register of Historic Places in 1973. The National Trust notes, "The St. Charles Line is the oldest continuously operated street railway line in the world today."

31. Cigliano and Landau, *The Grand American Avenue*, 15.

32. As a longtime observer and writer about cities and urban development, I have marveled at the staying power of these elegant landmark eateries, which have long succeeded in the most downscale, honkytonk neighborhoods, especially on Bourbon Street. According to accepted city planning norms, this should not happen.

33. Evans, *The Provincials*, 201.

34. No one, including Friedler's son, remembers when this talk was given, but a copy of this speech continues to circulate informally.

3. Fitting In

1. Klein, *Passion for Sharing*, 21.

2. Harris, *Merchant Princes*, 330.

3. Ascoli, *Rosenwald*, 62.

4. Harris, *Merchant Princes*, 325.

5. Harris, *Merchant Princes*, 332.

6. Harris, *Merchant Princes*, 325.

7. Klein, *Passion for Sharing*, 20.

8. Re "Israel": At this time, it was still Palestine, but Marion is remembering this years later, after the creation of the State of Israel in 1948. Harris, *Merchant Princes*, 326.

9. Klein, *Passion for Sharing*, 20.

10. Between the 1880s and 1920s, hundreds of settlement houses were established in many US cities in response to an influx of European immigrants who needed help with everything from navigating their new landscape to learning English. Hull House was one of the most famous.

11. Klein, *Passion for Sharing*, 30.

12. Baker, *Second Battle*, 48.

13. One of New Orleans's largest performance spaces is named in her honor.

14. Klein, *Passion for Sharing*, 40.

15. Stern, "Autobiography of a House."

16. Stern, "Autobiography of a House."

17. Schexnayder added the last name Machado after she married her second husband.

18. "By 1881 Jews lived in some 522 southern towns and cities, through which they circulated as they conducted business." Rabin, *Jewish South*, 129.

19. Harris, *Merchant Princes*, 327.

20. The larger Rosenwald family was divided over the founding of Israel.

21. Greene, *The Temple Bombing*, 57.

22. Greene, *The Temple Bombing*, 57.

23. Ferris, *Matzoh Ball Gumbo*, 90.

24. Wolf, *My New Orleans, Gone Away*, 46.

25. In some other southern cities, the Jewish community held a Purim Ball as their equivalent to Mardi Gras, donning costumes and masques to celebrate the deliverance of the Jews by Queen Esther and her cousin Mordechai.

26. Harris, *Merchant Princes*, 326. This was not unusual with country clubs elsewhere, where Jews were able to join at first, but later the membership became restricted.

27. Klein, *Passion for Sharing*, 57.

28. The first of two; the second one was built in 1939.

29. Margie Blumenthal, letter to Gerta Klein for her book *Passion for Sharing*, June 21, 1982, Longue Vue Archives.

30. The Playhouse is a building separate from the house where most parties and performances took place.

31. Harris, *Merchant Princes*, 327.

4. Like Father, Like Daughter

1. In 1939, Anderson first gained national attention when she gave a brave and stirring performance in front of the Lincoln Memorial after the Daughters of the American Revolution denied her the opportunity to sing in Constitution Hall.

2. Stern, "Autobiography of a House."

3. The Commission on Interracial Cooperation was founded in Atlanta in 1919 and merged with the Southern Regional Council in 1944; its aims were to oppose lynching and mob violence and to educate white southerners concerning the worst aspects of racial abuse. Fairclough notes: "It functioned as the principal vehicle of southern liberalism during the interwar period" (*Race and Democracy*, 11). Alexander was born in Missouri in 1884 and attended Vanderbilt University.

4. Stern, "Autobiography of a House."

5. Not that the rest of the country was integrated. Elsewhere segregation was a matter of custom but was not legally codified. And it would last longer in New Orleans than in many places.

6. Sybil Morial died on September 3, 2024.

7. Harris, *Merchant Princes,* 305.

8. Deutsch, *You Need a Schoolhouse,* 110. There are photographs of integrated parties in the Rosenwald home.

9. I make no attempt to explore the full diversity of Rosenwald's philanthropy, but he donated to many causes. He made, for example, the first contribution to the defense fund for Leo Frank, the Atlanta Jew falsely accused of murder, and years later, in 1931, he funded Admiral Richard Byrd's expedition to the South Pole. Byrd gave Rosenwald the US flag that he carried on the expedition. Quietly, Rosenwald took such actions as helping salvage a Black insurance company from imminent bankruptcy in 1924.

10. Deutsch, *You Need a Schoolhouse,* 153.

11. Kerner Commission Report on the Causes, Events and Aftermath of the Civil Disorders of 1967, issued in 1968.

12. Boorstin, vol. 3 of *The Americans.* By 1890, Sears was outpacing Montgomery Ward.

13. Barry, *The Great Influenza,* 134.

14. There were 395 Rosenwald Schools in Louisiana.

15. As Diner points out, "Jews had a long tradition of philanthropy. This tradition, which had theological roots in the Bible and in the Talmud, made charity not only a virtue, but a duty" (*In the Almost Promised Land,* 125).

16. Harris, *Merchant Princes,* 303.

17. The Stern Fund, 11.

18. Ascoli, *Rosenwald,* 2. (Ascoli is Rosenwald's grandson.)

19. She had the same name as JR's wife.

20. Spearie, "Springfield's Two Synagogues."

21. Dattel, *Reckoning with Race*, 94.

22. Travis, An Autobiography of Black Chicago, 7.

23. Lemann, *The Promised Land,* 160.

24. Lemann, *The Promised Land,* 6.

25. Lemann, *The Promised Land,* 81.

26. Ascoli, *Rosenwald,* 41.

27. Ascoli, *Rosenwald,* 50.

28. *The Stern Fund,* 115.

29. *The Stern Fund.*

30. Harris, *Merchant Princes,* 321.

31. Harris, *Merchant Princes,* 321.

32. Harris, *Merchant Princes,* 321.

33. Ascoli, *Rosenwald,* 53

34. Ascoli, *Rosenwald,* 54.

35. Ascoli, *Rosenwald*, 61.

36. Klein, *Passion for Sharing*, 24.

37. Davey and Reese, *Longue Vue House and Gardens*, 168.

38. Deutsch, *You Need a Schoolhouse*, 93.

39. Ascoli, *Rosenwald*, 77.

40. Klein, *Passion for Sharing*, 75.

41. Harris *Merchant Princes*, 304.

42. Harris, *Merchant Princes*, 304.

43. Lemann, *The Promised Land*, 81.

44. Davis, *American Heroine*, 56.

45. Davis, *American Heroine*, 57.

46. Davis, *American Heroine*, 6.

47. Klein, *Passion for Sharing*, 30.

48. Ascoli, *Rosenwald*, 79.

49. Ascoli, *Rosenwald*, 89.

50. Deutsch, *You Need a Schoolhouse*, 116.

51. Deutsch, *You Need a Schoolhouse*, 143.

52. Klein, *A Passion for Sharing*, 87.

53. Harris, *Merchant Princes*, 310

54. Du Bois, quoted in "History of *The Crisis*," NAACP website, https://naacp.org/find-resources/history-explained/history-crisis.

55. Embree, *Julius Rosenwald Fund*, 14.

56. Walker, "Foreword" to Buchanan, *Giving Done Right*, 3.

57. Fairclough, *Race and Democracy*, 38.

58. Harris, *Merchant Princes*, 306.

59. Perkins, *Edwin Rogers Embree*, 25.

60. Embree, *Julius Rosenwald Fund*, 6.

61. Harris, *Merchant Princes*, 306.

62. Harris, *Merchant Princes*, 307.

63. Embree, *Julius Rosenwald Fund*, 12.

64. Perkins, *Investment in Talent*, 115.

65. "More than two decades would pass before other philanthropic boards would begin to elect Black members in significant numbers," Alfred Perkins wrote in his biography of Embree, *Edwin Rogers Embree*, 81.

66. Perkins, *Edwin Rogers Embree*, 82.

67. Perkins, *Edwin Rogers Embree*, 82.

68. Embree, *Julius Rosenwald Fund*, 15.

69. Kluger, *Simple Justice*, 69.

70. Kluger, *Simple Justice*, 94.

71. Ascoli, *Rosenwald*, 95.

72. Ascoli, *Rosenwald*, 385.

73. Ciesla Foundation, *Rosenwald,* film.

74. Bluestone, "Framing Landscape," 506.

75. Alfred was the son of Edith's sister Marion and Alfred Stern Sr.

76. Ascoli, *Rosenwald,* 344–52.

77. *American City* 43 (November 1930), 151.

78. Bluestone to Gratz, email, 2/20/21.

79. Perkins, *Investment in Talent,* 105.

80. Shulman, *A Force for Change.*

81. Shulman, *A Force for Change,* 13.

82. Embree, *Julius Rosenwald Fund,* 16.

5. A Place to Live and a Place to Learn

1. Formerly the Delgado Museum, named for its founder, Isaac Delgado, a Sephardic Jew and a sugar planter.

2. Isaacson, foreword to Davey and Reese, *Longue Vue House and Gardens,* 6.

3. Both documents are in the Longue Vue Archives.

4. Stern, "Autobiography of a House."

5. Allured and Gentry, *Louisiana Women,* 253. Dormon "also worked tirelessly to protect Louisiana's ancient archeological sites, to create ethnographical records of modern Louisiana Native communities, and to provide those communities with economic assistance by promoting the sale of Native arts and crafts."

6. Davey and Reese, *Longue Vue House and Gardens,* 192.

7. Davey and Reese, *Longue Vue House and Gardens,* 209.

8. Stern, 1978 interview, Longue Vue Archives.

9. Stern, 1978 interview, Longue Vue Archives.

10. Davey and Reese, *Longue Vue House and Gardens,* 14.

11. Davey and Reese, *Longue Vue House and Gardens,* 14.

12. Stern, "Autobiography of a House."

13. Such as New Orleans Master Guild, run by John Ethan Hankins.

14. Stern, "Autobiography of a House."

15. Letter to Philip Stern, April 27, 1947, Longue Vue Archives.

16. Memo to Gerda Klein from Marjorie Stich, Sept. 12, 1982, Longue Vue Archives.

17. Stern, "Autobiography of a House."

18. Irma Barnett, n.d., Longue Vue Archives.

19. The clippings do not include the name of the newspaper.

20. Undated and untitled news clipping, probably the *New Orleans States-Item,* Longue Vue Archives.

21. Undated copy of Edith's remarks, Longue Vue Archives.

22. The members of the group were Mr. & Mrs. Edward B. Benjamin, Mrs. Ralph Boothby, Mrs. Russell Clark, Mrs. Thomas B. Denegre, Mrs. Stuart O. Landry, Mr. Thomas C. Nicholls,

Mrs. Dorothy Pigman, Mrs. Fort Pipes, Mrs. John G. Pratt, Mrs. James W. Reily, Mr. & Mrs. Edgar B. Stern, Mr. & Mrs. Walter J. Trautman, Mrs. C.S. Williams, Mrs. Robert M. Walmsley, Mr. & Mrs. A. M. Dantzler, and Mrs. Eli Watson.

23. Undated copy of Edith's remarks, Longue Vue Archives.

24. Undated copy of Edith's remarks, Longue Vue Archives.

25. Undated and untitled news clipping, probably the *New Orleans States-Item*, Longue Vue Archives.

26. Reportedly, the Metairie Park Country Day School charter copied the Tulane charter, which makes sense because Edgar was on the Tulane board. "Eh-la-bas" is a signature Cajun phrase meaning "Hey there."

6. A University Is Born

1. Stern to Embree, 4/9/30, Rosenwald files, box 140, folder 6, Amistad Research Center, Tulane University.

2. *New Orleans Times-Picayune*, April 1930.

3. Stern to Embree, 4/4/30, Rosenwald files, box 140, folder 6.

4. Stern to Embree, 1931, Rosenwald files, roll 26, box 191, folder 7.

5. Stern to Embree, 4/4/30.

6. Xavier University, the only historically Black Roman Catholic institution of higher education in the United States, was founded in 1925 by Katharine Drexel, daughter of banker-financier Francis Drexel. Xavier had started a decade earlier as a high school.

7. Danziger to Stern, 1/29/29, Rosenwald files, roll 26, box 191, folder 7.

8. Stern to Embree, 1/3/37, Rosenwald files, roll 5, boxes 76–77.

9. Mrs. Albert W. Dent, "Remembering Mr. and Mrs. Edgar B. Stern, Sr.: A Personal Tribute," Longue Vue Archives.

10. After desegregation, Flint-Goodridge, like many Black institutions, suffered a loss of patients. It closed in 1983.

11. Stern to Holgate, 1/8/1931, Rosenwald files, roll 26, box 191.

12. Stern to Holgate, 1/8/1931.

13. Stern to Brownlee, 3/16/31, Rosenwald files, roll 26, box 191.

14. Stern to Brownlee, 3/16/31.

15. Bernard and Randiclani, *Within These Walls*, 10–11.

16. Alexander was also a lecturer at the League of Nations on race relations and a recipient of the first Harmon Foundation award for distinguished service in American race problems.

17. He was a Rosenwald Fellow in hospital administration.

18. Davey and Reese, *Longue Vue House and Gardens*, 172.

19. Rosa Freeman Keller collection, taped interview, Keller with Kim Lacy Rogers, box 6, item 6, Amistad Research Center.

20. Stern to Embree, 11/13/31, Rosenwald files, roll 26, box 191.

21. Claire Perry and George Sessions Perry, "Penny-a-Day Hospital," *Saturday Evening Post*, September 2, 1939, 30.

22. Davey and Reese, *Longue Vue House and Gardens*, 178.

23. Arthur to Stern, 10/19/31, Rosenwald files, roll 26, box 188–91.

24. She received a Rosenwald Fellowship for piano.

7. Renewing the French Quarter

1. Baumbach and Borah, *Second Battle*, 222.

2. It was destroyed by fire nine years later.

3. Gehlman, *The Free People of Color*, 23.

4. It later spread to San Antonio, Providence, Miami Beach, Baltimore, New York, Alexandria, and Savannah.

5. Starr, quoted in Gratz, *We're Still Here*, 307.

6. Unpublished autobiography, Lester Kabacoff.

7. DeMers, *French Quarter Royalty*, 52.

8. DeMers, *French Quarter Royalty*, 60.

9. DeMers, *French Quarter Royalty*, 56.

10. Unpublished autobiography, Lester Kabacoff.

8. Legal Pathbreakers

1. Keller, taped autobiography, Amistad Research Center.

2. Baker, *The Second Battle*, 7.

3. Baker, *The Second Battle*, 426.

4. Baker, *The Second Battle*, 89.

5. Baker, *The Second Battle*, 89.

6. Baker, *The Second Battle*, 90.

7. Baker, *The Second Battle*, 96.

8. Medina, *Loyola University*, 84.

9. Earlier, they had met briefly in New York City.

10. Baker, *The Second Battle*, 94.

11. Baker, *The Second Battle*, 106.

12. He was appointed to the court with Judges Herbert Christenberry and William Borah.

13. Edith organized a similar action for Hale Boggs in 1952 as well.

14. Elliott Hebert, "At Your Service, Mr. Voter . . ." unpublished article, Longue Vue Archives, box 16, Edith Stern Committees, series 1, 55–66.

15. Hebert, "At Your Service, Mr. Voter. . . ."

16. "Cleaning Up the Voter Registration Rolls," Longue Vue Archives, box 16, Edith Stern Committees, series 1, 55–66.

17. Fairclough noted, "Successive governers, all of them from north Louisiana—Earl Long, Robert Kennon, and Jimmie Davis—used their power to appoint the Orleans Parish registrar as a means of restricting the Black vote in New Orleans" (*Race and Democracy*, 186).

18. Wright, quoted by Klein, *Passion for Sharing*, 164.

19. Klein, *Passion for Sharing*, 165.

20. Allured and Gentry, *Louisiana Women*, 307.

21. Fairclough, *Race and Democracy*, 148.

22. Stern, *Race & Education in New Orleans*, 230.

23. Warren Rogers, "The Man in the Fish Fry Parlor," *Look*, Oct. 17, 1967, 115.

24. Emanuel and Tureaud, *A More Noble Cause*, 62. Ernest Morial, later the first Black mayor of New Orleans, was the first Black graduate of the LSU Law School.

25. Fairclough, *Race and Democracy*, 109.

26. "This is a sad day for America. Today, for the first time in the two hundred years of our history, the executive department has succeeded in stopping the presses. It has enlisted the judiciary in the suppression of our most precious freedom. As if the long and sordid war in Southeast Asia had not already done enough harm to our people, it now is used to cut out the heart of our free institutions and system of government. I decline to follow my colleagues down this road and I must forcefully state my dissent." United States of America, Appellant, v. the Washington Post Company et al., 446 F. 2d 1322 (D.C. Cir. 1971). Twelve days later, June 30, 1971, his position was adopted by the US Supreme Court, which allowed publication by both the *New York Times* and the *Washington Post*.

27. Baker, *The Second Battle*, 52.

28. Baker, *The Second Battle*, 13.

29. Camelbacks are a style of shotgun house. They have a second story set back far enough from the street so as not to cause the house to be taxed as a two-story house.

30. Emanuel and Tureaud, *A More Noble Cause*, 10.

31. Baker, *The Second Battle*.

32. By 1951, Baker reports that there were six Black lawyers (*The Second Battle*).

33. The NAACP was founded in 1909 by W. E. B. Du Bois as an interracial group to fight for racial justice.

34. Emanuel and Tureaud, *A More Noble Cause*, 62.

35. As Baker notes in *The Second Battle*, 375, Mayor Chep Morrison denied Marshall use of the Municipal Auditorium to give a speech on the grounds "it would promote controversy and was not in the interest of the people of New Orleans," although the mayor raised no similar objections when Governor Orval Faubus of Arkansas asked to use it.

36. Mara, *Thurgood Marshall*, 36.

37. Baker, *The Second Battle*, 223.

38. Margolick, "The Day Louis Armstrong Made Noise."

39. Baker, *The Second Battle*, 330.

40. Baker, *The Second Battle*, 423.

41. Wisdom is probably best known for ruling on the case of James Meredith in 1961, who was denied admission to the University of Mississippi. Wisdom overruled the denial but eventually the case went to the US Supreme Court, which upheld his admission.

42. Fairclough, *Race and Democracy*, 218.

43. Friedman, *Champion of Civil Rights*, 19.

44. Baker, *The Second Battle*, 289.

45. Baker, *The Second Battle*, 291.

46. Baker, *The Second Battle*, 425.

47. Baker, *The Second Battle*, 425.

48. Feibleman was rabbi from 1935 to 1967.

9. An Upfront Activist

1. Baker, *The Second Battle*, 253.

2. Fairclough, *Race and Democracy*, 31.

3. Tyler, *Silk Stockings*, 207.

4. Much of the information on Rosa here is from her own unpublished story of her life on file at the Amistad Research Center.

5. Rosa Freeman Keller interview by Dorothy Schlesinger, July 7, 1977, transcript, 4–5, Special Collections, Howard-Tilton Memorial Library, Tulane University.

6. Tyler, *Silk Stockings*, 233.

7. Fairclough, *Race and Democracy*, 251.

8. Keller interview by Schlesinger, Amistad Research Center.

9. Baker, *The Second Battle*, 251.

10. Devlin, *A Girl Stands at the Door*, 70.

11. Baker, *The Second Battle*, 3.

12. Baker, *The Second Battle*, 329, 328.

13. Formerly the Commission on Interracial Cooperation, organized in 1919 in Atlanta to promote equality and voter registration, the Southern Regional Council functioned as the principal vehicle of southern liberalism during the interwar years. The Stern Fund was an early supporter.

14. Tyler, *Silk Stockings*, 226.

15. Tyler, *Silk Stockings*, 224.

16. Fairclough, *Race and Democracy*, 237.

17. Tyler, *Silk Stockings*, 229.

18. Fairclough, *Race and Democracy*, 237.

19. Peltason, *Fifty-Eight Lonely Men*, 239.

20. Fairclough, *Race and Democracy*, 284–85.

21. Postcard from Edith Stern, Rosa Freeman Keller Papers, Amistad Research Center.

10. Edith and the Arts

1. Fagaly, *Nightcrawler King,* 120.

2. Fagaly, *Nightcrawler King,* 119.

3. Fagaly, *Nightcrawler King,* 120.

4. Fagaly, *Nightcrawler King,* 120.

5. Stern, "Autobiography of a House."

6. Fagaly, *Nightcrawler King,* 125.

7. Klein, *Passion for Sharing,* 239.

8. Fagaly, *Nightcrawler King,* 123.

9. Fagaly, *Nightcrawler King,* 124–25.

10. Klein, *Passion for Sharing.*

11. Stern, Autobiography of a House."

12. Stern, Autobiography of a House."

13. Stitch remembrance, Longue Vue Archives.

14. Stitch remembrance, Longue Vue Archives.

15. Margo Miller interview, Longue Vue Archives.

16. Bernard oral history, Longue Vue Archives.

17. Margo Miller interview, Longue Vue Archives.

18. Stern to Bernard, March 1963, Longue Vue Archives.

11. Overcoming the Masque

1. Gratz, "The Demise of Charity Hospital," in *We're Still Here,* 199.

2. Gratz, *We're Still Here,* 123.

3. Eckstein, *Sustaining New Orleans,* 38–39.

4. Jed Horne, foreword to Borah and Baumbach, *The Second Battle of New Orleans,* xvi.

5. Goddard, *Getting There,* 126.

6. The full story of this court case can be found in Goddard, *Getting There.*

7. Goddard, *Getting There,* 126.

8. As quoted in Borah and Baumbach, *Second Battle,* 102.

9. Horne, foreword to Borah and Baumbach, *The Second Battle of New Orleans.*

10. The citizens group included John W. Lawrence, Arthur Q. Davis, Mark P. Lowrey, William J. Long, and city councilmen John J. Petre and James A. Moreau.

11. Local plaintiffs included Mark Lowrey, Martha Robinson, Harnett Kane, Raymond Boudreau, and William Long.

12. It said, in part, "In the face of ever-increasing extensions of urban centers, highways and residential, commercial and industrial developments, it is necessary and appropriate for the Federal Government to accelerate its historic preservation programs and activities."

13. *Business Week* article, n.d., private collection.

14. The fight in New York City to stop the Lower Manhattan Expressway, which would have destroyed SoHo, Chinatown, and much of Greenwich Village, was going on at the same time. It was killed before it became an official federal highway project.

15. Fairclough, *Race and Democracy,* 240.

16. *Electronic Media,* January 18, 1999, 76.

17. *Electronic Media,* January 18, 1999, 76.

18. *Newsweek,* November 25, 1968.

19. *Electronic Media,* January 18, 1999, 76.

20. Neither of Corporon's two sons had copies.

21. Edgar Stern Jr. to Edgar Stern Sr., n.d., Longue Vue Archives.

22. Edgar Stern Jr. to Edgar Stern Sr., Longue Vue Archives.

23. Private film made for the family.

24. Oral history, Longue Vue Archives.

25. *Electronic Media,* January 18, 1999, 76.

Conclusion

1. Diner, *In the Almost Promised Land,* 101.

2. Diner, *In the Almost Promised Land,* 3.

3. The jail terms of the defendants were of different lengths. Some were released or retried. Eighty years later the state exonerated them.

4. Although I only mention them briefly, the Rosenwald siblings were impressive philanthropists, as were other Stern children and grandchildren.

5. Diner, *In the Almost Promised Land,* 94–95.

6. Evans, *The Provincials,* 40.

7. New Orleans Data Center, report, 2023.

8. See Gratz, *We're Still Here,* chap. 1. Many Lower Nine residents were so poorly compensated after Katrina (unlike their upper-income neighbors) that they could not afford to rebuild. The government compensation went first to banks to cover the remaining mortgages, leaving little or nothing with which to build anew.

9. The pre–Super Bowl cleanup and the ongoing school story were and are covered more thoroughly by the online investigative journal *The Lens,* a post-Katrina invention of New Orleans resident Karen Gadbois, than by any other local print or online newspaper. I proudly sit on its board.

10. Bureau of Governmental Research, "The Lost Penny: BGR Analyzes the Orleans Parish Hotel Tax Structure," January 30, 2019, BGR website, https://www.bgr.org/report-index/bgr-analyzes-the-orleans-parish-hotel-tax-structure/.

11. See *We're Still Here.*

Selected Bibliography

Note: See the acknowledgments for a list of those interviewed for this book.

Allen, Carol. *Leah Chase: Listen, I Say like This.* Pelican Publishing, 2002.

Allured, Janet, and Judith F. Gentry, eds. *Louisiana Women: Their Lives and Times.* University of Georgia Press, 2009.

American City. 43 (November 1930). University of Michigan, Ann Arbor.

Ascoli, Peter M. *Julius Rosenwald: The Man Who Built Sears, Roebuck and Advanced the Cause of Black Education in the American South.* Indiana University Press, 2006.

Baker, Liva. *The Second Battle of New Orleans: The Hundred-Year Struggle to Integrate the Schools.* HarperCollins, 1996.

Barnard, Hollinger F., ed. *The Autobiography of Virginia Foster Durr.* University of Alabama Press, 1985.

Barry, John M. *The Great Influenza: The Epic Story of the Deadliest Plague in History.* Viking, 2004.

———. *Rising Tide: The Great Mississippi Flood of 1927 and How It Changed America.* Touchstone Books, 1997.

Bauman, Mark K., and Berkley Kalin, eds. *The Quiet Voices: Southern Rabbis and Black Civil Rights, 1880s to 1990s.* University of Alabama Press, 1997.

Baumbach, Richard O., Jr., and William E. Borah. *The Second Battle of New Orleans: A History of the Vieux Carré Riverfront Expressway Controversy.* 1981; rpr. University of Louisiana at Lafayette Press, 2019.

Bernard, Louise, and Clytus Randiclani. *Within These Walls: A Short History of Dillard University.* Offices of the President, Dillard University, 2000.

Bluestone, Daniel. "Framing Landscape While Building Density: Chicago Courtyard Apartments, 1891–1929." *Journal of the Society of Architectural Historians* 76, no. 4 (2017): 506–31.

Chapman, Peter. *Bananas: How the United Fruit Company Shaped the World.* Canongate, 2007.

Cigliano, Jan, and Sarah Bradford Landau, eds. *The Grand American Avenue (1850–1920).* Pomegranate Artbooks, 1994.

Cohen, Rich. *The Fish That Ate the Whale: The Life and Times of the Banana King.* Farrar, Straus and Giroux, 2012.

Cremin, Lawrence A. *American Education: The Metropolitan Experience, 1876–1980.* Harper & Row, 1988.

Dattel, Gene, *Reckoning with Race: America's Failure.* Encounter Books, 2017.

Davey, Charles, and Carol McMichael Reese. *Longue Vue House and Gardens.* Skira Rizzoli, 2015.

Davis, Allen F. *American Heroine: The Life and Legend of Jane Addams.* Ivan R. Dee, 1973.

DeLucca, Claire. "Both Sides of the Barbed Wire: Lives of German Prisoners of War and African Americans in Camp Claiborne, La., 1944–46." University of New Orleans Theses and Dissertations 245, 2018. https//scholarworks.uno.edu/id/2454/.

DeMers, John. *French Quarter Royalty: The Tumultuous Life and Times of the Omni Royal Orleans Hotel.* Omni Royal Orleans Hotel, 1993.

Deutsch, Stephanie. *You Need a Schoolhouse: Booker T. Washington, Julius Rosenwald, and the Building of Schools for the Segregated South.* Northwestern University Press, 2011.

Devlin, Rachel. *A Girl Stands at the Door: The Generation of Young Women Who Desegregated America's Schools.* Basic Books, 2018.

DeVore, Donald E., and Joseph E. Logsdon. *Crescent City Schools: Public Education in New Orleans, 1841–1991.* Orleans Parish School Board, 1991.

Dewey, John. *Reconstruction in Philosophy.* Beacon Press, 1964.

Diner, Hasia. *In the Almost Promised Land: American Jews and Blacks, 1915–1935.* Johns Hopkins University Press, 1977.

———. *Julius Rosenwald: Repairing the World.* Yale University Press, 2017.

Duis, Perry R. *Challenging Chicago: Coping with Everyday Life, 1837–1920.* University of Illinois Press, 1998.

Eaves, Marilee. *Singing Out Loud: A Memoir of an Ex-Mardi Gras Queen.* She Writes Press, 2019.

Eckstein, Barbara. *Sustaining New Orleans: Literature, Local Memory, and the Fate of a City.* Routledge, 2006.

Emanuel, Rachel L., and Alexander Tureaud Jr. *A More Noble Cause: A. P. Tureaud and the Struggle for Civil Rights in Louisiana.* LSU Press, 2011.

Embree, Edwin R. *Julius Rosenwald Fund: Review of Two Decades, 1917–1936.* Pamphlet, 1936.

Evans, Eli N. *Judah P. Benjamin: The Jewish Confederate.* Free Press, 1988.

———. *The Provincials.* University of North Carolina Press, 1973.

———. *The Lonely Days Were Sundays: Reflections of a Jewish Southerner.* University Press of Mississippi, 1993.

Fagaly, William. *The Nightcrawler King: Memoir of an Art Museum Curator.* William Morris, 2022.

Fairclough, Adam. *Race and Democracy: The Civil Rights Struggle in Louisiana, 1915–1972.* University of Georgia Press, 1995.

Feiler, Andrew. *A Better Life for Their Children: Julius Rosenwald, Booker T. Washington, and the 4,978 Schools That Changed America.* University of Georgia Press, 2021.

Ferris, Marcie Cohen. *Matzoh Ball Gumbo: Culinary Tales of the Jewish South.* University of North Carolina Press, 2005.

Ferris, Marcie Cohen, and Mark I. Greenberg. *Jewish Roots in Southern Soil: A New History.* Brandeis University Press, 2006.

Finkelstein, Norman H. *Schools of Hope: How Julius Rosenwald Helped Change African American Education.* Calkins Creek, 2014.

Friedman, Joel William. *Champion of Civil Rights: Judge John Minor Wisdom.* LSU Press, 2009.

Garvey, Joan B., and Mary Lou Widmer. *Beautiful Crescent: A History of New Orleans.* Pelican Publishing, 2013.

Gehlman, Mary. *The Free People of Color of New Orleans: An Introduction.* Margaret Media, Inc., 1994.

———. *Women and New Orleans: A History.* D'Ville Press, 2018.

Gill, James. *Lords of Misrule: Mardi Gras and the Politics of Race in New Orleans.* University Press of Mississippi, 1997.

Goddard, Stephen B. *Getting There: The Epic Struggle Between Road and Rail in the American Century.* Basic Books, 1994.

Green, Adam. *Selling the Race: Culture, Community and Black Chicago, 1940–1955.* University of Chicago Press, 2007.

Greene, Melissa Fay. *The Temple Bombing.* Addison-Wesley, 1996.

Haas, Edward F. *DeLesseps S. Morrison and the Image of Reform: New Orleans Politics, 1946–1961.* LSU Press, 1974.

Harris, Leon. *Merchant Princes: An Intimate History of Jewish Families Who Built Great Department Stores.* Harper & Row,1977.

Jarrette, Alfred Q. *Julius Rosenwald, Son of a Jewish Immigrant, a Builder of Sears,*

Roebuck and Company, Benefactor of Mankind: A Biography Documented. Southeastern University Press, 1975.

Keiler, Allan. *Marian Anderson: A Singer's Journey*. University of Illinois Press, 2002.

Kempner, Aviva, dir. *Rosenwald: The Remarkable Story of a Jewish Partnership with African American Communities*. Ciesla Foundation, 2015.

Khaton, Lionel. "The Wonder Years in Pontchartrain Park." *Preservation in Print*, June 2019.

Klein, Gerda Weissmann. *A Passion for Sharing: The Life of Edith Rosenwald Stern*. Rossel Books, 1984.

Kluger, Richard. *Simple Justice: The History of Brown v. Board of Education and Black America's Struggle for Equality*. Vintage Press, 2004.

Krist, Gary. *Empire of Sin: A Story of Sex, Jazz, Murder and the Battle for Modern New Orleans*. Broadway Books, 2014.

Lachoff, Irwin, and Catherine C. Kahn. *The Jewish Community of New Orleans*. Arcadia Publishing, 2005.

Lemann, Nicholas. *The Promised Land: The Great Black Migration and How It Changed America*. Alfred A. Knopf, 1991.

Lukes, Austin. "The Importance of Pontchartrain Park." *Preservation in Print*, June 2019.

Mara, Wil. *Thurgood Marshall: Champion for Civil Rights*. Franklin Watts, 2004.

Margolick, David. "The Day Louis Armstrong Made Noise," *New York Times*, September 23, 2007.

Medina, Maria Isabel. Loyola University New Orleans College of Law: A History. LSU Press, 2016.

Miller, Donald. *City of the Century: The Epic of Chicago and the Making of America*. Simon & Schuster, 1996.

Peltason, J. W. *Fifty-Eight Lonely Men: Southern Federal Judges and School Desegregation*. University of Illinois Press, 1971.

Perkins, Alfred. *Edwin Rogers Embree: The Julius Rosenwald Fund, Foundation Philanthropy, and American Race Relations*. Indiana University Press, 2011.

Pierce, Wendell, with Rod Dreher. *The Wind in the Reeds: A Storm, a Play, and the City That Would Not Be Broken*. Penguin, 2015.

Powell, Lawrence N. *Troubled Memory: Anne Levy, the Holocaust, and David Duke's Louisiana*. 2nd ed. University of North Carolina Press, 2019.

Rabin, Shari. *The Jewish South: An American History*. Princeton University Press, 2025.

Rothstein, Richard. *The Color of Law: A Forgotten History of How Our Government Segregated America*. W. W. Norton, 2017.

Satter, Beryl. *Family Properties: How the Struggle over Race and Real Estate Transformed Chicago and Urban America*. Henry Holt, 2009.

Shulman, Daniel, ed. *A Force for Change: African American Art and the Julius Rosenwald Fund*. Northwestern University Press, 2009.

Spearie, Stephen. "Springfield's Two Synagogues Share a Common History." *State Journal Register [Illinois]*, March 1, 2013.

Starr, S. Frederick. *New Orleans Unmasqued: Being a Wagwit's Sketches of a Singular American City*. Dedeaux Pub., 1985.

Stern, Mrs. Edgar B. "Autobiography of a House." Typescript, no date. Longue Vue Archives.

The Stern Fund: The History of a Progressive Family Foundation. Institute for Media Analysis, 1992.

Stevenson, Bryan. *Lynching in America: Targeting Black Veterans*. Equal Justice Initiative, 2017.

Travis, Dempsey. *An Autobiography of Black Chicago*. Bolden Books, 2013.

Tyler, Pamela. *Silk Stockings & Ballot Boxes: Women & Politics in New Orleans, 1920–1965*. University of Georgia Press, 1996.

Urban League of Greater New Orleans. *State of Black New Orleans: 10 Years Post-Katrina*. Urban League of Greater New Orleans, 2015.

Walker, Darren. "Foreword." In Phil Buchanan, *Giving Done Right*. Public Affairs, 2019.

Washington, Booker T. *Up from Slavery*. Dover, 1995.

Williams, T. Harry. *Huey Long*. Vintage, 1981

Wolf, Peter M. *My New Orleans, Gone Away: A Memoir of Loss and Renewal*. Delphinium Books, 2013.

Wolff, Jane, and Carol McMichael Reese, eds. *Pontchartrain Park + Gentilly Woods: Landscape Manual*. Longue Vue House & Gardens, 2009.

Index

Academy of the Sacred Heart, 41
actuaries, 28
Addams, Jane, 5, 49, 82, 83–85
Adler, Dankmar, 74, 81
Adler, Lee, 206
affordable housing, 13–14, 95–96
Agam, Yaacov, 106
Agate, Ralph, 15
Aida (opera), 199
Airbnbs, 227
air-conditioning system, 106
Alexander, Will W., 68, 141
Alexandria, LA, 10
Algiers, 9, 16, 20
An American Citizen (Brooks), 85
American Legion, 154
The Americans (Boorstin), 70
Anderson, Marian, 3, 67–68, 234n1
Angelou, Maya, 93–94
Angola, 184
antilynching legislation, 164, 174–75
antisemitism, 3, 39, 55, 72, 79–80, 175–76, 216–18, 219
Antoine's, 41
Armstrong, Louis, 42, 49–50, 169
Armstrong, Mrs. Thomas, 196
Arnaud's, 41
Arp, Jean, 106, 189
Arthur, George R., 91, 138, 139, 143
Arts Quarterly (magazine), 52
Aschaffenburg, Susan Okun, 55
Aspen, CO, 61, 217–18
assimilation, 35
Association of Southern Women for the Prevention of Lynching (ASWPL), 175
Atlanta, GA, 17, 32, 43, 79, 99, 145, 180, 219–21, 226, 234n3, 241n13
Aubert, Linda, 8, 63–64
Audubon Park, 17
"Autobiography of a House" (Stern), 50–51, 68, 101, 108, 111, 188, 193

Baker, Liva, 34, 158–59, 166, 172–73, 177, 179, 240n35
Baldwin, James, 98
Baldwin, William H., Jr., 85–86
Barnett, Irma, 112
Barry, John, 26, 71
Barthé, Richmond, 98
Bartholemew, Joseph, 20
Bartholomew, Joseph M., 10–11
Baruch, Bernard, 71
"Battle of New Orleans" (Von Eckardt), 208–9
Baumbach, Richard O., Jr., 6, 154, 202, 203, 207–11
Bayon, Mrs. Maurice, *123*
Bayou Road School, 165
Belmont, Mrs. August, 196
Berea, KY, 90
Bernard, Annabelle, 98–99, 197–200
Bethune, Mary McLeod, 175
Bezou, Henry C., 177
Black, Hugo, 156
Black community: art and culture of, 68, 97–99, 196–200; and Black advancement, 200, 228–29; Black women, 36, 142–43, 176,

Black community (*continued*)
180; craftsmen in, 108; and Dillard University, 131–45; economic standing and failing of the, 226–29; Edgar's views of, 139–41; Edith's aide of, 62–64; and education, 5, 30, 44, 85–88; and employment at Sears & Roebuck, 78–79; and failure of government, 33; and Flint-Goodridge Hospital, 131–45, 177; fundraising within the, 138; golfers, 10–12; and the Great Migration, 49–50, 76–77, 95; homeowners and businesses in, 14; and the Jews, 223–26; Keller's activism in, 175–77; and middle class, 19, 22; and neighborhoods, 181–82, 203–4, 205–6, 227; newspapers, 9; and police, 12, 17, 38; and protests, 38; and Rosenwald Fund, 86–87, 90–91; and Rosenwald Schools, 71–72, 93–94; and Rosenwald's philanthropy, 71–72, 82–83; and Save Our Schools (SOS), 180–81; servicemen from, 9–10, 158; Stern family's involvement with, 222–23; and Voters' Registration League, 160–61; voters/voting rights of, 29–30, 37–38, 133, 158, 160–62; Washington and Du Bois, 92–93; working with whites, 167; Wright's impact on, 163–64. *See also* integration
Black Creoles, 22, 165–66
Blackstone Hotel, 69
Black YMCAs, 82–83, 93
Blanchard, Terence, 12
Bloom, Edgar, 29
Blue Room, 105–6, 107
Bluestone, Daniel, 96
Blumenthal, Margie, 60
Boggs, Hale, 211
Bond, Horace Mann, 98
Bond, Julian, 93–94
Bond, Max, 98
Boorstin, Daniel, 70
Boothby, Ralph E., 114–15
Borah, Bill, 6, 154, 201–11, 216
Borah, Wayne G., 201
Boston Club, 3–4, 25, 31
Bousfield, M. O., 91
Boy Scouts of America, 88, 142, 144
Brandeis, Louis, 71
"Bring Estelle Home" campaign, 190
Bronzeville neighborhood, 95
Brooks, John Graham, 85
broom brigade, 160, 221
Broussard's, 41
Brown, Emma, 8–9, 13, 18, 53, 63–64, 67–68, *124*
Brownlee, Fred L., 140
Brown v. Board of Education, 37, 91, 155–56, 164, 168, 169–70, 178–79, 180, 211
Bullard, John, 187, 190, 191
Bunche, Ralph, 98
Burnham, Daniel, 74, 75
buses, 2, 38, 158, 164, 202, 205
Bush, Benjamin, 178
Bush v. Orleans Parish School Board, 178–79
Business Week (magazine), 211
Byrd, Richard, 235n9
Byrnes, James, 189
Bywater neighborhood, 39

Cahn, Gladys, 181
Camellia Walk, 111
Campanella, Richard, 28, 203
Camp Claiborne, 10
Canal Garden, 111
Carnival, 32
carpetbaggers, 37
Catholic Church, 38
Catlett, Elizabeth, 98, 200
CB Radio Booths series, 184
Central City neighborhood, 138
Century of Progress Exposition, 94
challenge grants, 83, 86, 88–89, 111–12
Chapman, Peter, 36–37
Charity Hospital, 34, 135, 201, 230
Chicago, IL: and Addams, 49, 83–85; affordable housing in, 95–96; Edith's early life in, 45–47; and the Great Migration, 49–50; and poverty, 76–77; and Rosenwald's philanthropy, 80–83; and Sears & Roebuck, 77–79; and urban pride, 74–76
Chicago Daily Defender, 9
Chicago-Examiner, 69
Chicago Hebrew Institute, 85
Chicago Housing Authority, 96
Chicago Museum of Science and Industry, 94

Citizens' Committee to Test the Constitutionality of the Separate Car Law, 37
City Beautiful movement, 75
City Park, 10, 17, 100, 164
city planning, 75
civil rights movement, 10, 38–39, 154
Civil War, 52, 147–48
Claiborne Avenue, 181–82
Claiborne Expressway, 203–4
Clark, Kenneth B., 98
Clark Atlanta University, 134
class distinctions, 52
clubs, 3–4, 25–26, 31–32
Cohen, Rich, 35
College of New Orleans, 135
The Color of Law (Rothstein), 14
Columbian Exposition (Chicago World's Fair), 74–75, 94
Commission Council, 140
Commission on Interracial Cooperation, 141, 234n3, 241n13
Committee for Public Education (COPE), 181
Confederate Underground, 221
Congo Square, 41
Convention Center, 229, 230
Corporon, John, 212, 213
corruption, 37
Cotton Exchange, 32
Council of National Defense, 71
Country Day Founders group, 114
Country Day type of school, 114
courtyard apartments, 95–96
craftsmanship, 107–8
craftsmen, 166
Crawford, Hamilton, 19
Crescent City Connection, 227
Crescent City imagery, 24–25
The Crisis, 88, 93, 143
Cultural Attractions Fund, 194
Curtis, Nathaniel, 153
Cuzcanian Spanish colonial paintings, 190–91

Danziger, A. D., 135
Davey, Charles, 107, 141
Davies, Richard, 159
Davis, Arthur Q., 153–54, 190–91
Davis, Jimmie, 179
DeDeaux, Dawn, 52, 184–85
Degas, Edgar, 189–90
Dennery, Phyllis, 110, 187
Dent, Albert, 136–37, 141, 143–44, 180
Dent, Ernestine Jesse Covington, 137, 144
Dent, Tom, 144
department stores, 225
desegregation, 17, 159, 170, 172–73, 177, 181
Desire Housing Project, 18–19
Detroit, MI, 205
Dewey, John, 85, 112–13, 114
Dillard, James Hardy, 137–38
Dillard University, 23, 30, 99, 131–45, 177, 200, 226
Diner, Hasia, 27, 219–20
Discovery Garden, 111
disenfranchising amendments, 29–30
D'Orlando, Alberto, 64
Dormon, Caroline, 102, 109–10, 237n5
downtowns, 203, 204, 206, 208
Dresden, Germany, 48
Drew, Charles, 98
Drexel, Katharine, 238n6
Dryades Street, 225
Du Bois, W. E. B., 88, 92–94, 98, 99, 132, 134, 240n33
due process clause, 17
Dunham, Katherine, 98
Durr, Virginia Foster, 174–75
Dwyer Canal, 19

Eastern European immigrants, 34–36, 55, 57, 76
Eastland, James, 174–75
Eaves, Marilee, 26
Education Committee of the Conference on Human Welfare, 115
Eisenhower, Dwight D., 169, 173, 205, 221
Electronic Media, 212, 213, 217
Ella West Freeman Matching Fund, 189
Ellender, Allen J., 170
Ellis, Frank B., 170–71
Ellison, Ralph, 98
Embree, Edwin Rogers, 78–79, 87, 90–91, 93, 97–99, 134–36, 143
Emmet, Mrs. Christopher Temple, 195

Engman, Robert, 111
enslaved people, 41
Equal Protection Clause of the Fourteenth Amendment, 167, 220
Essex, Karen, 59
European Jewry, 55
Evans, Eli, 42
Evans, Robert, 198
Exodus (ship), 36
expressways, 203–4, 207–9, 211, 216, 243n14

Fagaly, William, 186–87, 189–92
Fairclough, Adam, 38, 39, 171, 175, 182, 234n3
Fair Employment Practices Committee, 164
Faubus, Orval, 169, 213, 240n35
Favrot, Gervais, 15
FBI, 218
Federal Housing Authority (FHA), 7, 14–15, 21, 22. *See also* Pontchartrain Park
Fee, John G., 90
Feibelman, Rabbi, 173
Fellowship Program, 97–99, 197
Fenner, Darwin, 152
Ferris, Marcie Cohen, 57
Fichter, Joseph, 181
Fifteenth Amendment, 29–30
Fifth Circuit Court, 2, 159, 162, 163, 170, 171, 173
Finley, Joseph, 15
Firestone Company, 205
First African Baptist Church, 68
Fisk University, 86, 132, 134
Flint-Goodridge Hospital, 131–45, 177
Florida, 13
Florsheim, Lillian, 189
food, 57
Forcia, Clarence, 63
Forcia, Natalie, 62–63, *124*, *125*
Ford, Henry, 79–80
Ford Foundation grant, 183
Foreman, Clark, 90–91
Forrest, Nathan Bedford, 38
Fourteenth Amendment, 17
Francis, Muriel Bultman, 187
Francis, Sam, 189
Frank, Leo, 79, 219–20, 235n9
Frankfurter, Felix, 29
Franklin, John Hope, 98
Franzen, August, 107
Free Fall (DeDeaux), 184
Freeman, A. B., 152, 175
Freeman, Edgar, 183
Freeman, Ella, 175
Freeman, Richard, 182–83
free people of color, 41
The Free People of Color (Gehlman), 149
French Creoles, 148–49
French Jews, 57
French Quarter, 4–6, 24, 41–42, 133, 146–54, 188, 201, 202–3, 207–8, 216, 227
Friedler, Frank, Jr., 42–43
From Degas to Picasso exhibit, 186

Gabo, Naum, 106
Gadbois, Karen, 243n9
Galatoire's, 31, 41
garden club movement, 102
Garden Club of America, 110
Garden District, 40, 41, 43
Garden Lane, 101, 102
garden rooms, 103, 111
gardens, 109–11
Garden Study Club of New Orleans, 109–10
Garrison, William Lloyd, Jr., 82
Gehlman, Mary, 149
General Education Board (GEB), 85, 99, 138
General Motors, 204–5
Gentilly Woods, 12, 17, 19, 20, 22, 133
German Jews, 27, 28–29, 35, 41, 54–55, 57, 73
German prisoners of war, 10
Getting There (Goddard), 204–5
GI Bill, 21
Gilded Age, 74, 76
Girl Scouts, 176
Goddard, Stephen B., 204–5
Goldfish Pond, 104
Goldman, Henry, 78
Goldovsky, Boris, 197
Goldstein, Moise H., 102
golf, 10–12, 15–16, 20
Gompers, Samuel, 71
Greater Gentilly Civic Improvement Association, 17

Great Fire, 75
Great Migration, 49–50, 76–77, 95, 166
Greek Revival style, 104
Greene, Melissa Fay, 56
Greene, Thomas, 193
greenhouse, 111
Greyhound and Yellow Coach bus companies, 205
Gropius, Walter, 190
Gutheim, Rabbi James Koppel, 27
Gwathmey, Virginian Robert, 98

Haas, Edward F., 16
Hammerslough, Julius, 73
Hammerslough brothers, 72–73
Hammerslough Brothers Clothiers, 73
Hampton College, 134
Hampton Institute, 86
Hand, Learned, 29
Harahan (New Orleans suburb), 10–11
Hardwick, Elizabeth, 98
Harris, Leon, 45, 47, 54–55, 64–65, 87–88
Harvard University, 193
Hebert, Elliott, 160
Helis, William G., 152
Henry, Troy, 22
Hepworth, Barbara, 106
Hess, Anne, 52–53, 61–62
Hess, Bill, 53, 54–55, 56–57, 65, 215
Hess, Susan, 53, 55
Hess, Thomas B., 144, 186, 188, 190, 223
Hess, Tom, 64–65, 109
Higgins Boats, 32–33
highways, 6, 201–11
Hill, Patty Smith, 112
Hirsch, Rabbi Emil, 5, 86
Hirsch, Rabbi Emil G., 80–82
historically Black colleges and universities (HBCUs), 134
historic preservation movement, 41, 149–50
Holgate, Thomas F., 139
Holmes, Oliver Wendell, Jr., 114
Horne, Jed, 209
House & Garden (magazine), 103
housing crisis, 95–96
housing developments, 7–23
Houston, Charles H., 91
Houston, Charles Hamilton, 166, 168
Howard Law School, 166
Howard University, 134
Huey Long (Williams), 34
Hughes, Charles Evans, Sr., 114
Hughes, Langston, 98
Hull, Mrs. Lytle, 196
Hull House, 83–85, 233n10
Hunter, David, 209–10
Hunter, Howard, 114
Hurricane Katrina, 201, 227–28, 230
Hurston, Zora Neale, 97–98

Ickes, Harold, 90–91
Illinois Central Railroad, 49
illiteracy, 89
Independent Women's Organization, 160, 176
Indiana, 51
integration: Black community divided over, 19; of Boy Scouts, 142; and *Brown v. Board of Education*, 164, 168, 169–70, 178–79, 211; *Bush v. Orleans Parish School Board*, 178–79; and Federal Housing Authority (FHA), 14–15; and Flint-Goodridge Hospital, 135, 142; impact on New Orleans, 146; and Keller's activism, 177–78; and Marshall, 168; of Metairie Park Country Day School, 116; and Morrison, 12–13, 18, 182–83; and NAACP, 38, 167–68; of neighborhoods in New Orleans, 39–40; and Rosenwald Fund, 88, 90–91; and Save Our Schools (SOS), 3, 173, 180–81; of Tulane University, 182–83; and WDSU radio and TV, 4, 6, 179, 211–13; and Wisdom, 170–73; and women, 179–81; Wright's impact on, 2, 156, 162–64, 171
Interstate Highway Act of 1956, 207
interstate highway system, 205, 210–11
investigative journalism, 50
Irish Channel neighborhood, 157
Iris Walk, 111
Isaacson, Walter, 100
Isidore Newman, 23

Jackson, Mahalia, 50
jazz, 41–42

jewelry, 60
Jews: and antisemitism, 79–80, 175–76, 216–18; Black community and, 223–26; and challenge grants, 83; and Frank, 219–20; and Garden Club of America, 102, 110; hiring practices, 80; immigrants, 223–26; immigrants from Eastern Europe, 34–36, 55, 57; and Jewishness, 54–55, 64–65, 81, 215; Jewish refugees, 35–36; in New Orleans, 26, 27, 56–58; non-government appointees, 71; and non-Jews, 31–32; peddling, 223–26; as philanthropists in New Orleans, 222–23; and Reform Judaism, 81–83; and Save Our Schools (SOS), 173; and Scottsboro Boys, 220; on St. Charles Avenue, 40–41; and Temple bombing, 221; and Zionist cause, 71
Jim Crow, 9, 37, 133, 144, 158, 165
John Dewey Laboratory School in Chicago, 112–13
Johnson, Charles S., 91
Johnson, Hiram, 114
Johnson, James Weldon, 98
Johnson, Lyndon B., 91, 168
Just, E. E., 98
Juvenile Court Committee, 85

Kabacoff, Lester "Kabby," 5, 12, 150–54, 212
Kabacoff, Pres, 150–51
Kandinsky, Wassily, 105, 189, 192
Keller, Charles, 8–9, 12, 14, 174, 175–76, 178
Keller, Rosa Freeman, 8–9, 12, 14, 18, 142, 155, 174, 175–78, 181–83, 230
Kempner, Aviva, 72
Kennedy, John F., 1–2, 164, 170
Kennon, Robert, 161
Khaton, Lionel, 21
Klein, Gerda Weissmann, 2, 162, 191, 194
Knoblock, Gertrude, 110
Koch, Richard, 153
Ku Klux Klan (KKK), 38–39, 79, 212–13, 217, 220

Labatt, David Cohen, 171
labor, 18
La Follette, Robert, 114
Landmarks Illinois, 96
Landrieu, Moon, 150
landscape design, 103
Lawrence, Jacob, 98, 190
League of Classroom Teachers, 177
League of Women's Voters, 160–61, 176
Leibowitz, Samuel, 220–21
Lemann, Monte, 4, 12, 29, 31, 53, 116, 132, 140, 142
Lemann, Nettie Hyman, 12
Lemann, Nicholas, 53–54, 76–77, 84, 150
Lemann, Tommy, 191
Lenox, MA, 198
The Lens, 243n9
Le Parc, Julio, 189
Levy, Adele Rosenwald, 45–46, 69, 97, *118*, 186
Lewis, John, 93–94
liberal groups, 218
Liberman, Alexander, 106
libraries, 106, 177
Life magazine, 195
Lillian, Sara May, 29
Lincoln, Abraham, 73
Little Rock, AR, 179
Long, Earl, 161, 212
Long, Huey, 11, 33–37
Long, Russell, 170
Longue Vue House and Gardens, 2–3, 7, 100–111; and Anderson, 67; artful décor in, 188; and Bernard performance, 198; craftsmanship and purpose of, 107–9; as first house, 102; gardens of, 109–11; as Jewish home, 54; livability of, 105–7; memories of, 61–62; move from Longue Vue I to Longue Vue II, 102; photographs of, *126–30;* and the Platts, 104–5; and Shipman, 103–4; and tree from Israel, 71
Longue Vue House and Gardens (Davey and Reese), 100
Longworth, Mrs. Nicholas, 195–96
Look magazine, 163
Lorando, Mark, 212
Louisiana Club, 25
Louisiana Department of Transportation, 202
Louisiana Landmarks Society, 208
Louisiana politics, 33–37, 157–58
Louisiana Purchase, 147

Louisiana Weekly, 9, 154
Loving Cup award, 58, *126*, 137, 139–40, 223
Lower Manhattan Expressway, 243n14
Loyola University, 41
LSU Law School, 163
lynchings, 38, 133, 164, 174–75, 220

MacIver, Sandra, 60–62, 64, 215–18
mantle, 107
Mardi Gras: krewes, 25, 171–72, 182, 229; society, 8, 25–26, 32, 35, 216
Marigny neighborhood, 39
Marshall, Thurgood, 38, 167, 168, 240n35
Marx, Dr. David, 56
masques, 25
Matzoh Ball Gumbo (Ferris), 57
Mayo, William J., 131
Mayor's Advisory Committee, 18–19
McGill, Ralph, 89–90, 98
McKelpin v. Orleans Parish School Board, 167
Merchant Princes (Harris), 45
Metairie (New Orleans suburb), 7, 182
Metairie Country Club, 10
Metairie Park Country Day School, 100–101, 113–16, 194
mezuzah, 54
Michigan Boulevard Garden Apartments, 95–96
middle-class white neighborhoods, 19
midwives, 142–43
Migration Series (Lawrence), 98
Miller, Margo, 197, 199
Milling, Anne, 58
Milling, King, 58
Mississippi River, 40
Mitchell, Joan, 189
model homes, 9, 20–21
Monroe, Bill, 212, 213
Montgomery Ward, Aaron, 78
Montgomery Ward and Company, 70, 78, 80
Morehouse College, 134
Morial, Ernest Nathan "Dutch," 14, 22, 68, 146
Morial, Jacques, 14, 18, 19
Morial, Leonie (Moore), 146
Morial, Marc Haydel, 146
Morial, Sybil, 68, 136, 145, 235n6
Morial, Walter Etienne, 146
Morrison, deLesseps S. (Chep), 10, 12–20, 23, 160, 177, 181–82, 207, 240n35
Moses, Robert, 201–2, 206–7
Moses, Stephen, 60
Moss, A. L., 140
Mothers Club, 143
MotherShip series (DeDeaux), 184
Murvison, Peggy, 181
Museum of Modern Art (MOMA), 186
Museum of the Southern Jewish Experience, 223
Music Inside Out (radio program), 12
My New Orleans, Gone Away (Wolf), 57–58

NAACP, 38, 133–34, 163–64, 166, 167–68, 240n33
National City Lines (NCL), 205
National Historic Preservation Act, 211
National Trust for Historic Preservation, 211
The Negro Woman (Catlett), 98
Nelson, John P., 181, 182–83
Nelson, William Stuart, 141
Newcomb Nursery School, 100, 112
Newgas, Bernard, 27
Newman, Isidore, *123*, 161
New Orleans, LA, 1–6; Black art and culture in, 67–68; economy of, 32–33, 42–44; Edith's move to, 51–54; failing the Black community, 226–29; food, culture of, 57; and neighborhood integration, 39–40; segregation in, 1–2, 39, 52, 169–70, 178–79; social hierarchy of, 229; and society, 51–52
New Orleans City Council, 149–50
New Orleans Civic Council, 160
New Orleans Community Chest, 138
New Orleans Country Club, 101
New Orleans Data Center, 226
New Orleans Garden Study Club, 102
New Orleans Item, 20
New Orleans Museum of Art (NOMA), 52, 54, 108, 185, 187, 188, 189, 190, 191, 200
New Orleans Philharmonic Symphony, 192–94
New Orleans Recreation Department (NORD), 17
New Orleans school board. *See* Orleans Parish School Board

New Orleans States-Item, 15
New Orleans Times-Picayune, 42, 58, 131, 137, 139, 140, 156, 223
Newsweek, 213
New York, 50–51, 197–98, 207
New Yorker, 25
New York Times, 164
Ninth Ward, 227
Ninth Ward Civic League (NWCL), 162
Nixon, Richard, 204
non-Jews, 31–32
Norman, Sunny, 187
nursery school movement, 112–13
Nussbaum, Aaron, 77

Oberdorfer, Louis F., 210–11
Ochsner, Alton, 142, 177
Ochsner Hospital, 142
Old Metairie, 113
Oliver, Raymond, 192
Olmsted, Frederick Law, 75
Omni Royal Orleans. *See* Royal Orleans Hotel
on-air editorials, 6, 179, 211–14, 218
Orlando, Mark, 217
Orleans Parish Medical Society, 177
Orleans Parish School Board, 30–31, 163, 167, 171, 173, 178–80, 181
Ouanga (opera), 197

Palestine, 36, 54–55, 71
Pan Garden, 7, 110
panic peddlers, 77
The Park. *See* Pontchartrain Park
Parker, Dorothy, 29
Parks, Gordon, 98
parks for Black citizens, 10, 17–18, 20
A Passion for Sharing (Klein), 2
Peabody, Mrs. Malcolm, 196
Peabody Award, 4
Pearson, Drew, 156
peddling, 223–26
Perez, Leander H., 179
Perkins, Alfred, 89
"A Personal Tribute" (Dent), 137
Phagan, Mary, 219
Pickwick Club, 25
Pierce, Wendell, 11, 22
Pitot House, 153
Pittsburgh Courier, 9
Planer, Ed, 212, 213
Planer, Marcy, 213
Platt, Charles A., 103–4
Platt, Geoffrey, 104
Platt, William, 2–3, 104, 105, 108, 111
Playhouse, 3, 8, 62, 64, 67, 104, 136, 234n30
Plessy, Homer, 37–39
Plessy v. Ferguson, 37, 133, 161–62, 163, 168
Pontalba, Micaela, 149
Pontchartrain Hotel, 107, 190
Pontchartrain Park, 7–23, 95, 202
porches, 105–6
Portico Garden, 110
Port of New Orleans, 151
Portrait of Estelle Musson Degas (Degas), 189–90
Prairie style, 46, 74
preschool education, 112–13
Progressive Education movement, 114–15
The Provincials (Evans), 42
PTA, 176
public housing, 13–15, 18–19, 38, 207
public schools, 38, 114, 163, 168, 171, 173, 179, 180, 190, 228. See also *Brown v. Board of Education*; Save Our Schools (SOS)

Race and Democracy (Fairclough), 38
race and racism: and antilynching legislation, 164, 174–75; attitudes and actions in the Rosenwald and Stern families, 30–32; Edgar's views on, 139–41; and the Great Migration, 76–77; and Keller's activism, 175–76; and Scottsboro Boys, 220–21; and socializing between races, 68, 132, 136–37; and Wright, 158–59
race riots, 76
Radcliffe, 36, 103
"Raised to the Trade" exhibition, 108
Ravinia, IL, 47, 51
Reconstruction, 37, 134
Reese, Carol McMichael, 107, 141
Reform Jews, 56, 58
Reform Judaism, 35, 81–83, 223

refugees, 71
Reily, Gladys, *123*
restaurants, 31
Riverfront Expressway, 203–4, 207–9, 211, 216
Rockefeller, John D., Jr., 50, 82, 86
Rockefeller, John D., Sr., 50, 69, 85, 87–88
Rockefeller Foundation, 97
Rockefeller Foundation Board, 87
Roosevelt, Eleanor, 97, 115, 175
Root, John Wellborn, 74
Rose Hill, 137, 140
Rosenberg, Sam, 173
Rosenwald (film), 72
Rosenwald, Augusta ("Gussie") (née Nussbaum), 5, 45–47, 48, 50, 69, 71, 85, 97, *118*, *126*
Rosenwald, Augusta (née Hammerslough), 72–73, 107
Rosenwald, Helen ("Leni"), 186
Rosenwald, Julius, 4–5, 235n9; and Addams, 83–85; and affordable housing, 95–96; antisemitism, confronting, 79–80; and Chicago Lab School, 112; early life of, 72–73; as Edith's role model, 68–71; education of, 85–90; family life of, 45; focus on the needs of the Black community, 71–72, 82–83; magazine articles about, 87–88; and museums, 94–95; photograph of, *118;* and Reform Judaism, 81–82; and Rosenwald Fund, 90–91; and Rosenwald Schools, 71–72, 86–89, 91–92, 93–94; and Sears & Roebuck, 77–79
Rosenwald, Lessing, 45, 97, *118*, 186, 216–18
Rosenwald, Marion, 45–47, 48, 81, *118*
Rosenwald, Philip, 186
Rosenwald, Samuel, 72–73, 79, 225
Rosenwald, William, 45–47, *118*
Rosenwald Court Apartments, 96
Rosenwald Fund, 30, 33, 44, 69–70, 72, 86–91, 93, 97, 134–35, 138, 139, 143, 186
Rothschild, Rabbi Jacob, 221
Rothstein, Richard, 14
Royal Orleans Hotel, 5–6, 133, 146, 150–54, 202, 216
Russian Jews, 57, 82, 85
Rustin, Bayard, 39
Sachs, Paul J., 85
Saint Augustine, 23
Saint-Gaudens, Augustus, 103
Sanchez, George I., 91
Sauvinet, Felix, 188
Savage, Augusta, 98
Save Our Schools (SOS), 3, 173, 180–81
Scheuering, W. Ray, 15–16
Schexnayder, Vilma, 52, 59
Schiff, Jacob, 5, 36, 87, 93
Schlesinger, Lee, 101
scholarships, 86
School and Society (Dewey), 113
Scottsboro Boys, 220–21
Sears, Richard, 77
Sears & Roebuck, 58, 70, 77–79, 86, 214
The Second Battle of New Orleans (Baker), 240n35
The Second Battle of New Orleans (Borah and Baumbach), 209
segregation: and *Brown v. Board of Education*, 37, 91, 155–56, 164, 168, 169–70, 178–79, 180, 211; in Chicago, 76; in hotels, 154; and housing, 13–15; NAACP, 134; in New Orleans, 1–2, 39, 52, 169–70, 178–79; and *Plessy V. Ferguson*, 37, 133, 161–62, 163, 168; and Pontchartrain Park, 19, 23; and separate but equal, 23, 37, 133, 163, 168; and Tureaud, 164, 166; during World War II, 10; Wright's impact on, 163–64
Segue, Taylor, 10–11, 15–16
Selig, Lucille, 219
separate but equal, 23, 37, 133, 163, 168
settlement houses, 49, 233n10
Seventh Ward, 227
Several Circles (Kandinsky), 189
Shipman, Ellen Biddle, 2–3, 102, 103–4, 107, 109–10, 188
Shipman, Louis, 103
Shulman, Daniel, 97
Shushan, Dorothy, 187
Sibley, Mrs. Harper, 196
Sidwell Friends School, 65
Sinclair, Upton, 50
Singing Out Loud (Eaves), 26
slave auctions, 148

Sloan, Alfred P., 204–5
slum clearance, 13
Smith v. Allwright, 162
Snowden, George A., 15
Sobel, Rabbi Ronald, 55
social activism, 49–50
social justice, 2, 52, 68, 81–83
social stratification, 42–44
Sokolsky, Harvey, 172
Sokolsky, Saul (Stone), 172
Sonnabend, Roger, 152
South Rampart Street, 41
Southern Conference for Human Welfare, 175
Southern Regional Council, 175, 180, 241n13
Spanish Court, 110
Springfield, IL, 72–73
S. Rosenwald & Co., 73
Standard Oil Company, 32, 50, 205
Starr, Ellen, 84
Starr, Frederick, 24–25, 149
State of Israel, 36
St. Charles Avenue, 40–41
St. Charles Hotel, 148
Steiner, David, 64
Stern, Alfred K., 95, 97
Stern, Anne, 112
Stern, Audrey, 64–65, 109, 112, *120*, 186, 223
Stern, Charles, 31
Stern, David, 64
Stern, Edgar Bloom, 3–6; and Anderson, 67–68; Black community involvement, 222; and Black education, 30, 44; and Brown, 63–64; on Committee for Public Education (COPE), 181; and Davis, 190; and Dillard University, 99, 131–45; early life of, 26–28; and Edith's interest in art, 185–86; education of, 89; entertaining Black guests, 156–57; exclusionary policies, 43; financial success and social advancement, 28–30; fundraising campaigns, 131–33, 138, 193; and gardens, 104; impact on New Orleans, 221–23; Jewishness, 4, 54–55, 81, 215; and Julius Rosenwald, 69; and Longue Vue House and Gardens, 100–111; and Loving Cup award, 139–40; marriage to Edith, 51, 59; and Metairie Park Country Day School, 115; and Morrison, 160; and the NAACP, 163; New York estate of, 197–98; photograph of, *117, 119, 120, 122;* and Pontchartrain Park, 7–23, 95; progressivism of, 58–59; race-related attitudes and actions, 30–32; and Rosenwald Fund, 97; and Royal Orleans Hotel, 150–54, 202; and the Save our Schools organization, 173; and son Edgar, 214–15; standing out, 59–62; on St. Charles Avenue, 40–41; and Stern legacy, 229–30; and St. Louis Hotel, 148, 153–54; and Urban League, 168; and Vieux Carré Commission (VCC), 150; and WDSU radio and TV, 212; and women's efforts, 149; in the world of New Orleans, 44
Stern, Edgar, Jr., 4–6; and anti-highway campaign, 203, 208–9; birth of, 112; Black community involvement, 222; and Borah and Baumbach, 203, 208, 210; and Jewishness, 64, 215–16; as partner to parents, 58–59, 214–15; photograph of, *120;* relocation to Aspen, 217–18; retribution against, 216–18; and Royal Orleans Hotel, 152–54, 202; and Stern legacy, 229–30; and WDSU radio and TV, 179, 211–14
Stern, Edith Rosenwald, 1–6, 7–8; and Addams, 84–85; and affordable housing, 14; and Anderson, 67–68; and art and art collecting, 105–6, 185–91; and Bernard, 98–99, 196–200; Black community involvement, 222; and Borah and Baumbach, 210; and Brown, 63–64; and challenge grants, 111–12; childhood antics of, 48–49; and citywide support for the arts, 194–95; and Committee for Public Education (COPE), 181; and Cuzco collection, 190–91; and Degas, 189–90; dinner parties of, 191–92; early life of, 45–48; education of, 89; entertaining Black guests, 132; and exclusionary policies, 43; first marriage of, 50–51; and Forcia, 62–64; impact on New Orleans, 58–59, 221–23; and integration, 3, 160, 183; and Jewishness, 4, 54–55, 64–65, 81, 215; and Julius Rosenwald, 68–71; and Keller, 174; and Longue Vue House and Gardens, 100–111; and Loving Cup award, 140; and marriage to Edgar, 51, 59; and Metairie Park Country Day School, 113–16; mixing the refined with

the kitsch, 60–61; and Morrison, 12, 160; and the NAACP, 163; and Newcomb Nursery School, 103; and New Orleans Garden Study Club, 102; and New Orleans Philharmonic Symphony, 192–94; and New York estate, 197–98; and nursery school movement, 112–13; photographs of, *118, 119, 120, 121, 122, 123;* and Pontchartrain Park, 23, 95; and Rosenwald Fund, 97; and the Save our Schools organization, 173; social standing of, 195–96; son Edgar, 214–16; standing out, 59–62; on St. Charles Avenue, 40–41; and Stern legacy, 229–30; and voter registration programs, 160–61, 162, 164; in the world of New Orleans, 44, 51–54; and Wright, 156
Stern, Eva, 65
Stern, Hannah Bloom, 27–29, 54–55, *117*
Stern, Isaac, 193
Stern, Maurice, 27–28, 54–55, *117*, 225
Stern, Pauline (Polly) (née Stewart), 60, 64, 215–18
Stern, Philip, 64–65, 100, 109, 112, *120*
Stern, Sara May, *117*
Stern, Solomon, *117*
Stern, Walter, 28, 29–30
Stern Fund/Stern Family Fund, 33, 44, 58, 139, 175, 180, 188, 209–10, 218, 241n13
Stevenson, Adlai, 215
Stewart, Pauline (Polly). *See* Stern, Pauline (Polly) (née Stewart)
Stich, Margery, 110, 187, 194–95
St. Louis Cathedral, 149
St. Louis Hotel, 148, 153–54
Storyville, 41
Straight College, 135
streetcars, 40, 74, 164, 202, 205, 209, 233n30
St. Regis Hotel, 55
suburbs, 9, 21
Sullivan, Louis, 74, 81
Sulzberger, Germon F., 50–51
Super Bowl, 227, 243n9
synagogues, 41

Talmadge, Eugene, 92
Tanglewood, 197–98
Tarbell, Ida, 50
Taylor, Robert, 87
Temple bombing, 221
Temple Sinai, 28, 41, 54, 58, 80–81, 82
Thomas, Jeff, 11, 22–23
Thompkins, Gwen, 12, 21, 24, 229
Title I of the 1949 Housing Act, 206–7
Torkanowsky, David, 193–94
Torkanowsky, Werner, 193–94
Touro Infirmary, 36
Touro Synagogue, 41
Tremé neighborhood, 42, 182, 203–4, 207
Trillin, Calvin, 25
trolley systems, 204–5
Trujillo, Rafael, 36
Truman, Harry, 159
Tulane University, 36, 41, 182–83, 193
Tureaud, Alexander Pierre, 17, 38, 164–66, 167–68, 178
Tureaud, A. P., Jr., 167
Tureaud, Louis and Eugenie (DeJean), 165–66
Tureaud, Lucille, 167
Tuskegee Institute, 68, 85–88, 92

United Nations resolution, 36
University of Chicago, 112
University of Chicago Laboratory School, 85
University of Mississippi, 241n41
University of Oklahoma, 163
University of Texas, 163
Up from Slavery (Washington), 30, 69, 85
Uptown, 41, 135, 147, 179
urban development, 75
Urban League of New Orleans, 133, 168, 171, 178, 181
urban renewal, 13–15, 181–82, 206–9
US Attorney's Office, 158–59
US Court of Appeals for the District of Columbia Circuit, 164, 170
US Supreme Court, 37, 90, 116, 133, 146, 155–56, 162, 164, 168, 169–70, 178, 220–21

Vasarely, Victor, 106, 189
VCPORA, 208
Victory Garden, 111
Vieux Carré Commission (VCC), 149–50

Villard, Oswald Garrison, 82
Volpe, John, 204, 211
Von Eckardt, Wolf, 208–9
voter fraud, 158, 160–61
Voters' Registration League, 160–61
voting rights, 29–30, 37–38, 133, 158, 160–62

Walker, Darren, 69–71, 87, 97
Walker, Madame C. J., 82
Walled Garden, 111
Wall Street Journal, 181
Walter, Solomon, 29
Warren, Earl, 168, 169
Washington, Booker T., 5, 30, 68–69, 85–87, 92–93, 132
WDSU radio and TV, 4, 6, 152, 179, 211–14, 216
Weaver, Robert C., 91
Weizmann, Chaim, 36
Wellford, Robert, 107
West End, 42
Whim House, 104, 110–11
White, Charles, 98
White, Clarence Cameron, 197
White, Edward Douglass, 29
White, Michael, 62–64
White, Natalie, 63
White Citizens' Council, 179
white-collar jobs, 206
white flight, 14
white-only primaries, 161–62
white supremacy, 38
Wild Flowers of Louisiana (Dormon), 102
Wild Garden, 111
Wilding, Dorothy, *121*
Williams, Edwin, 9
Williams, Kemper, 152
Williams, T. Harry, 33–34
Wilson, Samuel, Jr., 153–54
Wilson, Woodrow, 71
Wisdom, Betty, 180
Wisdom, John Minor, 170–73, 182, 241n41
Wolf, Peter, 57–58
women, 3, 45, 49–50, 84–85, 103, 149–50, 160–61, 179–81
Wood, Robert Elkington, 80
Woodward, William, 188
Woolworth's, 60–61, 106
World War I, 71
World War II, 9–10, 111, 204
Wright, Frank Lloyd, 74
Wright, Helen (née Patton), 155–56, 158–59, 167, 176–77
Wright, James, 155–56, 170
Wright, James E., III, 155–56
Wright, J. Skelly, 1–3; and desegregation of City Park, 17; early life and career of, 157–58; and Edith, 156; and Fifth Circuit Court, 170; impact of, 163–64; and Keller, 176–77; retribution against, 155; transformative moment, 158–59; and voting rights, 161–62; and Wisdom, 170–73
Wright, Katherine, 180

Xavier University of Louisiana, 63, 197, 199–200, 226, 238n6

Yellow Garden, 110–11
YMCAs, 82–83
Young, Andrew, 134, 144–45
YWCAs, 83, 176

Zemurray, Sam, 26, 33–37
Zionist cause, 71